The Human Rights Challenge to Immunity in International Law

"This timely and thoroughly researched book makes an important contribution to the topical issue of when, if at all, states and their leaders should be granted immunity for their actions which violate certain universally recognised fundamental human rights standards. The study constitutes a significant step along the path towards full accountability of international players for their conduct."

—Brice Dickson, *Emeritus Professor of International and Comparative Law, Queen's University Belfast, UK*

"I commend to prospective readers Selman Özdan's considerations of the tension between immunities and impunity within the rarefied air of *jus cogens* norms within an international human rights law paradigm. Dr Özdan does well to set out a possible road forward towards an international rule of law which ensures the absolute protection of those fundamental rights of a peremptory character."

—Jean Allain, *Professor of International Law, Monash University, Australia*

"The ratification and signing of international human rights conventions are one of the landmark achievements of the twentieth century, signalling the global necessity of respecting human dignity by protecting fundamental entitlements. This book significantly advances such debates with its rigorous analysis and defence of *jus cogens* norms to brilliantly argue that these norms must prevail over state immunity and impunity."

—Alison MacKenzie, *Senior Lecturer and a member of Centre for Children's Rights, Queen's University Belfast, UK*

"Selman Özdan's *The Human Rights Challenge to Immunity in International Law* makes a strong contribution to the field. The monograph shines a light directly onto the existing challenges, tensions and contradictions surrounding human rights and immunities. It draws on a rich body of research, is very well written and cogently argued. A must-read for all those interested in international law and, specifically, human rights."

—Faith Gordon, Associate Professor, *ANU College of Law, The Australian National University*

Selman Özdan

The Human Rights Challenge to Immunity in International Law

palgrave
macmillan

Selman Özdan
Ondokuz Mayıs University
AFB School of Law
Samsun, Turkey

ISBN 978-3-030-92922-0   ISBN 978-3-030-92923-7 (eBook)
https://doi.org/10.1007/978-3-030-92923-7

This Palgrave Macmillan imprint is published by the registered company Springer Nature Switzerland AG.
The registered company address is: Gewerbestrasse 11, 6330 Cham, Switzerland

To my daughter Bilge and my wife Zeycan

Contents

Abbreviations

ECtHR	European Court of Human Rights
IACtHR	Inter-American Court of Human Rights
ICC	International Criminal Court
ICJ	International Court of Justice
ICTY	International Criminal Tribunal for the former Yugoslavia
SCSL	Special Court for Sierra Leone
UN	United Nations

CHAPTER 1

Introduction

The development of international human rights as a distinct and unique field within the boundaries of public international law has become the significant and notable battleground regarding challenges to jurisdictional immunities. These challenges have appeared within the areas of State immunity, Head of State immunity, and diplomatic immunity. This book's title is formulated to evoke a main research question: Does immunity equate to impunity when violations of fundamental human rights recognised as *jus cogens* norms (peremptory norms of general international law) are committed by States, Heads of State, and diplomatic agents?

This book is an enquiry into the tensions that exist between the protection of fundamental human rights on the one hand and the bestowal of immunities on States and their representatives on the other. A number of cases that are currently before international and national courts demonstrate that the protection of fundamental human rights poses significant challenges to State, Head of State, and diplomatic immunities. There is an inevitable and irrefutable tension between human rights protection and the defence of States, Heads of State, and diplomatic agents as a consequence of the propounding of jurisdictional immunity. This book considers the extent to which this tension affects the sovereign structure of the State, and seeks to ascertain how these immunities can be chipped away if not abolished in order to ensure a fuller protection of fundamental human rights under international law.

This book argues that the immunities of States, Heads of State, and diplomatic agents should be rescinded when they interfere with respect for fundamental human rights recognised as peremptory norms of general

S. Özdan, *The Human Rights Challenge to Immunity in International Law*, https://doi.org/10.1007/978-3-030-92923-7_1

international law. These immunities will be carefully differentiated from those identified largely in the legal literature as absolute immunity or limited immunity in relation to the protection of human rights. Because of the sensitive nature of the contradictions arising from this tension, the challenges from human rights to these immunities will be analysed. The central argument is the assertion that immunity should not equate to impunity when violations of fundamental human rights recognised as *jus cogens* norms are at stake. While the doctrine of State immunity should be maintained, this doctrine should no longer extend to circumstances where there has been a violation of fundamental human rights guaranteed by a peremptory norm of general international law. The viability and validity of immunity should not imply impunity and to sustain this assertion, a systematic analysis and examination will be undertaking on: the theory of sovereignty; the concept of international and fundamental human rights; the theory of immunity; recent case law; and State practice concerning violations of fundamental human rights.

Background

International human rights law has developed considerably since the Second World War. The devastation wrought by the Second World War, and the atrocities committed by some State actors, affected the international system in terms of generating new methods of international human rights advocacy with irreversible consequences for the international community. The extra-judicial actions of both State and non-State actors led a great many people to be tortured, raped, and deliberately eliminated and killed on an industrial scale hitherto unknown in violation of international human rights norms. However, because of political considerations, the perpetrators of these acts mostly benefited from immunities.[1] Mario Bettati has emphasised that until the middle of the twentieth century, States and their agents 'had succeeded in juridically protecting their free will; or more precisely, their free wilfulness'.[2] However, in the contemporary world order, States and their representatives cannot ignore international human rights norms under the pretext of absolute or exclusive sovereignty. In fact, they neither completely reject international human rights norms nor precisely abide by international human rights law. As Jean Allain rightly states, at the international level, 'the nature of the anarchic legal system allows states much more leeway to construct human rights in their image as opposed to those they are meant to protect—the individual'.[3]

There are two fundamental interests in international law: State interests and international human rights interests. Both State and international human rights interests have become crucial concepts in the international system. The relationship between State interests and international human rights interests has to be properly balanced. Allain has noted that for 'the international community of states, human rights were to be accorded as a type of a pressure-valve that could regulate the extent to which individuals might be protected from the abuse of states'.[4] States became the primary actors in the international legal system. Louis Henkin has asserted that human rights 'have revolutionized the international system and international law. The law now reflects human values in addition to state values, or allows human values to modify state values. We have seen a revolution in the content of international law to include a growing field directly relevant to the lives of five billion people, every one of them [sic] now a subject of international law'.[5] Since immunity derives from the sovereign right of the State, there will inevitably be a conflict of interest between the State's right to immunity and citizens' right to claim or assert justice. In this sense, the concept of immunity becomes an important subject of analysis in the context of the aforementioned challenge.

Sovereign immunity, which derives from the sovereign rights of States, is based on a common law principle. It is derived from English jurisprudence which assumes that *the King can do no wrong*. Sovereign immunity appears to be the exclusive jurisdiction of the State and its own territory; therefore, a foreign State needs an express licence to exercise its national jurisdiction.[6] Sovereign immunity is a crucial interest for the State and its representatives.

International law is concerned with both protecting immunity from foreign jurisdiction and with preventing violations of fundamental human rights. Sovereign immunity is best read, not as a particular rule of customary international law, but as a legally binding principle. If States and their representatives are not bound by detailed obligations of treaties, they are free to frame and designate the range of immunity within their domestic law according to their interpretation of the ambits determined by principles of international law. Under the principle of immunity, international courts 'may only scrutinize whether a state has violated the boundaries set by international law that a state must observe when balancing its territorial sovereignty and the sovereign independence of foreign states. These limits of international law restrict not only the freedom of states to grant, but also their freedom to deny, sovereign immunity to foreign states within their jurisdiction'.[7]

The principle of immunity is a considerable obstruction to the enforcement of international law. However, lately, there has been a growing inclination for a human rights-oriented approach in international law to question this fundamental element of statecraft. After the Second World War, one of the most important developments in international law was the leverage of human rights norms in approaching issues 'traditionally dealt with through the principle of non-intervention in the domestic jurisdiction of states'.[8] This evolution towards a human rights-oriented approach has been clearly emerging and marked out before the Appeals Chamber of the International Criminal Tribunal for the former Yugoslavia (ICTY) in the *Prosecutor v Tadíc* case which was about the prosecution of Bosnian-Serb Dušan Tadić for committing war crimes against Bosnian Muslims and Bosnian Croats at a Serb-run concentration camp in Bosnia-Herzegovina during the Bosnian War. It noted that a 'State-sovereignty-oriented approach has been gradually supplanted by a human-being-oriented approach [...] the distinction between interstate wars and civil wars is losing its validity as far as human beings are concerned'.[9] Likewise Antônio Cançado Trindade, the Judge of the International Court of Justice (ICJ) and the former president of the Inter-American Court of Human Rights (IACtHR), also emphasised that grave 'breaches of human rights and of international humanitarian law, amounting to international crimes, are anti-juridical acts, are breaches of *jus cogens*, that cannot simply be removed or thrown into oblivion' by reliance on immunities.[10]

Motivation and Approach of the Book

The issue of whether the protection of fundamental human rights recognised as *jus cogens* norm prevails over the State, Heads of State, and diplomatic immunities still exists in the contemporary international order. As a matter of course, the relationship between human rights interests and State interests is quite contentious, and the tension between the two remains far from settled. Although international society tends to favour the protection of human rights, the literature has emphasised on the main procedural application of the principle of immunity, while the problem of the substantive application of the prohibition of fundamental human rights violations has not been adequately explored. The principle of immunity (procedural nature) should not amount to impunity when fundamental human rights deemed to be *jus cogens* norms (substantive nature) are breached. However, the distinction between procedural immunity and substantive nature of *jus cogens* norms becomes artificial when *jus cogens* norms are violated.[11] When procedural immunity prevails over substantive *jus cogens* norms, States, Heads of State, and diplomatic agents who have allegedly perpetrated grave violations of *jus cogens* norms could thereby be exempt from punishment. It is my contention that in cases of *jus cogens* violations that impunity should not be permitted.

Further, the discussions over immunity *versus* impunity in cases of violations of fundamental human rights are not yet fully fledged from the perspective of academic discourse. The issue of the superiority of fundamental human rights which are recognised as *jus cogens* norms over the procedural application of the immunity principle is still at an embryonic stage, since those fundamental human rights have an organic structure. Therefore, the relationship between State and human rights interests requires further study and a broader focus in order to drive the point home. In this sense, assessing the immunity principle and characterising the nature of human rights are critical conceptualisations for approaching this challenge. Therefore, this book aims to present a detailed analysis of the immunity *versus* impunity debate within the framework of a human rights-based challenge to immunities. In achieving this aim, the organic structure of the concept of sovereignty and human rights will be delineated. To do so, the human rights-based challenge will be examined from three perspectives: State immunity, Head of State immunity, and diplomatic immunity. In so doing, this book puts the concept of fundamental human rights at the centre of the immunity *versus* impunity debate, and the transition from a State-centric system to a human-centric system is placed under the microscope.

This book draws from both international law and domestic case-law. In particular, it considers the issue of diplomatic immunity *versus* impunity for fundamental human rights violations primarily in reference to the decisions of domestic courts. Domestic courts necessarily serve by default as agents of the international judicial order.[12]

With respect to the importance of decisions of domestic courts, Lauterpacht underscored that the foundational element of international law is the consent of States. Decisions of domestic courts thus assist by creating both *opinio juris*[13] and State practice which establishes customary international law.[14] Furthermore, the decisions of domestic courts may be deemed important for future developments in international law. Domestic courts have become an important part of the international legal system for developing or changing norms of international law as they are seemingly endowed with an international legal function and may be regarded as the natural or first-instance judges of international law.[15] For example, in the case of *Jurisdictional Immunities of the State*, the issue of respect due to State immunity originates in the decisions of Italian and Greek domestic courts to reject Germany's claim to State immunity for serious human rights violations during the Second World War.[16] In this case, the ICJ's decision contributes to the development of international law by offering 'an interpretation of the law contrary to that proffered by the Italian courts'.[17] Therefore, it should be noted that domestic courts have a substantial mission in judicial evolution and development of international law.

There are few studies which deeply consider and examine the challenges posed to State, Head of State, and diplomatic immunity, by those human rights which fall within the domain of *jus cogens* norms. This book aims to address this deficiency in the literature by assessing various international and national case-law, legal reports, international conventions, and related documents. It also fills this gap by focusing on the principal interests in international law: preserving the immunity of States and those who represent them and protecting fundamental human rights recognised as *jus cogens*. In so doing, the distinction between immunity and impunity in terms of States, Heads of State, and diplomatic agents, when transgressions of peremptory norms are at stake, will be examined. The self-evident contradiction between the claim of absolute immunity by States, Heads of State, and diplomatic agents before a judicial body, and the claim of the *jus cogens* character of fundamental human rights by the victims of the implementation of that absolute immunity are addressed. To examine this contradiction, this study applies Kelsen's understanding of the law as a hierarchical perspective of legal order in order to demonstrate the unquestioned superiority of peremptory norms of general international law over all other norms. This study illustrates, therefore, the contentious issue on immunity *versus* impunity when fundamental human rights which have *jus cogens* character are transgressed. It seeks to differentiate between immunity and impunity and also to determine how the hierarchical framework can be established between *jus cogens* nature human rights and the principle of immunity.

Structure of the Book

This book considers the tension between the bestowal of immunities and the protection of fundamental human rights by exploring the distinction between immunity and impunity in cases of violations of fundamental human rights. It is divided into the following chapters. Following this Introduction, Chap. 2 explores the concept of State sovereignty. It further demonstrates how international law imposes on States the obligation to protect fundamental human rights, and how the State-oriented approach has gradually given way to a human rights-oriented approach. The main purpose of this chapter is to provide a theoretical framework for immunities, as the immunity principle is derived from the concept of State supremacy and from the need to have effective functioning inter-State relations. Thus Chap. 2 provides and explains the link between State sovereignty and immunities.

Sovereignty has always been a controversial issue in international law, as it reflects the paradox of power to enact laws and the law which limits that power.[18] Although State sovereignty is a contentious topic in international law and, as such, it is often described in vague and conflicting terms, it nevertheless remains the main structure of, and the intellectual framework for, international law. Through analysis of the transition from Westphalian to post-Westphalian sovereignty, and by a reappraisal of the relationship between State sovereignty and human rights, Chap. 2 considers the contradictions between State sovereignty and international law and provides a theoretical framework for immunities. Noting that the principle of sovereign immunity is derived from the concept of State supremacy and the need for smooth-functioning inter-State relations,[19] this chapter also explores the question of how to protect human rights under international law as part of its analysis of the relationship between human rights and State sovereignty. To take this task in hand, this chapter charts the evolution of the concept of State sovereignty, particularly in the post-Second World War period, in parallel with the development of international human rights.

Chapter 3 examines fundamental human rights, which fall within the domain of peremptory norms of general international law. To that end, the chapter elucidates the notion of human rights and its international legal aspects. It also examines the notion of *jus cogens* by paving the way for identifying those human rights that are recognised as *jus cogens* norms. Further, it discusses whether a hierarchy can be established among human rights regarding *jus cogens* norms. Following this hierarchic relationship, Chap. 3 evaluates the differentiation of fundamental human rights which fall within the scope of *jus cogens* norms from non-derogability. Finally, this chapter sets out fundamental human rights that have been established as *jus cogens* norms and considers jus cogens norms as a declaration to secure the absolute protection of fundamental human rights for all human beings.

The following chapters engage respectively with State immunity (Chap. 4), Head of State immunity (Chap. 5), and diplomatic immunity (Chap. 6). The central aim of these chapters is to examine the distinction between immunity and impunity based on the decisions of international and national courts in cases involving violations of fundamental human rights.

For its part, Chap. 4 explores the debate over State immunity *versus* State impunity in cases of violations of fundamental human rights. The concept of immunities has a long history under international law.[20] These immunities are required whenever a ruler or an organisation has been attributed a public duty under the requirements of international law. Even before 'the establishment of modern sovereign States, it was recognised that if State-like entities were effectively to interact in commercial, diplomatic and other fields, there was a need for a formula ensuring their official representatives' freedom from'[21] proceedings in the foreign State. Despite its deep roots in history and the legal or natural necessity for jurisdictional immunities, the law of State immunity is not settled under contemporary international law; in other words, the 'law of State immunity is not static'.[22]

Chapter 4 analyses State immunity with regard to customary international law. It conducts a general examination of State immunity under international law, charting its progress and explaining its rise within the international order and offers new considerations as to the basis of State immunity. Additionally, this chapter explores the transition from absolute to restrictive immunity with reference to the increasing tension between State immunity and human rights.

States are vested with coercive powers and enjoy jurisdictional immunity in regard to their own property from the proceedings of other States' courts[23]; therefore, 'a State cannot be impleaded in the courts of another State without its express consent'.[24] On this point, Bankas states that the 'State is a means to an end, hence State immunity exists as a veritable consequence of sovereignty'.[25] Those consequences are found in the general principle of foreign State immunity, first expression in the *Schooner Exchange v McFaddon* case of 1812. This historic decision of Chief Justice

Marshall of the United States Supreme Court formulated sovereign immunity thus:

> This perfect equality and absolute independence of sovereigns, and this common interest impelling them to mutual intercourse, and an exchange of good offices with each other, have given rise to a class of cases in which every sovereign is understood to waive the exercise of a part of that complete exclusive territorial jurisdiction, which has been stated to be the attribute of every nation.[26]

The principle of State immunity creates an obstacle to suing foreign States in national courts.[27] It finds its contemporary manifestation in the 2004 United Nations (UN) Convention on Jurisdictional Immunities of States and Their Property (Article 5), which states: 'A State enjoys immunity, in respect of itself and its property, from the jurisdiction of the courts of another state'.[28] The principle of State immunity is therefore crucial to the development of international law, because it applies to each nation State and therefore functions as a neutral way of 'denying jurisdiction to States over the international administration of another State and diverting claims to settlement in the courts of that State'.[29]

In considering the relationship between State sovereignty and State immunity, Chap. 4 introduces a different perspective on whether the concept of State sovereignty creates an obstacle to foreign investigation. In this context, an important question is what impact the clash between State interests and human rights has had on State immunity. To answer this question, this chapter both analyses the human rights challenge to the State immunity and re-examines the relationship between State sovereignty and State immunity.

Chapter 5 explores the tension between immunity and impunity, when violations of fundamental human rights are committed by Heads of State. With regard to jurisdictional immunity, a general rule of public international law is that 'certain holders of high-ranking office in a State, such as the Head of State, Head of Government and Minister for Foreign Affairs, enjoy immunities from jurisdiction in other States, both civil and criminal'.[30] In international law, there is interest both in protecting the immunities of Heads of State from foreign jurisdictions, but also in the protection of fundamental human rights. Giving Head of State immunity as a principle, international courts 'may only scrutinize whether a [Head of] State has violated the boundaries set by international law that a [Head of] state must observe when balancing [the possessed] sovereignty and the sovereign independence of foreign States. These limits of international law restrict not only the freedom of States to grant, but also their freedom to deny head of state immunity'.[31]

The development of international law has raised the question of whether Head of State immunity can prevail over protection of fundamental human rights. This question has been made a subject of litigation in the *Pinochet*[32] cases put before the United Kingdom House of Lords. This case not only raised the problem of Head of State immunity, but also embedded Head of State immunity in judicial and academic discourse. In the 1990s, the creation of ad hoc international criminal tribunals by the UN Security Council became a novel avenue for proceedings against a Head of State.

The political aspects of international society and the development process of international human rights have always influenced the implementation of Head of State immunity. As a consequence, Head of State immunity is a puzzling feature of international law. Chapter 5 traces the evolution of the concept of Head of State immunity as it applies under international law. Through analysis of statutes, treaties, and customary international law, the chapter provides a background to, and rationale for, the practices of international courts. Additionally, it contributes to the debate over the extent to which international courts can interfere in immunities of Heads of States. Finally, Chap. 5 identifies and describes the legal basis of and rationale for Head of State immunity and considers the position of Head of State immunity in cases of violations of fundamental human rights.

Chapter 6, for its part, explores the question of whether the immunity of diplomatic agents leads to impunity when they are responsible for violations of fundamental human rights. Diplomatic immunity is traditionally deemed to be a fundamental principle of customary international law that 'originated to protect representatives of foreign governments based abroad from retaliation in time of international conflicts'.[33] Furthermore, diplomatic immunity is a necessary principle in reinforcing and sustaining international relations. The ICJ has emphasised its 'cardinal importance for the maintenance of good relations between States in the interdependent world of today. There is no more fundamental prerequisite for the conduct of relations between States [...] than the inviolability of diplomatic envoys and embassies, so that throughout history nations of all creeds and cultures have observed reciprocal obligations for that purpose'.[34] According to a study by Hazel Fox, diplomatic immunity is given '(i) as recognition of the sovereign independent status of the sending State and of the public nature of the acts which render them not subject to the jurisdiction of the receiving State; (ii) as protection to the diplomatic mission and staff to ensure their efficient performance of functions free from interference from the receiving State'.[35]

The human rights challenge to diplomatic immunity is also discussed in Chap. 6. A brief overview of the concept of diplomacy serves as an introduction to a discussion of the immunities which diplomatic agents benefit from when abroad. The theoretical basis of diplomatic immunity, its historical development, and its codification process will be considered in the context of an evaluation of diplomatic law.

Diplomatic law can be described as a bedrock of the modern international legal order.[36] So as to analyse contemporary issues regarding the relationship between diplomatic immunity and violations of fundamental human rights, the identification of diplomatic immunity under modern international law will be evaluated as well. By examining related cases and issues, Chap. 6 considers whether or not diplomatic immunities breach fundamental human rights. Abuses of such diplomatic immunities and privileges will also be discussed. Chapter 6 concludes by considering whether diplomatic immunity is superior to fundamental human rights in the event of a conflict between the two norms and asserts that absolute diplomatic immunity from legal proceedings is irreconcilable with international human rights law.

Finally, Chap. 7 brings together questions of jurisdictional immunity in relation to the protection of fundamental human rights and summarises the argument that immunity does not equate to impunity when violations of fundamental human rights are at stake. As stated earlier, the doctrine of immunity should be kept. However, it should be no longer applied to situations where a violation of fundamental human rights recognised as a peremptory norm of general international law has occurred.

Notes

1. M. Cherif Bassiouni, 'Combating Impunity for International Crimes', *University of Colorado Law Review* 71, no. 2 (2000): 409–22.
2. Mario Bettati, 'The International Community and Limitations of Sovereignty', in *Tolerance Between Intolerance and the Intolerable*, ed. Paul Ricoeur (Oxford: Berghahn Books, 1996), 91.

3. Jean Allain, 'International Human Rights Law in Theory and Practice', in *The Tension Between Group Rights and Human Rights: A Multidisciplinary Approach*, ed. Koen De Feyter and George Pavlakos, vol. 13 (Portland, OR: Hart Publishing, 2008), 271.
4. Allain, 271.
5. Louis Henkin, 'Human Rights and State Sovereignty', *Georgia Journal of International and Comparative Law* 25, no. 1 (1996): 43–44.
6. Ian Brownlie, *Principles of Public International Law*, 7th ed. (Oxford: Oxford University Press, 2008), 323.
7. Jasper Finke, 'Sovereign Immunity: Rule, Comity or Something Else?', *European Journal of International Law* 21, no. 4 (2010): 853.
8. R. E. Vinuesa, 'Interface, Correspondence and Convergence of Human Rights and International Humanitarian Law', *Yearbook of International Humanitarian Law* 1 (1998): 108.
9. *Prosecutor v. Tadić (IT-94-1-AR72), Decision on The Defence Motion for Interlocutory Appeal on Jurisdiction*, Appeals Chamber (ICTY 2 October 1995) at para 97.
10. Judge Antônio Augusto Cançado Trindade, *The Construction of a Humanized International Law: A Collection of Individual Opinions (1991–2013)* (Leiden: Brill Nijhoff and Hotei Publishing, 2015), 1519.
11. Selman Özdan, 'State Immunity or State Impunity in Cases of Violations of Human Rights Recognised as Jus Cogens Norms', *The International Journal of Human Rights* 23, no. 9 (2019): 1528–30.
12. Richard Falk, 'The Role of Domestic Courts in the International Legal Order', *Indiana Law Journal* 39, no. 3 (1964): 436.
13. *Opinio juris* is an essential element of customary international law and it 'requires that custom should be regarded as state practice amounting to a legal obligation, which distinguishes it from mere usage'. Elizabeth A. Martin, *A Dictionary of Law*, 7th ed. (Oxford: Oxford University Press, 2009), 385.
14. Hersch Lauterpacht, 'Decisions of Municipal Courts as a Source of International Law', *British Yearbook of International Law* 10 (1929): 80.
15. See Antonios Tzanakopoulos, 'Domestic Courts in International Law: The International Judicial Function of National Courts', *Loyola of Los Angeles International and Comparative Law Review* 34 (2011): 159.
16. *Jurisdictional Immunities of the State (Germany v. Italy: Greece Intervening), Judgment*, ICJ Reports 99 (2012) at 113–116.
17. Tzanakopoulos, 'Domestic Courts in International Law: The International Judicial Function of National Courts', 162.
18. Graham Burchell, Colin Gordon, and Peter Miller, eds., *The Foucault Effect: Studies in Governmentality* (Chicago: University of Chicago Press, 1991), 87–104.

19. McGregor states that if 'immunity derives from sovereignty, its meaning, extent, and impact must also be contingent on the current scope of sovereignty. Yet, by simply restating the origins of immunity in sovereignty, courts have failed to acknowledge the restrictions on the scope of immunity caused by the evolution of sovereignty over time'. Lorna McGregor, 'Torture and State Immunity: Deflecting Impunity, Distorting Sovereignty', *European Journal of International Law* 18, no. 5 (2007): 916.
20. Linda S. Frey and Marsha L. Frey, *The History of Diplomatic Immunity* (Columbus: Ohio State University Press, 1999).
21. Ilias Bantekas and Susan Nash, *International Criminal Law*, 2nd ed. (London: Cavendish Publishing, 2003), 165.
22. Hazel Fox QC and Philippa Webb, *The Law of State Immunity*, 3rd ed. (Oxford: Oxford University Press, 2013), 3.
23. Hersch Lauterpacht, *Recognition in International Law* (Cambridge: Cambridge University Press, 2013).
24. Ernest K. Bankas, *The State Immunity Controversy in International Law: Private Suits Against Sovereign States in Domestic Courts* (Berlin: Springer, 2005), 37.
25. Bankas, 37.
26. *The Schooner Exchange v. McFaddon & Others*, 11 U.S. (7 Cranch) 116 (Supreme Court of the United States 1812) at 137.
27. Hazel Fox, 'International Law and Restraints on the Exercise of Jurisdiction by National Courts of States', in *International Law*, ed. Malcolm Evans, 3rd ed. (Oxford: Oxford University Press, 2010), 340–79.
28. UN General Assembly, 'United Nations Convention on Jurisdictional Immunities of States and Their Property', A/RES/59/38 (2004) Article 5.
29. Hazel Fox, 'In Defence of State Immunity: Why the UN: Convention on State Immunity Is Important', *International and Comparative Law Quarterly* 55, no. 02 (2006): 405.
30. *Arrest Warrant of 11 April 2000 (Democratic Republic of the Congo v. Belgium), Judgment,* ICJ Reports 3 (2002) at 21.
31. Finke, 'Sovereign Immunity', 877.
32. *R v. Bow Street Metropolitan Stipendiary Magistrate and Others, ex parte Pinochet Ugarte (No. 1)*, 4 AII ER 897 (House of Lords 1998); *R v. Bow Street Metropolitan Stipendiary Magistrate and Others, ex parte Pinochet Ugarte (No. 2)*, 2 W.L.R. 272 (House of Lords 1999); *R v. Bow Street Metropolitan Stipendiary Magistrate and Others, ex parte Pinochet Ugarte (No. 3)*, 1 A.C. 147 (House of Lords 2000).
33. Mitchell Ross, 'Rethinking Diplomatic Immunity: A Review of Remedial Approaches to Address the Abuses of Diplomatic Privileges and

Immunities', *American University International Law Review* 4, no. 1 (1989): 173–74.

34. *United States Diplomatic and Consular Staff in Tehran, Judgment,* ICJ Reports 3 (1980) at 42.
35. Fox QC and Webb, *The Law of State Immunity*, 580.
36. Eileen Denza, *Diplomatic Law: Commentary on the Vienna Convention on Diplomatic Relations*, 2nd. (Oxford and New York: Oxford University Press, 2004).

References

Allain, Jean. 'International Human Rights Law in Theory and Practice'. In *The Tension Between Group Rights and Human Rights: A Multidisciplinary Approach*, edited by Koen De Feyter and George Pavlakos, 13:271–86. Portland, OR: Hart Publishing, 2008.

Arrest Warrant of 11 April 2000 (Democratic Republic of the Congo v. Belgium), Judgment, ICJ Reports 3 (2002).

Bankas, Ernest K. *The State Immunity Controversy in International Law: Private Suits Against Sovereign States in Domestic Courts.* Berlin: Springer, 2005.

Bantekas, Ilias, and Susan Nash. *International Criminal Law*. 2nd ed. London: Cavendish Publishing, 2003.

Bassiouni, M. Cherif. 'Combating Impunity for International Crimes'. *University of Colorado Law Review* 71, no. 2 (2000): 409–22.

Bettati, Mario. 'The International Community and Limitations of Sovereignty'. In *Tolerance Between Intolerance and the Intolerable*, edited by Paul Ricoeur, 91–110. Oxford: Berghahn Books, 1996.

Brownlie, Ian. *Principles of Public International Law*. 7th ed. Oxford: Oxford University Press, 2008.

Burchell, Graham, Colin Gordon, and Peter Miller, eds. *The Foucault Effect: Studies in Governmentality*. Chicago: University of Chicago Press, 1991.

Denza, Eileen. *Diplomatic Law: Commentary on the Vienna Convention on Diplomatic Relations*. 2nd. Oxford and New York: Oxford University Press, 2004.

Falk, Richard. 'The Role of Domestic Courts in the International Legal Order'. *Indiana Law Journal* 39, no. 3 (1964): 429–45.

Finke, Jasper. 'Sovereign Immunity: Rule, Comity or Something Else?' *European Journal of International Law* 21, no. 4 (2010): 853–81.

Fox, Hazel. 'In Defence of State Immunity: Why the UN: Convention on State Immunity Is Important'. *International and Comparative Law Quarterly* 55, no. 02 (2006): 399–406.

———. 'International Law and Restraints on the Exercise of Jurisdiction by National Courts of States'. In *International Law*, edited by Malcolm Evans, 3rd ed., 340–79. Oxford: Oxford University Press, 2010.

Fox QC, Hazel, and Philippa Webb. *The Law of State Immunity*. 3rd ed. Oxford: Oxford University Press, 2013.

Frey, Linda S., and Marsha L. Frey. *The History of Diplomatic Immunity*. Columbus: Ohio State University Press, 1999.

Henkin, Louis. 'Human Rights and State Sovereignty'. *Georgia Journal of International and Comparative Law* 25, no. 1 (1996): 31–46.

Jurisdictional Immunities of the State (Germany v. Italy: Greece Intervening), Judgment, ICJ Reports 99 (2012).

Lauterpacht, Hersch. 'Decisions of Municipal Courts as a Source of International Law'. *British Yearbook of International Law* 10 (1929): 65–95.

———. *Recognition in International Law*. Cambridge: Cambridge University Press, 2013.

Martin, Elizabeth A. *A Dictionary of Law*. 7th ed. Oxford: Oxford University Press, 2009.

McGregor, Lorna. 'Torture and State Immunity: Deflecting Impunity, Distorting Sovereignty'. *European Journal of International Law* 18, no. 5 (2007): 903–19.

Özdan, Selman. 'State Immunity or State Impunity in Cases of Violations of Human Rights Recognised as Jus Cogens Norms'. *The International Journal of Human Rights* 23, no. 9 (2019): 1521–45.

Prosecutor v. Tadić (IT-94-1-AR72), Decision on The Defence Motion for Interlocutory Appeal on Jurisdiction, Appeals Chamber (ICTY 2 October 1995).

R v. Bow Street Metropolitan Stipendiary Magistrate and Others, ex parte Pinochet Ugarte (No. 1), 4 All ER 897 (House of Lords 1998).

R v. Bow Street Metropolitan Stipendiary Magistrate and Others, ex parte Pinochet Ugarte (No. 2), 2 W.L.R. 272 (House of Lords 1999).

R v. Bow Street Metropolitan Stipendiary Magistrate and Others, ex parte Pinochet Ugarte (No. 3), 1 A.C. 147 (House of Lords 2000).

Ross, Mitchell. 'Rethinking Diplomatic Immunity: A Review of Remedial Approaches to Address the Abuses of Diplomatic Privileges and Immunities'. *American University International Law Review* 4, no. 1 (1989): 173–205.

The Schooner Exchange v. McFaddon & Others, 11 U.S. (7 Cranch) 116 (Supreme Court of the United States 1812).

Trindade, Judge Antônio Augusto Cançado. *The Construction of a Humanized International Law: A Collection of Individual Opinions (1991–2013)*. Leiden: Brill Nijhoff and Hotei Publishing, 2015.

Tzanakopoulos, Antonios. 'Domestic Courts in International Law: The International Judicial Function of National Courts'. *Loyola of Los Angeles International and Comparative Law Review* 34 (2011): 133–68.

UN General Assembly. 'United Nations Convention on Jurisdictional Immunities of States and Their Property', A/RES/59/38 (2004).

United States Diplomatic and Consular Staff in Tehran, Judgment, ICJ Reports 3 (1980).

Vinuesa, R. E. 'Interface, Correspondence and Convergence of Human Rights and International Humanitarian Law'. *Yearbook of International Humanitarian Law* 1 (1998).

CHAPTER 2

From a State-Oriented to a Human-Oriented Approach

The Human Rights Challenge to Immunity in International Law begs the question of whether international law chips away at the power of the State in cases of conflict between State sovereignty and fundamental human rights. This chapter thus charts the transition from Westphalian sovereignty to post-Westphalian sovereignty and explains how State sovereignty has evolved into its current manifestation. The meaning of classic sovereignty is considered and the new structure of State sovereignty is explained by emphasising a post-Westphalian form. This analysis forms the background against which to explain the inherent contradiction between State sovereignty and contemporary international law. Analysing this contradiction is important in allowing a consideration of the tension between fundamental human rights and State sovereignty. Further, the main purpose in engaging with the concept of State sovereignty is to provide a theoretical framework for immunities, given that the principle of sovereign immunity is derived from the concept of State supremacy and is meant to ensure the smooth functioning of inter-State relations. This chapter will evaluate how international law controls and limits State sovereignty. It goes on to explore the growing tension between human rights and State sovereignty and examines the position of human rights under international law. This serves as an important gateway to the issue of the human rights' challenge to immunities which will be discussed in Chaps. 4, 5, and 6.

S. Özdan, *The Human Rights Challenge to Immunity in International Law*, https://doi.org/10.1007/978-3-030-92923-7_2

Sovereignty

Sovereignty is a charming, controversial, and provocative concept of social science, and as a phenomenon, it has dominated national and international relations of States over the course of the past five centuries. Sovereignty is an inclusive concept which combines the State elements and qualifications: permanent population, defined territory, government, and capacity to enter into relations with other States.[1] In addition, the State is the main actor of international relations and the main subject of international law. Sovereignty is the bedrock of the social construct which is the State, and is recognised as one of the most fundamental concepts of international law and political science.[2]

Sovereignty has a variety of meanings because of its relative context. There are two main reasons why there are many meanings, concepts, and connotations of sovereignty: namely the circumstances of the period when sovereignty is conceptualised, and the ideology and benefits of the person who conceptualises sovereignty. First, sovereignty has constantly been reconceptualised and reconceived over time because of changes in the context in which this takes place, and is, therefore, often dependent on historical and environmental conditions. Jean Bodin, for example, developed and defined the concept of absolute sovereignty in the context of religious wars in Europe that were destroying the stability of the polity with regard to supreme power.[3] Second, Carl Schmitt, for his part, stated, four centuries later, that of 'all juristic concepts, the concept of sovereignty is the one most governed by actual interests'.[4] Here then, we can begin to see the malleability of the concept of sovereignty; in the context of discussions about change and transformation of sovereignty, there are at least twenty conceptualisations of sovereignty in international law and international relations literatures, including Westphalian, absolute, popular, pooled, legal, political, *de facto*, and *de jure*, among others. As there are many connotations of sovereignty, it follows that sovereignty is itself an organic concept, lacking static structure or meaning.

However, despite its many conceptualisations and for the purposes of the analysis of this book, sovereignty has a settled core feature: Sovereignty is a supreme power. The predominant contention for the continuous discussions about change and transformation of sovereignty is the influence and dominance of Westphalian sovereignty on international law and international relations.

Classic Conception of Sovereignty

Jean Bodin, considered the father of the modern theory of sovereignty, states that 'sovereignty is that absolute and perpetual power vested in a commonwealth... [and] is the highest power of command'.[5] For him, monarchy is the best form of sovereign power, and 'all the laws of nature point towards monarchy, whether we regard the microcosm of the body, all of whose members are subject to a single head on which depend will, motion, and feeling, or whether we regard the macrocosm of the world, subject to the one Almighty God. If we look at the heavens, we see only one sun'.[6] Bodin conceptualised sovereignty as absolute and perpetual power, but at the same time he considered that it was not limitless, as sovereignty was subject to divine and natural law.[7] Likewise, Thomas Hobbes argued that sovereignty was absolute and perpetual.[8] However, for Hobbes, unlike Bodin, sovereignty was not subject to any kind of law.[9] Sovereignty as conceptualised by Bodin and Hobbes has been accepted as a classic conceptualisation of sovereignty in international law and international relations. From this perspective, classical sovereignty is to be understood as being the supreme, absolute, and perpetual authority[10] and as such is not subject to any worldly authority.[11] By considering Bodin and Hobbes, Emerich de Vattel turned his attention to the State, noting that 'every nation that governs itself, without dependency on any foreign power, is a sovereign state'.[12] In addition, Georg Wilhelm Friedrich Hegel argued that States are independent entities in relation to other States, and that the sovereign authority of the State is the absolute power on earth.[13]

The 1791 French Constitution may be regarded as a prominent written source for this classic conceptualisation of sovereignty. After the French Revolution, which adopted popular sovereignty as its main discourse, the French Constitution particularly emphasised the meaning of sovereignty as an exclusive power by specifying that power can only be exercised by the Nation. The French Constitution of 1791 explicitly stated that sovereignty is 'one, indivisible, inalienable, and imprescriptible: it belongs to the Nation: no section of the people nor any individual can attribute to himself the exercise thereof'.[14]

Despite this classic understanding of sovereignty, this concept was challenged in the twentieth century. Over the last 100 years, sovereignty has been re-conceptualised from three different perspectives. First, in its classic sense, sovereignty symbolises the absolute power of the State. Second, sovereignty represents absolute independence beyond the State. Third, it is one's absolute power, as a legal entity, under international law. The first two perspectives, in some sense, may seem arbitrary, as the State resorts to its power to exploit its citizens with impunity. Concerning the third one, *jus cogens* norms appear to challenge the very sovereign rights of the State.[15] Let us consider these perspectives in more depth.

Using differing nomenclature and approaches, many authors have concluded that the concept of sovereignty represents the highest authority of the State. In this regard, sovereignty generally correlates with power and is considered absolute. Albert Venn Dicey describes sovereignty as 'the power of law-making unrestricted by any legal limit'.[16] For Dicey, sovereign power is legally held by the possessor of a constitutional power to legislate, so long as the constitution imposes no restrictions on the implementation of the power in question. Therefore, this power is held independently over certain territory and is not subject to any restriction by a superior power.[17] In this context, Saul Newman, a contemporary political theorist, considers that sovereignty 'is always the rule of One, the moment of unicity, indivisibility, absolutism and the singular exception'.[18] Such conceptions in respect of the absolute characteristic of sovereignty are based on Bodin's sovereign theory. Such absolutism centres on the internal sovereignty of the State through which it has supreme power over the people and the political structure.[19]

As for the second perspective, absolute independence beyond the State is referred to as external sovereignty and the relation between States. Christian Wolff, the Eighteenth Century German international jurist, argued that 'no nation has the right to any act which belongs to the exercise of the sovereignty of another nation, for sovereignty, as it exists in a people, or originally in a nation, is absolute'.[20] The concept of sovereignty often connotes external sovereignty in international law. External sovereignty is the State's freedom from outside influence upon its domestic policies and freedom of action by the State in relation to other States, also known as sovereign equality.[21]

The third perspective related to the conceptualisation of sovereignty is a State's absolute capacity under international law. According to this perspective, the State's capacity is subject to framed limits by international law. In this sense, *jus cogens* norms become determining for the capacity of a State.

One of the most important reasons for the continuity of the sovereignty debate is the tension between political and legal aspects of sovereignty. On this point, there are two main commentaries about sovereignty:

Hans Kelsen's hierarchical view of law and Carl Schmitt's idea of political sovereignty. These commentaries may be applied to all three perspectives. Kelsen and Schmitt, as two leading political and legal theorists of the twentieth century, dealt with politics and international law through sovereignty; yet their conceptualisations of sovereignty are far apart.

On the basis of his hierarchical view of the law (legal order), Kelsen underscores the idea of the State as the personification of a legal system, but that it is not 'the total legal order that regulates the behaviour of all individuals living within its territorial sphere of validity'.[22] From the perspective of Kelsen, the sovereign competence of the State is the result of legal order; namely, the legal order 'pre-exists the sovereignty of the State and remains in control thereof'.[23] It follows that sovereignty is vested in the State, but it is legally limited. This situation is perhaps best voiced by Martti Koskenniemi, in *From Apology to Utopia*: 'The Prince cannot legitimize his action by referring to his sovereignty if this action conflicted with the law. [...] Even if Bodin did stress the scope of the Prince's authority, he did not give up the idea that such authority was derived from a normative code which remained controlling'.[24]

Schmitt, however, approaches sovereignty from a political perspective. According to Schmitt, the political perspective enables independent discussion of concepts.[25] From his ideal political perspective, the denotation of sovereign has never been interpreted as a person or an institution that enjoys perpetual power. Rather, as Schmitt stated famously, the sovereign 'is he who decides on the exception'. The exception, 'which is not codified in the existing legal order, can at best be characterized as a case of extreme peril, a danger to the existence of the state, or the like'.[26] States adopt sovereignty, which is basically an indispensable feature of the State to maintain territorial order.

The link between Kelsen and Schmitt is that while Schmitt considers that sovereignty is a 'matter of fact-description and law a normative consequence thereof',[27] Kelsen insists that 'the law is normative and sovereignty [is] merely a descriptive shorthand for the rights, liberties and competences which the law has allocated to the State'.[28]

From the foregoing review, it can be seen that there are different doctrinal concepts of sovereignty. Some authors read sovereignty as absolute and perpetual power, while others describe it as the power necessary to safeguard human safety. Hereby, an aim of this chapter is to determine whether there is any conflict between State sovereignty and the protection of human rights. As can be seen, the various conceptions of sovereignty mean that its meaning has never been fixed, and yet the concept of sovereignty endures. In this regard, sovereignty has gone through two main phases. The first, known as the Westphalian phase, addresses the international order of sovereign States that emerged after the Peace of Westphalia, ending the Thirty Years War in 1648. The second phase, which has emerged recently, is the post-Westphalian phase. The latter is increasingly concerned with international human rights and the ability of international law to trump Westphalian sovereignty.

Westphalian Phase

The Peace of Westphalia (1648) has been considered a turning point indicating the end of an epoch and the start of another.[29] Westphalia is a historical fact, and also a concept and a phenomenon. The Peace of Westphalia is accepted as the main root of classical sovereignty, the modern State system, and of the international order. This discourse is widely accepted as the orthodoxy in political science and international law. For this reason, despite some critics who speak of a *Westphalian Myth*, the Peace of Westphalia remains central to discussions of State sovereignty.[30]

The Peace of Westphalia ended the Thirty Years' War (1618–1648) by the treaties of Osnabrück and Münster. These two treaties gave birth to the modern States system.[31] Leo Gross, 'the Homer of the Westphalian discourse', states that the Peace of Westphalia 'represents the majestic portal which leads from the old into the new world'.[32] As such, it is accepted as the starting point of sovereign equality and non-interference principles of contemporary international law.[33] The external and internal aspects are the main dynamics of Westphalian sovereignty.[34] For four centuries, most of the political theorists and jurists (Hugo Grotius, Samuel von Pufendorf, Jean Bodin, Thomas Hobbes, etc., as well as contemporary scholars) have discussed the character and concept of sovereignty in terms of its internal and external aspects.

Internal sovereignty refers to a State's power or competence within its own territory, and this internal sovereignty confers upon the State a monopoly on authority to use coercive power within its territory.[35] Internal sovereignty refers to 'the idea that a political authority or community has [an] undisputed right to determine the framework of rules, regulations and policies in a given territory and to govern accordingly'.[36] With regard to the internal aspect of State sovereignty, the State ultimately is a legal entity which organises certain rules of public life; therefore, the purpose of the internal aspect of sovereignty is to protect the State's own interests. External sovereignty, on the other hand, refers to the independence of States in international relations, as sovereign equals.[37] In this relationship, the State also endeavours to balance foreign relations with other States.

Considerations of sovereignty are to be found in the constitution of the international system. Although Article 2(1)[38] of the 1945 UN Charter signals the sovereign equality principle of all States, in fact this principle of international law harks back to the Peace of Westphalia, by which 'the hierarchical system organized around the Church and the Holy Roman Empire was disbanded in preference to a horizontal system based on the recognition of the equality of nation states'.[39] On this point, the international jurist Vattel remarked that a 'dwarf is as much a man as a giant [is]; a small republic is as much a sovereign state as the most powerful kingdom'.[40] In the legal sense, the principle of sovereign equality was clearly emphasised by Judge Shahabuddeen in 1992 before the ICJ: Whatever 'the debates relating to its precise content in other respects, the concept of equality of states has always applied as a fundamental principle to the position of states before the Court'.[41]

For Benjamin Schiff, the Peace of Westphalia is 'conventionally regarded by international relations theorists as the beginning of an international system based on collective acceptance by governments of the institution of sovereignty'.[42] In the contemporary international system, the notion *nation State* arose after the signing of the Peace of Westphalia. As a result, nation States engaged in internal integration and organisation, through which they effectively created a monopoly, enhancing and improving their power over external relations.[43]

In terms of the external aspect of sovereignty, a number of cases have been heard before the Permanent Court of International Justice and the ICJ. However, the 1928 *Island of Palmas* case is the source, and the most authoritative judgement on sovereignty disputes; as a result, most subsequent cases refer to it. Thus, what follows is a consideration of the *Island of Palmas* case, so as to better understand the external aspect of sovereignty.

In the *Island of Palmas* (*United States of America v Netherlands*) case, the US, as a successor State to Spain's rights over the Philippines,[44] claimed that Spain had discovered the Islands. Therefore, the US as a successor State had sovereign title over the territory. For the other side, the Netherlands asserted that the claim that Spain had discovered the Island of Palmas was not effectively established, and so Spain never had sovereign title over the territory. The Arbitrator, Max Huber, stated that the Netherlands Government's 'main argument endeavours to show that the Netherlands, represented for this purpose in the first period of colonisation by the East India Company, have possessed and exercised rights of sovereignty from 1677, or probably from a date prior even to 1648, to the present day'.[45] Max Huber believed that 'there were unchallenged acts of peaceful display of Netherlands sovereignty in the period from 1700 to 1906, and which [...] may be regarded as sufficiently proving the existence of Netherlands sovereignty'.[46] Max Huber went on to state that 'sovereignty in the relations between States signifies independence. Independence [...] is right to exercise to the exclusion of any other state'.[47] In his arbitral award, Max Huber observed that the right to exercise in question is the other face of the absolute character of the territorial aspect of sovereignty. Therefore, Max Huber held that the Island of Palmas had belonged to the Netherlands. This case demonstrates that sovereignty over a territory can exclusively be held by an effective power which can both protect the rights of the inhabitants of that territory and ensure that the interests of other States will not be infringed. Therefore, this becomes an exemplar case for the external characteristic of sovereignty by unveiling the contradiction between States in relation to their sovereign rights over territory.

The correlation between State and nation is a crucial element of the Westphalian sovereign system, as Falk has highlighted: 'The invention of militant nationalism in the 18th century served to consolidate state power, enhancing its mobilising capacity, as well as accentuating the contrasts between inside and outside, between citizen and alien, and even between civilised and barbaric'.[48] Since the rise of the nation state after the Peace of Westphalia, the sovereignty concept has evolved pursuant to the relationship among States. In other words, the concept of sovereignty is deemed to be significant only when other States exist in the international order. As Janice Thomson has observed, sovereignty 'is not an attribute of the state but it is attributed to the state by other states or state rulers'.[49] In other words, State sovereignty derives from other States in the contemporary order. On this point, Hedley Bull rightly noticed that sovereignty principles have international bases: the principle of non-intervention, the principle of the equality of States, and the rights of States before domestic jurisdiction.[50]

Ultimately, Westphalian sovereignty may be seen as an institutional machine letting States attune to a new political life. As such, sovereignty is based on two principles, namely territoriality and the exclusion of foreign actors from internal authority systems; and Westphalian sovereignty is contravened when external actors impact on, or determine, internal authority structures.[51] However, the increasing influence of international law on internal authorities has come to challenge the very meaning of Westphalian sovereignty.

Post-Westphalian Phase

> *Every new age and every new epoch in the coexistence of peoples, empires, and countries, of rulers and power formations of every sort, is founded on new spatial divisions, new enclosures, and new spatial orders of the earth.*[52]

Post-Westphalian sovereignty should not be considered as a substitution for Westphalian sovereignty but can be read as a re-conceptualisation of sovereignty when the concept of Westphalian sovereignty remains inadequate to interpret contemporary affairs. For instance, the concept of Westphalian sovereignty falls short when discussing violations of fundamental human rights because of the characteristics attributed to States by Westphalian sovereignty. Under these circumstances, a new conceptualisation of sovereignty is required by international society.

The post-Westphalian model of sovereignty is better attuned to address the requirements of the contemporary world order. It must be underscored that the post-Westphalian order does not mark the end of State sovereignty; rather, it is an inception which holds traces of the past. Namely, the post-Westphalian order does not fully abolish the concept of State sovereignty, but this order offers a new understanding for State sovereignty as this section will now explain.

The Westphalian sovereign model has surely had a significant place in the international order; however, continued challenges to the Westphalian model show that the world order is transitioning to a post-Westphalian sovereign model, which tends to set aside the claims of States to absolute sovereignty in an anarchical world order. In this regard, increasing responsibility for, and violations of, international human rights will likely transform the structure of the Westphalian model. Accordingly, Falk emphasises that the twenty-first century will be 'characterized by the challenge of institutionalizing responsibility for serious abuses of human rights by leaders and others in positions of authority'.[53] As a consequence, this situation 'erodes the Westphalian image of a world of territorial sovereign states by insisting that even adherence to the superior orders of the state does not override the most solemn humanitarian obligations of international law'.[54]

Increasing concerns related to international human rights issues may be said to have prompted review of the sovereign power of the State. The world system has shifted from state-centric to international human rights-centric. Since the end of the Cold War in 1989, the influence of international courts, non-governmental organisations, and international organisations over the foreign and domestic relations of States has increased. This period can be named as the age of post-Westphalian sovereignty. As claimed by Bjorn Hettne, post-Westphalian rationality implies that the State 'has lost its historical usefulness, and the new solutions to problems of security and welfare therefore must be found increasingly in transnational, multilateral or [...] regional structures'.[55] In other words, although the State maintains its status in the international arena, its role has qualitatively transformed from the meaning of the State sovereignty principle in the post-Westphalian model.

Sovereignty is a script whose prominent line is that a State bears the legitimate right to apply its authority. An international intervention in a State's affairs diminishes its legal rights; however, international problems enforce the State to criticise and revisit its sovereign authority.[56] In this sense, violations of international human rights can be deemed to be the main dissipating influence over sovereignty.

Wendy Brown has summed up how the system works in a post-Westphalian order and thereby makes a rational distinction between the Westphalian and post-Westphalian phases. In a post-Westphalian system, sovereign States 'no longer exclusively define the field of global political relations or monopolize many of the powers organizing that field, yet states remain significant actors in that field, as well as symbols of national identification'.[57] The traditional concept of sovereignty is no longer a viable concept for considering the State either as an actor of international relations or as a principle of internal affairs. Sir Francis Jacobs explains the ineffectuality of the traditional concept of sovereignty as follows. In terms of international politics, the concept of sovereignty is not feasible; no State can act independently in today's world. The concept is not viable in a legal sense, either, because all States willingly or unwillingly accept and obey the restrictions of international law.[58]

Regarding the internal aspect, Jacobs underscores that the traditional concept of sovereignty is defunct; politically, 'it has been replaced by some form of the separation of powers, often divided between legislature, executive and judiciary. Legally, it is difficult, if not impossible, to identify today a State in which a sovereign legislature is not subject to legal limitations on the exercise of its powers'.[59]

Thus, sovereignty is essential in that it confers on the State the authority to maintain the existing system within its territory; however, the State does not embody power. In other words, sovereignty means that 'the State is treated as the entity that represents a group of people in relation to each other and in relation to other States. Sovereignty is a matter of authority, not control'.[60] Ultimately, in the contemporary world order, each State's main objective is to protect its own interests and its intention is to govern its own territory without being exposed to foreign intervention. States naturally resist giving up their own sovereign rights, but they also desire to be regarded as legitimate actors on the international stage. In such circumstances, States' interests could conflict with each other, leading to chaos in the international arena.

State Sovereignty Under International Law

Since the end of the Cold War, international scholars have raised the question of whether State sovereignty has diminished in an interdependent world.[61] In the sense of contemporary international law, sovereignty may be conceptualised as the fundamental international legal status of a state which is not subject, within the bounds of its territorial jurisdiction, to the jurisdiction of a foreign state or to foreign law other than international law.[62]

State sovereignty is one of the principal pillars of international law. States are the essential actors in the international order 'where they seek to maximize power and/or security, and to pursue their interests in competition with other states'.[63] The fundamental part of the world system consists of sovereign States; thus international law has been created and developed thanks to sovereign States. Rene Provost argues that 'being a system based on the formal equality and sovereignty of states, [it] has arisen largely out of the exchange of reciprocal rights and duties between states'.[64] That said, sovereignty has always been a controversial issue in international law.

Even though State sovereignty appears to be a contentious subject in international law and is demonstrably so in an indeterminate and fluctuating manner, the sovereign State is a basic structure and an intellectual framework of international law.[65] That international order is ruled by

States, international law is based on the relationship between States, diplomacy has a meaning as long as states exist, and international organisations and international courts fulfil their role in the State system; therefore, the sovereign State is the crucial component of the international organism.[66] Provost states that despite 'some inroads over the last few decades, the whole edifice of international law remains built on and around the state. Considerations of state sovereignty mean that each state may make a preliminary appreciation for itself of any situation of fact or law in all areas of international law, including human rights'.[67] The State appears at the very centre of the international system and it can be taken that international law is an invention of sovereign States.

Koskenniemi has emphasised that the most 'universally acclaimed principles of international law continue to be those of sovereignty, self-determination, territorial integrity, non-intervention, and consent, each of which is a reaffirmation of statehood as the law's creative centre'.[68] The field of interest of international law has grown in conjunction with recent international problems, such as fundamental human rights violations; however, international law continues to exist as law which is applicable between States. That said, even though the concept of sovereignty has been evolving, and is no longer unlimited, nevertheless, its core remains intact.

There is a tension between State sovereignty and international law. Regarding this tension, Hans Kelsen claims that the sovereignty of the State is not at odds with international law since 'international law is valid for the state only if recognized by this state, and hence is not superior to the state, is quite compatible with the fact that a state, in recognizing international law by virtue of its sovereignty [...] restricts its sovereignty'.[69] However, there is a structural tension between State sovereignty and international law and its obligations. This tension is evident especially in the case of major national and international concerns, such as protecting State governance over the domestic legal system and avoiding external pressures in respect of international affairs. Accordingly, this tension is revealed when preventing fundamental human rights violations and prosecuting the perpetrators of those violations. In this sense, fundamental human rights is a critical point between State sovereignty and international law.

The 1923 *S.S. Wimbledon* case provides an important illustration of how international law prevails over State sovereignty. In that case, the German government refused, on 21 March 1921, to allow a British steamship, *The Wimbledon*, which was chartered by a French company, to travel through the Kiel Canal which connects the North Sea to the Baltic Sea. The Canal is in German territory and the German government chose to be neutral in the Russian-Polish armed conflict and avoid supporting either side. For this reason, the government refused to allow the *S.S. Wimbledon* to traverse the Canal.[70] The plaintiffs (the French, British, Japanese, and Italian governments) claimed that the German government had violated Article 380 of the Treaty of Versailles: 'The Kiel Canal and its approaches shall be maintained free and open to the vessels of commerce and of war of all nations at peace with Germany on terms of entire equality'.

According to the majority decision of the Permanent Court, Article 380 unambiguously obligated Germany to allow free passage to all vessels without distinguishing between vessels of commerce and war vessels, with a condition that the vessels in question must be at the disposal of States at peace with Germany.[71] The Permanent Court also considered that the 'terms of article 380 are categorical and give rise to no doubt'.[72]

The Permanent Court held that 'the German authorities on March 21st, 1921, were wrong in refusing access to the Kiel Canal to the S.S. Wimbledon'.[73] *The Wimbledon* case reveals some limitations on State sovereignty by deciding that the German government violated international law. Ultimately, this case demonstrates that international law prevails over State sovereignty. Pleadings of the German government were taken to remark that 'the abandonment [...] of a personal and imprescriptible right, which forms an essential part of [State] sovereignty and which [State] neither could nor intended to renounce by anticipation'.[74] In response to this argument, the Permanent Court stated that

> The Court declines to see in the conclusion of any Treaty by which a State undertakes to perform or refrain from performing a particular act an abandonment of its sovereignty. No doubt any convention creating an obligation of this kind places a restriction upon the exercise of the sovereign rights of the State, in the sense that it requires them to be exercised in a certain way. But the right of entering into international engagements is an attribute of State sovereignty.[75]

The Permanent Court, in this case, consented to handle the case on the ground of the concept of sovereignty by stating that any convention brings an obligation and such an obligation requires a restriction of sovereign rights. The Court furthermore stated that consenting to international law is not loss of sovereignty, but rather it is an attribute of State sovereignty; it is a manifestation of that very sovereignty.

The Court therefore rejected the conclusion that placing restrictions on State's autonomy violates sovereign rights. This decision was also restated by the Permanent Court in the advisory opinion relating to the *Jurisdiction of the European Commission of the Danube*, in which the Court stated that 'restrictions on the exercise of sovereign rights accepted by treaty by the State concerned cannot be considered as an infringement of sovereignty'.[76]

In *The Wimbledon* case, the Permanent Court also referred to restrictive interpretation and stated that

> [T]he fact remains that Germany has to submit to an important limitation of the exercise of the sovereign rights which no one disputes that she possesses over the Kiel Canal. This fact constitutes a sufficient reason for the restrictive interpretation, in case of doubt, of the clause which produces such a limitation. But the Court feels obliged to stop at the point where the so-called restrictive interpretation would be contrary to the plain terms of the article and would destroy what has been clearly granted.[77]

Placing restrictions on the sovereign rights of a State is a characteristic of State sovereignty due to States' consent to rules of international law. It follows that entering into international agreements or engagements does not imply the relinquishment of sovereignty. This relationship between the concept of sovereignty and international law was underscored by Judge Weiss, in his dissenting opinion to the 1927 *Lotus* case: 'If States were not sovereign, no international law would be possible, since the purpose of this law precisely is to harmonize and reconcile the different sovereignties over which it exercises its sway'.[78]

Sovereignty, from a legal perspective, is distinguished by 'an uneasy tension between an effort legally to define, and therefore limit, the powers of the person or body who claims to be sovereign, and that sovereign's [...] efforts to evade the control exerted by legal rules [...] or change the law according to his interests'.[79] Sovereign States always claim or decline their sovereign rights in the case of political crisis, war, civil war, and party controversies. Nevertheless, sovereignty plays an important role in international legal and contemporary constitutional theory as well as in politics.

The contradictions of sovereignty are an important facet of the 'very discipline of international law, which is confronted by the analogous problem of how the omnipotent sovereign that creates the law can be simultaneously constrained by that law'.[80] International law and State sovereignty are co-constitutive; in other words, 'international law accords the recognition, standing and rules of behaviour for sovereign states; sovereign states are a key source of international law'.[81] At the same time, international law restrains and conducts State sovereignty. The aforementioned tension between State sovereignty and international law is also found out when preventing violations of human rights and bringing legal proceedings against the perpetrators of those violations. The notion of human rights becomes a crucial issue regarding this tension. The growing concern for the protection of human rights in the international community has led to a tension between the principles of State sovereignty and human rights which will be explained in the next section.

Growing Tension Between Human Rights and State Sovereignty

Because it is impossible to avoid debate with regards to the challenge presented by human rights to State sovereignty, it is best to start with Louis Henkin's conceptualisation of sovereignty and his description of the ideal relationship between human rights and sovereignty. The discussion which follows should be read with reference to Henkin's assertion that sovereignty

> should not mean isolationism. It should not mean resistance to cooperation. It should not mean indifference to, or forfeiture of responsibility for, what happens elsewhere. It should not mean refusal to assume obligations. It should not mean failure to comply with obligations we have assumed. Sovereign states, one has to remind governments, can adhere to human rights treaties, and they can do so without reservations. And they can cancel reservations they have entered.[82]

International law can be distinguished from intra-organisational legal orders by the deficiency of central administration authority, the significance of which comes to light in the field of fundamental human rights protection. The sovereignty of states is identified as the principal agent responsible for such a lamentable situation with respect to the internationally regulated and controlled implementation and enforcement of human rights.[83]

Sovereign States have a role in creating the international norms that serve to protect human rights; however, whether or not they decide individually to consent to those norms depends entirely on their sovereign will; it is therefore evident that there is a tension between international protection of human rights and State sovereignty.[84] This tension is significant because any international intervention in the affairs of a State is fundamentally at odds with the concept of State sovereignty. For those who see international human rights norms as universal values, human rights constitute a serious and critical challenge to State sovereignty, because the obligation to protect fundamental human rights presents a significant obstacle for the State in the exercise of its political and legal authority.

The steady advance of human rights as a shared value is challenging the concept of State sovereignty. In this sense, it is possible to say that international obligations to protect human rights have chipped away at State sovereignty and accordingly an international legal aspect of human rights has penetrated the once-nonpermeable State organisation and today addresses human rights issues within every state.[85]

State sovereignty and human rights may not be in sharp contrast to each other; however, it is obvious that there is a serious tension between these two norms. Human rights have been used to challenge sovereign States by those who would assert that the settlement of a world community that rises above the system of sovereign States is essential to liberate humankind.[86] Adapting the sovereign structure of the State may be the most convenient method of decreasing the negative effects of this problematical issue. Despite Jack Donnelly's contention that 'over the past two decades, dominant understandings of sovereignty have become less absolutist and more human rights-friendly',[87] a decrease in the absolute power of State sovereignty does not always indicate that the human rights situation within a State will improve.

While the sovereignty principle is deemed a basic norm of international society, international human rights norms are regarded as a compensatory international system which aims to restrict and prevent human rights violations by sovereign authorities. International human rights norms draw the line, therefore, with regard to States' attitudes towards their peoples, compromising absolute sovereign rights in the name of international standards of legitimate State conduct.[88]

Given the increasing impact of human rights on sovereign powers, the approach of the political philosopher John Rawls provides an important lens through which to reflect on the tension between human rights and

State sovereignty. He interprets the transformation of State sovereignty from the perspective of human beings. According to Rawls, human beings, as opposed to States, have become an essential, determinant, element with respect to the changing sovereign structure.[89]

In today's world, there are increasing concerns over the international human rights challenge to the sovereign structure of the State. International human rights and State sovereignty are mostly 'considered separate, mutually contradictory regimes in international society'.[90] Kathryn Sikkink clearly highlights the conflict between State sovereignty and international human rights: The 'debate over human rights forms part of a more fundamental debate over the changing nature of sovereignty, since the doctrine of internationally protected human rights offers one of the most powerful critiques of sovereignty as the concept is currently understood, and the practices of human rights law offer concrete examples of shifting understandings of the limits of sovereignty'.[91] Viewed from this aspect, we may deduce that international human rights should be enshrined as much as State sovereignty in international law. Neither creating a challenge to nor decreasing the effect of State sovereignty is enough to enshrine human rights. Given that the abuse of sovereign rights may lead to violations of internationally recognised human rights, State sovereignty may present a challenge to the protection of human rights.

In the twentieth century, the concept of sovereignty was both justified and criticised depending on whether or not the State was viewed as an appropriate guarantor of fundamental human rights and fundamental freedoms, 'supplanting the politically impotent legitimating principle of divine rights'.[92] International human rights norms, beyond their embryonic stage, became highly effective in increasing the role of the new sovereign States in the development of a new world order. This modern sovereign system is best explained by Robert Jackson: The new sovereignty concept is 'complicated by the emergence of a cosmopolitan regime which seeks to establish the legal status of humans in international relations against [...] the sovereign Leviathan. This norm [...] is a reaction to [classical sovereignty]: human rights are intended to curb sovereign rights'.[93]

Over the last two decades, the immunity that States once enjoyed in relation to their treatment of their own people has been chipped away by the increasing legitimisation of human rights and the growing discourse on the importance of international human rights norms. On this point, Reisman notes that international law is 'still concerned with the protection of sovereignty, but, in its modern sense, the object of protection is not the power base of the tyrant who rules directly by naked power or through the apparatus of a totalitarian political order, but the continuing capacity of a population freely to express and effect choices about the identities and policies of its governors'.[94] In response to increasing emphasis on human rights values, the concept of sovereignty has begun to evolve. Although sovereign power is still held by the State, it is the people of that State who designate an executive unit to exercise that power. Thus, it is clear that sovereignty has never disappeared under international law, but rather it has been relocated and applied elsewhere.

For many centuries, the principle of State sovereignty was considered to be both preeminent and unconditional under international law. States trumped any endeavours to curb or even question the absolutism of their sovereign capacity.[95] However, the increasing number of human rights violations obliged the international community to conceive a form of sovereignty which no longer alienates, but rather integrates, the concept of human rights. Following such integration, the State would be unable to exercise absolute sovereignty unless it acknowledges its obligation to protect its people's rights.

States, the UN, and all other inter-governmental organisations are therefore faced with a complicated and thorny question: namely, how to balance two sensitive issues, human rights and State sovereignty. In this regard, Stanley Hoffmann has remarked that the State that asserts its sovereignty deserves respect only as long as it safeguards human rights.[96] When the State attempts to violate them, 'the presumption of fit between the government and the governed' disappears.[97]

As the importance of human rights has evolved and developed, the perception of State sovereignty no longer correlates with the right of kings, governments, presidents, or sheikhs to govern; their sovereign rights depend, in part, on whether they respect human rights in the performance of their duties.[98] Reflecting on this point, John Rawls argues that it is wrong that sovereign power vests a State with absolute autonomy when dealing with its own people. Rawls claims that 'a government as the political organisation of its people is not, as it were, the author of all of its own powers. The war powers of governments, whatever they might be, are only those acceptable within a reasonable Law of Peoples'; it is necessary to 'reformulate the powers of sovereignty in light of a reasonable Law of Peoples and deny to states the traditional rights to war and to unrestricted internal autonomy'.[99]

The sovereign right of the State can no longer be defined as an absolute power exercised within a certain territory. Instead, this right has become a complicated, legal obligation to exercise power ethically. Although State-centric discourse still continues, international law is more liberal and non-restrictive concerning cross-border considerations for protecting fundamental human rights.

The inviolable and inalienable principle of State sovereignty has been gradually challenged by the increasing power of the rules designed to protect human rights. Although some developments in the name of human rights have arisen previously in the international order, the sovereignty principle of the State has taken precedence over human rights. However, reconceptualising State sovereignty has led to a new understanding of the relationship between human rights and State sovereignty. Kofi Annan described this new conceptualisation as follows:

> State sovereignty, in its most basic sense, is being redefined—not least by the forces of globalisation and international co-operation. States are now widely understood to be instruments at the service of their peoples, and not vice versa. At the same time individual sovereignty—by which I mean the fundamental freedom of each individual, enshrined in the Charter of the UN and subsequent international treaties—has been enhanced by a renewed and spreading consciousness of individual rights. When we read the Charter today, we are more than ever conscious that its aim is to protect individual human beings, not to protect those who abuse them.[100]

The focus of academic discourse in this field has evolved from clarifying the conflict between human rights and State sovereignty, to indicating that human rights movements play a crucial role in the evolution of the concept of State sovereignty. This evolution can be observed when fundamental human rights recognised as *jus cogens* norms are at stake. To that end, the next chapter examines human rights which fall within the domain of *jus cogens* norms.

Conclusion

This chapter provides an important opening discussion regarding the human rights challenge to immunities as it focuses on the tension between human rights and State sovereignty. Following the Second World War, growing interest in, and concern for, the protection of human rights compelled an examination of the sovereign structure of the State. Sovereignty may not have a self-adjusting system for adapting to the requirements of each century; however, inadequate human rights protections and fundamental human rights violations without doubt strengthen the power of international law to restrict the ultimate sovereign power of the State. With regards to the protection and endorsement of human rights, the sovereign structure of States no longer embraces the notion of absolute power.

The mummification of the structure of absolute sovereignty intrinsically hinders the development of human rights. If the concept of sovereignty is misapplied, it may protect perpetrators who are responsible for fundamental human rights violations. Hierarchically, it is certainly difficult to determine the dominant principle between State sovereignty and international human rights norms, because sovereignty is the preeminent authority to create and impose laws within a predetermined territory and the State technically holds the supreme power in its own territory. However, increasing concerns over international human rights issues have led to a review and criticism of the sovereign power of the State. Ultimately, it can be observed that considering human rights as determinant over the international system has exerted considerable influence on international law.

Notes

1. Malcolm N. Shaw, *International Law*, 7th ed. (Cambridge: Cambridge University Press, 2014), 144.
2. Jens Bartelson, *A Genealogy of Sovereignty* (Cambridge: Cambridge University Press, 1996), 23.
3. Jean Bodin, *On Sovereignty: Four Chapters from the Six Books of the Commonwealth*, ed. Julian H. Franklin (Cambridge: Cambridge University Press, 1992).
4. Carl Schmitt, *Political Theology: Four Chapters on the Concept of Sovereignty* (Chicago: University of Chicago Press, 2005), 16.
5. Bodin, *On Sovereignty*, 1.
6. Jean Bodin, *Six Books of the Commonwealth*, ed. M. J. Tooley (Oxford: Alden Press, 1955), 207.
7. Bodin, *On Sovereignty*, 34.
8. Thomas Hobbes, *Leviathan*, ed. J. C. A. Gaskin (Oxford: Oxford University Press, 1998), 138.
9. Hobbes, 116.

10. Francis Harry Hinsley, *Sovereignty*, 2nd ed. (Cambridge: Cambridge University Press, 1986), 36.
11. Sir Robert Jennings and Sir Arthur Watts, eds., *Oppenheim's International Law – Vol. I, Peace – Introduction and Part I*, 9th ed. (Harlow: Longman, 1992), 122.
12. Emer de Vattel, *The Law of Nations, or, Principles of the Law of Nature, Applied to the Conduct and Affairs of Nations and Sovereigns*, ed. Bela Kapossy and Richard Whatmore (Indianapolis, IN: Liberty Fund, 2008), 83.
13. G. W. F. Hegel, *Elements of the Philosophy of Rights*, ed. Allen W. Wood, trans. H. B. Nisbet, 8th ed. (Cambridge: Cambridge University Press, 2003), 366–67.
14. National Assembly of France, 'The Constitution of 1791' (1791) Title III Article 1.
15. Timothy Endicott, 'The Logic of Freedom and Power', in *The Philosophy of International Law*, ed. Samantha Besson and John Tasioulas (Oxford and New York: Oxford University Press, 2010), 245–46.
16. Albert Venn Dicey, *Introduction to the Study of the Law of the Constitution* (London: Liberty Classics, 1915), 27.
17. Neil MacCormick, *Questioning Sovereignty: Law, State, and Nation in the European Commonwealth* (Oxford and New York: Oxford University Press, 2001), 129; Neil MacCormick, 'On Sovereignty and Post-Sovereignty: Questioning Sovereignty', in *Readings in the Philosophy of Law*, ed. Keith C. Culver, 2nd ed. (Toronto: Broadview Press, 2008), 418.
18. Saul Newman, 'Introduction: Re-Encountering Stirner's Ghosts', in *Max Stirner*, ed. Saul Newman (New York, NY: Palgrave Macmillan, 2011), 6.
19. Jacques Maritain, 'The Concept of Sovereignty', in *In Defense of Sovereignty*, ed. W. J. Stankiewicz (London: Oxford University Press, 1969), 62.
20. Christian Wolff, *The Laws of Nations Treated According to a Scientific Method*, ed. Thomas Ahnert, trans. Joseph Drake (Carmel, IN: Liberty Fund, 2017), 188.
21. Stephen D. Krasner, *Sovereignty: Organized Hypocrisy* (Princeton, NJ: Princeton University Press, 1999), 20–23.
22. Hans Kelsen, *Pure Theory of Law*, trans. Max Knight (Clark, NJ: The Lawbook Exchange, Ltd., 2005), 293.
23. Martti Koskenniemi, *From Apology to Utopia: The Structure of International Legal Argument* (Cambridge: Cambridge University Press, 2006), 228.
24. Koskenniemi, 229.
25. Carl Schmitt, *The Concept of the Political*, ed. George Schwab (Chicago: University of Chicago Press, 1996), 26.

26. Schmitt, *Political Theology*, 5–6.
27. Koskenniemi, *From Apology to Utopia: The Structure of International Legal Argument*, 227.
28. Koskenniemi, 227.
29. Leo Gross, 'The Peace of Westphalia: 1648–1948', *The American Journal of International Law* 42, no. 1 (1948): 28.
30. Stéphane Beaulac, 'The Westphalian Legal Orthodoxy–Myth or Reality?', *Journal of the History of International Law* 2 (2000): 148–77.
31. Jeremy Larkins, *From Hierarchy to Anarchy: Territory and Politics before Westphalia* (New York, NY: Palgrave Macmillan, 2010), 3.
32. Gross, 'The Peace of Westphalia: 1648–1948', 28.
33. Janice E. Thomson, 'State Sovereignty in International Relations: Bridging the Gap between Theory and Empirical Research', *International Studies Quarterly* 39, no. 2 (1995): 227.
34. Peter Malanczuk, *Akehurst's Modern Introduction to International Law*, 7th ed. (London: Routledge, 1997), 17.
35. Jack Donnelly, 'State Sovereignty and International Human Rights', *Ethics & International Affairs* 28, no. 02 (2014): 226.
36. David Held and Anthony McGrew, 'Globalization and the Liberal Democratic State', *Government and Opposition* 28, no. 2 (1993): 265.
37. Robert Owen Keohane, 'Sovereignty, Interdependence, and International Institutions', in *Ideas & Ideals: Essays on Politics in Honor of Stanley Hoffmann*, ed. Linda B. Miller and Michael Joseph Smith (Boulder: Westview Press, 1993), 91–107.
38. Article 2(1) of the UN Charter states that: 'The Organization is based on the principle of the sovereign equality of all its Members'. UN, 'Charter of the United Nations', 1 UNTS XVI (1945) Article 2(1).
39. Gideon Boas, *Public International Law: Contemporary Principles and Perspectives* (Cheltenham and Northampton: Edward Elgar Publishing, 2012), 159.
40. Emer de Vattel, *The Law of Nations: Or, Principles of the Law of Nature, Applied to the Conduct and Affairs of Nations and Sovereigns* (London: Printed for J. Newbery [etc.], 1760), 6.
41. *Certain Phosphate Lands in Nauru (Nauru v. Australia), Preliminary Objections, Judgment*, ICJ Reports 240 (1992) at 270.
42. Benjamin N. Schiff, 'Universalism Meets Sovereignty at the International Criminal Court', in *Negotiating Sovereignty and Human Rights: Actors and Issues in Contemporary Human Rights Politics*, ed. Noha Shawki and Michaelene Cox (Surrey: Ashgate, 2009), 59.
43. Tom Lansford, 'Post-Westphalian Europe? Sovereignty and the Modern Nation-State', *International Studies* 37, no. 1 (2000): 2–4.

44. By the 'Treaty of December 10th, 1898, Spain ceded the Philippines to the United States'. *The Island of Palmas Case, United States of America v. Netherlands,* Reports of International Arbitral Awards 829 (Permanent Court of Arbitration 1928) at 837.
45. *The Island of Palmas Case, United States of America v. Netherlands,* Reports of International Arbitral Awards at 837.
46. *The Island of Palmas Case, United States of America v. Netherlands,* Reports of International Arbitral Awards at 870–71.
47. *The Island of Palmas Case, United States of America v. Netherlands,* Reports of International Arbitral Awards at 838.
48. Richard Falk, 'Revisiting Westphalia, Discovering Post-Westphalia', *The Journal of Ethics* 6, no. 4 (2002): 319–20.
49. Thomson, 'State Sovereignty in International Relations', 219.
50. Hedley Bull, *The Anarchical Society: A Study of Order in World Politics,* 4th ed. (New York, NY: Palgrave Macmillan, 2012), 35.
51. Krasner, *Sovereignty,* 20.
52. Carl Schmitt, *The Nomos of the Earth in the International Law of the Jus Publicum Europaeum* (New York, NY: Telos Press Publishing, 2003), 79.
53. Richard Falk, *Human Rights Horizons: The Pursuit of Justice in a Globalizing World* (New York, NY: Routledge, 2000), 9.
54. Falk, 9.
55. Bjorn Hettne, 'The Fate of Citizenship in Post-Westphalia', *Citizenship Studies* 4, no. 1 (2000): 38.
56. Stephen D. Krasner, 'Problematic Sovereignty', in *Problematic Sovereignty: Contested Rules and Political Possibilities,* ed. Stephen D. Krasner (Chichester, NY: Columbia University Press, 2001), 6.
57. Wendy Brown, *Walled States, Waning Sovereignty* (Brooklyn, NY: Zone Books, 2010), 24.
58. Francis G. Jacobs, *The Sovereignty of Law: The European Way* (Cambridge: Cambridge University Press, 2007), 4–5.
59. Jacobs, 5.
60. Gus Van Harten, 'The Public—Private Distinction in the International Arbitration of Individual Claims against the State', *International and Comparative Law Quarterly* 56, no. 02 (2007): 376.
61. See Antony Anghie, 'Rethinking Sovereignty in International Law', *Annual Review of Law and Social Science* 5, no. 1 (2009): 291–310; Christoph Schreuer, 'The Waning of the Sovereign State: Towards a New Paradigm for International Law?', *European Journal of International Law* 4, no. 1 (1993): 447–71.
62. Helmut Steinberger, 'Sovereignty', in *Encyclopedia of Public International Law: States: Responsibility of States: International Law and Municipal*

Law, ed. Rudolf Dolzer et al., vol. 10 (Amsterdam: North-Holland Publishing Company, 1987), 414.
63. Thomas W. Smith, *History and International Relations* (London: Routledge, 1999), 34.
64. René Provost, *International Human Rights and Humanitarian Law* (Cambridge: Cambridge University Press, 2004), 121.
65. Schreuer, 'The Waning of the Sovereign State', 447.
66. Robert McCorquodale, 'The Individual and the International Legal System', in *International Law*, ed. Malcolm D. Evans, 2nd ed. (Oxford: Oxford University Press, 2006), 321.
67. Provost, *International Human Rights and Humanitarian Law*, 277.
68. Martti Koskenniemi, 'The Future of Statehood', *Harvard International Law Journal* 32, no. 2 (1991): 406.
69. Hans Kelsen, 'Sovereignty and International Law', *Georgetown Law Journal* 48, no. 4 (1960): 637.
70. *S.S. Wimbledon (United Kingdom, France, Italy & Japan v. Germany), Judgment*, No. (ser. A) No. 1 (Permanent Court of International Justice 17 August 1923) at 16.
71. *S.S. Wimbledon (United Kingdom, France, Italy & Japan v. Germany), Judgment* at 22.
72. *S.S. Wimbledon (United Kingdom, France, Italy & Japan v. Germany), Judgment* at 22.
73. *S.S. Wimbledon (United Kingdom, France, Italy & Japan v. Germany), Judgment* at 33.
74. *S.S. Wimbledon (United Kingdom, France, Italy & Japan v. Germany), Judgment* at 25.
75. *S.S. Wimbledon (United Kingdom, France, Italy & Japan v. Germany), Judgment* at 25.
76. *Jurisdiction of the European Commission of the Danube between Galatz and Braila, Advisory Opinion*, No. (Ser. B) No. 14 (Permanent Court of International Justice 8 December 1927) at 36.
77. *S.S. Wimbledon (United Kingdom, France, Italy & Japan v. Germany), Judgment* at 24–25.
78. *Case of the SS Lotus, Judgment*, No. (Ser. A) No. 10 (Permanent Court of International Justice 7 September 1927) at 44.
79. Bardo Fassbender, 'Sovereignty and Constitutionalism in International Law', in *Sovereignty in Transition*, ed. Neil Walker (Portland, OR: Hart Publishing, 2006), 115–16.
80. Anghie, 'Rethinking Sovereignty in International Law', 306.
81. Jean L. Cohen, 'Whose Sovereignty? Empire Versus International Law', *Ethics & International Affairs* 18, no. 3 (2004): 15.

82. Louis Henkin, 'That S Word: Sovereignty, and Globalization, and Human Rights, Et Cetera', *Fordham Law Review* 68 (1999): 12.
83. Jost Delbrueck, 'International Protection of Human Rights and State Sovereignty', in *Third World Attitudes Toward International Law: An Introduction*, ed. Frederick E. Snyder and Surakiart Sathirathai (Dordrecht: Martinus Nijhoff Publishers, 1987), 263.
84. See Richard Falk, 'Responding to Severe Violations', in *Enhancing Global Human Rights*, ed. Jorge I. Domínguez (New York: McGraw-Hill, 1979), 245.
85. Louis Henkin, 'Human Rights and State Sovereignty', *Georgia Journal of International and Comparative Law* 25, no. 1 (1996): 33.
86. Robert Jackson, *Sovereignty: The Evolution of an Idea* (Cambridge: Polity, 2007), 114.
87. Donnelly, 'State Sovereignty and International Human Rights', 225.
88. Christian Reus-Smit, 'Human Rights and the Social Construction of Sovereignty', *Review of International Studies* 27, no. 04 (2001): 519.
89. See John Rawls, *The Law of Peoples: With, The Idea of Public Reason Revisited* (Cambridge: Harvard University Press, 2001).
90. Reus-Smit, 'Human Rights and the Social Construction of Sovereignty', 519.
91. Kathryn Sikkink, 'The Power of Principled Ideas: Human Rights Policies in the United States and Western Europe', in *Ideas and Foreign Policy: Beliefs, Institutions, and Political Change*, ed. Judith Goldstein and Robert Owen Keohane (Ithaca, NY: Cornell University Press, 1993), 141.
92. Reus-Smit, 'Human Rights and the Social Construction of Sovereignty', 520.
93. Robert H. Jackson, *Quasi-States: Sovereignty, International Relations and the Third World* (Cambridge: Cambridge University Press, 1993), 44–45.
94. W. Michael Reisman, 'Sovereignty and Human Rights in Contemporary International Law', *American Journal of International Law* 84, no. 4 (1990): 872.
95. Vesselin Popovski, 'Sovereignty as Duty to Protect Human Rights', *UN Chronicle* 41, no. 4 (2004): 16.
96. Stanley Hoffmann, *World Disorders: Troubled Peace in the Post-Cold War Era* (Lanham, MD: Rowman & Littlefield Publishers, 1998), 159.
97. Hoffmann, 159.
98. Popovski, 'Sovereignty as Duty to Protect Human Rights', 17.
99. Rawls, *The Law of Peoples*, 25–27.
100. Kofi Annan, 'Two Concepts of Sovereignty', *The Economist*, 18 September 1999.

References

Anghie, Antony. 'Rethinking Sovereignty in International Law'. *Annual Review of Law and Social Science* 5, no. 1 (2009): 291–310.

Annan, Kofi. 'Two Concepts of Sovereignty'. *The Economist*, 18 September 1999.

Bartelson, Jens. *A Genealogy of Sovereignty*. Cambridge: Cambridge University Press, 1996.

Beaulac, Stéphane. 'The Westphalian Legal Orthodoxy–Myth or Reality?' *Journal of the History of International Law* 2 (2000): 148–77.

Boas, Gideon. *Public International Law: Contemporary Principles and Perspectives*. Cheltenham and Northampton: Edward Elgar Publishing, 2012.

Bodin, Jean. *On Sovereignty: Four Chapters from the Six Books of the Commonwealth*. Edited by Julian H. Franklin. Cambridge: Cambridge University Press, 1992.

———. Six Books of the Commonwealth. Edited by M. J. Tooley. Oxford: Alden Press, 1955.

Brown, Wendy. *Walled States, Waning Sovereignty*. Brooklyn, NY: Zone Books, 2010.

Bull, Hedley. *The Anarchical Society: A Study of Order in World Politics*. 4th ed. New York, NY: Palgrave Macmillan, 2012.

Case of the SS Lotus, Judgment, No. (Ser. A) No. 10 (Permanent Court of International Justice 7 September 1927).

Certain Phosphate Lands in Nauru (Nauru v. Australia), Preliminary Objections, Judgment, ICJ Reports 240 (1992).

Cohen, Jean L. 'Whose Sovereignty? Empire Versus International Law'. *Ethics & International Affairs* 18, no. 3 (2004): 1–24.

Delbrueck, Jost. 'International Protection of Human Rights and State Sovereignty'. In *Third World Attitudes Toward International Law: An Introduction*, edited by Frederick E. Snyder and Surakiart Sathirathai, 263–74. Dordrecht: Martinus Nijhoff Publishers, 1987.

Dicey, Albert Venn. *Introduction to the Study of the Law of the Constitution*. London: Liberty Classics, 1915.

Donnelly, Jack. 'State Sovereignty and International Human Rights'. *Ethics & International Affairs* 28, no. 02 (2014): 225–38.

Endicott, Timothy. 'The Logic of Freedom and Power'. In *The Philosophy of International Law*, edited by Samantha Besson and John Tasioulas, 245–60. Oxford and New York: Oxford University Press, 2010.

Falk, Richard. *Human Rights Horizons: The Pursuit of Justice in a Globalizing World*. New York, NY: Routledge, 2000.

———. 'Responding to Severe Violations'. In *Enhancing Global Human Rights*, edited by Jorge I. Domínguez. New York: McGraw-Hill, 1979.

———. 'Revisiting Westphalia, Discovering Post-Westphalia'. *The Journal of Ethics* 6, no. 4 (2002): 311–52.

Fassbender, Bardo. 'Sovereignty and Constitutionalism in International Law'. In *Sovereignty in Transition*, edited by Neil Walker, 115–44. Portland, OR: Hart Publishing, 2006.

Gross, Leo. 'The Peace of Westphalia: 1648–1948'. *The American Journal of International Law* 42, no. 1 (1948): 20–41.

Hegel, G. W. F. *Elements of the Philosophy of Rights*. Edited by Allen W. Wood. Translated by H. B. Nisbet. 8th ed. Cambridge: Cambridge University Press, 2003.

Held, David, and Anthony McGrew. 'Globalization and the Liberal Democratic State'. *Government and Opposition* 28, no. 2 (1993): 261–88.

Henkin, Louis. 'Human Rights and State Sovereignty'. *Georgia Journal of International and Comparative Law* 25, no. 1 (1996): 31–46.

———. 'That S Word: Sovereignty, and Globalization, and Human Rights, Et Cetera'. *Fordham Law Review* 68 (1999): 1–14.

Hettne, Bjorn. 'The Fate of Citizenship in Post-Westphalia'. *Citizenship Studies* 4, no. 1 (2000): 35–46.

Hinsley, Francis Harry. *Sovereignty*. 2nd ed. Cambridge: Cambridge University Press, 1986.

Hobbes, Thomas. *Leviathan*. Edited by J. C. A. Gaskin. Oxford: Oxford University Press, 1998.

Hoffmann, Stanley. *World Disorders: Troubled Peace in the Post-Cold War Era*. Lanham, MD: Rowman & Littlefield Publishers, 1998.

Jackson, Robert. *Sovereignty: The Evolution of an Idea*. Cambridge: Polity, 2007.

Jackson, Robert H. *Quasi-States: Sovereignty, International Relations and the Third World*. Cambridge: Cambridge University Press, 1993.

Jacobs, Francis G. *The Sovereignty of Law: The European Way*. Cambridge: Cambridge University Press, 2007.

Jennings, Sir Robert, and Sir Arthur Watts, eds. *Oppenheim's International Law – Vol. I, Peace – Introduction and Part I*. 9th ed. Harlow: Longman, 1992.

Jurisdiction of the European Commission of the Danube between Galatz and Braila, Advisory Opinion, No. (Ser. B) No. 14 (Permanent Court of International Justice 8 December 1927).

Kelsen, Hans. *Pure Theory of Law*. Translated by Max Knight. Clark, NJ: The Lawbook Exchange, Ltd., 2005.

———. 'Sovereignty and International Law'. *Georgetown Law Journal* 48, no. 4 (1960): 627.

Keohane, Robert Owen. 'Sovereignty, Interdependence, and International Institutions'. In *Ideas & Ideals: Essays on Politics in Honor of Stanley Hoffmann*, edited by Linda B. Miller and Michael Joseph Smith, 91–107. Boulder: Westview Press, 1993.

Koskenniemi, Martti. *From Apology to Utopia: The Structure of International Legal Argument*. Cambridge: Cambridge University Press, 2006.

———. 'The Future of Statehood'. *Harvard International Law Journal* 32, no. 2 (1991): 397.

Krasner, Stephen D. 'Problematic Sovereignty'. In *Problematic Sovereignty: Contested Rules and Political Possibilities*, edited by Stephen D. Krasner. Chichester, NY: Columbia University Press, 2001.

———. *Sovereignty: Organized Hypocrisy*. Princeton, NJ: Princeton University Press, 1999.

Lansford, Tom. 'Post-Westphalian Europe? Sovereignty and the Modern Nation-State'. *International Studies* 37, no. 1 (2000): 1–15.

Larkins, Jeremy. *From Hierarchy to Anarchy: Territory and Politics before Westphalia*. New York, NY: Palgrave Macmillan, 2010.

MacCormick, Neil. 'On Sovereignty and Post-Sovereignty: Questioning Sovereignty'. In *Readings in the Philosophy of Law*, edited by Keith C. Culver, 2nd ed., 414–24. Toronto: Broadview Press, 2008.

———. *Questioning Sovereignty: Law, State, and Nation in the European Commonwealth*. Oxford and New York: Oxford University Press, 2001.

Malanczuk, Peter. *Akehurst's Modern Introduction to International Law*. 7th ed. London: Routledge, 1997.

Maritain, Jacques. 'The Concept of Sovereignty'. In *In Defense of Sovereignty*, edited by W. J. Stankiewicz. London: Oxford University Press, 1969.

McCorquodale, Robert. 'The Individual and the International Legal System'. In *International Law*, edited by Malcolm D. Evans, 2nd ed., 307–34. Oxford: Oxford University Press, 2006.

National Assembly of France. The Constitution of 1791 (1791).

Newman, Saul. 'Introduction: Re-Encountering Stirner's Ghosts'. In *Max Stirner*, edited by Saul Newman, 1–20. New York, NY: Palgrave Macmillan, 2011.

Popovski, Vesselin. 'Sovereignty as Duty to Protect Human Rights'. *UN Chronicle* 41, no. 4 (2004).

Provost, René. *International Human Rights and Humanitarian Law*. Cambridge: Cambridge University Press, 2004.

Rawls, John. *The Law of Peoples: With, The Idea of Public Reason Revisited*. Cambridge: Harvard University Press, 2001.

Reisman, W. Michael. 'Sovereignty and Human Rights in Contemporary International Law'. *American Journal of International Law* 84, no. 4 (1990): 866–76.

Reus-Smit, Christian. 'Human Rights and the Social Construction of Sovereignty'. *Review of International Studies* 27, no. 04 (2001): 519–38.

Schiff, Benjamin N. 'Universalism Meets Sovereignty at the International Criminal Court'. In *Negotiating Sovereignty and Human Rights: Actors and Issues in Contemporary Human Rights Politics*, edited by Noha Shawki and Michaelene Cox, 59–80. Surrey: Ashgate, 2009.

Schmitt, Carl. *Political Theology: Four Chapters on the Concept of Sovereignty.* Chicago: University of Chicago Press, 2005.

———. *The Concept of the Political.* Edited by George Schwab. Chicago: University of Chicago Press, 1996.

———. *The Nomos of the Earth in the International Law of the Jus Publicum Europaeum.* New York, NY: Telos Press Publishing, 2003.

Schreuer, Christoph. 'The Waning of the Sovereign State: Towards a New Paradigm for International Law?' *European Journal of International Law* 4, no. 1 (1993): 447–71.

Shaw, Malcolm N. *International Law.* 7th ed. Cambridge: Cambridge University Press, 2014.

Sikkink, Kathryn. 'The Power of Principled Ideas: Human Rights Policies in the United States and Western Europe'. In *Ideas and Foreign Policy: Beliefs, Institutions, and Political Change*, edited by Judith Goldstein and Robert Owen Keohane. Ithaca, NY: Cornell University Press, 1993.

Smith, Thomas W. *History and International Relations.* London: Routledge, 1999.

S.S. Wimbledon (United Kingdom, France, Italy & Japan v. Germany), Judgment, No. (ser. A) No. 1 (Permanent Court of International Justice 17 August 1923).

Steinberger, Helmut. 'Sovereignty'. In *Encyclopedia of Public International Law: States: Responsibility of States: International Law and Municipal Law*, edited by Rudolf Dolzer, Robert E. Hollweg, Peter M. Lawrence, Steven Less, and Peter Macalister-Smith, 10:397–417. Amsterdam: North-Holland Publishing Company, 1987.

The Island of Palmas Case, United States of America v. Netherlands, Reports of International Arbitral Awards 829 (Permanent Court of Arbitration 1928).

Thomson, Janice E. 'State Sovereignty in International Relations: Bridging the Gap between Theory and Empirical Research'. *International Studies Quarterly* 39, no. 2 (1995): 213–33.

UN. Charter of the United Nations, 1 UNTS XVI § (1945).

Van Harten, Gus. 'The Public—Private Distinction in the International Arbitration of Individual Claims against the State'. *International and Comparative Law Quarterly* 56, no. 02 (2007): 371–93.

Vattel, Emer de. *The Law of Nations: Or, Principles of the Law of Nature, Applied to the Conduct and Affairs of Nations and Sovereigns.* London: Printed for J. Newbery [etc.], 1760.

———. *The Law of Nations, or, Principles of the Law of Nature, Applied to the Conduct and Affairs of Nations and Sovereigns.* Edited by Bela Kapossy and Richard Whatmore. Indianapolis, IN: Liberty Fund, 2008.

Wolff, Christian. *The Laws of Nations Treated According to a Scientific Method.* Edited by Thomas Ahnert. Translated by Joseph Drake. Carmel, IN: Liberty Fund, 2017.

CHAPTER 3

Human Rights Recognised as Jus Cogens

Evolving Human Rights to International Legal Dimension

Human rights may be best understood as the rights one possesses because one is a human being.[1] Human rights have some agreed upon characteristics. First, human rights are based on respect for human dignity. Second, human rights are inalienable, meaning that they cannot be given away because they are bound up with the very fact of human existence and are therefore inherent in humankind. However, though inalienable, they may be limited in particular conditions. For instance, the right to liberty can be restricted when one is found guilty of a crime by a court of law. Third, human rights are universal and based on equality; in other words, they appertain equally to all human beings everywhere in the world, and are not subject to any time limit. As Article 2 of the 1948 Universal Declaration of Human Rights states, every human is entitled to benefit from her or his human rights 'without distinction of any kind, such as race, colour, sex, language, religion, political or other opinion, national or social origin, property, birth or other status'. Fourth, human rights are indivisible, interrelated and interdependent, meaning that various human rights are intrinsically dependent on each other.[2]

Article 55(c) of the 1945 UN Charter also states that:

> With a view to the creation of conditions of stability and well-being which are necessary for peaceful and friendly relations among nations based on respect for the principle of equal rights and self-determination of peoples, the United Nations shall promote [...] universal respect for, and observance

S. Özdan, *The Human Rights Challenge to Immunity in International Law*, https://doi.org/10.1007/978-3-030-92923-7_3

of, human rights and fundamental freedoms for all without distinction as to race, sex, language, or religion.

The international community witnessed a further significant step forward in respect of international human rights in the form of the 1993 Vienna World Conference on Human Rights. The first major international conference in the field of human rights after the collapse of the Eastern Bloc, the Conference hosted an important debate on the status of human rights around the world. The Vienna Declaration and Programme of Action (hereafter referred to as *the 1993 Vienna Declaration*) adopted at this Conference identified human rights as universal norms and emphasised that all human rights are indivisible, interrelated, and interdependent. The 1993 Vienna Declaration, by reaffirming the commitment to the purpose and principles of the UN Charter and Universal Declaration of Human Rights, recognised and affirmed that:

> [A]ll human rights derive from the dignity and worth inherent in the human person, and that the human person is the central subject of human rights and fundamental freedoms, and consequently should be the principal beneficiary and should participate actively in the realization of these rights and freedoms.

Since, at the centre of those provisions or statements is a human being, accordingly, the concept and scope of human rights have an organic character. This concept covers a broad spectrum of issues. The notion of human rights is not only a moral and political concept but also a legal one. Human rights, not surprisingly, have been the subject of an ever-expanding body of jurisprudential literature. Since the UN Charter was adopted, a new academic discourse has emerged around the argument that international law favours the rights of individuals over those of the State and its recognised representatives. A plethora of international conventions, covenants, treaties, and UN resolutions[3] can be put forward as manifestations of this idea.[4]

While the concept of human rights is deeply rooted in history,[5] the idea of international human rights is much more recent. In the past, international law was perceived to be concerned with governing and ruling relations among States exclusively; in other words, only States were seen as subjects of international law. Before the Second World War, human beings had not been regarded as having international legal rights; in fact, they were deemed to be objects rather than subjects of international law. Furthermore, the idea of universal human rights appeared only as an embryonic statement in customary international law and international treaties.[6] The systematic codification of universal human rights 'at the international level has largely, though not exclusively, been a twentieth century development'.[7]

The Second World War may, therefore, be considered a milestone with regards to the development of human rights doctrines after which the concept of human rights took on an international dimension. Thereafter, human rights issues were no longer considered only a national or domestic issue, international human rights were recognised as an essential component of public international law. As a matter of fact, there is a plausible argument for human rights 'being considered as a distinct branch of international law as respect for human rights is not primarily a characteristic of inter-state obligations, but rather a reflection of the state's undertakings in respect of its population'.[8]

The horrors of the Second World War, the establishment and development of the UN, and the rules of the UN Charter and subsequent international covenants, conventions, and treaties have brought human rights to the fore in the international arena and made them the foremost values for the international community. Indeed, the UN Charter was the first to consider fundamental international human rights as subjects of international law. Issued in 1945, the Preamble to the UN Charter expresses a resolution to reaffirm faith in fundamental human rights. Highlighting the problem of inadequate protection of human rights, the UN declared that 'promoting and encouraging respect for human rights and for fundamental freedoms for all without distinction as to race, sex, language, or religion'[9] was one of its primary purposes.

One of the remarkable breakthroughs in international law during the post-War period has been the development of international human rights values outlined in the 1948 Universal Declaration of Human Rights and other international instruments. Modern international human rights law was leveraged when the UN General Assembly adopted the Universal Declaration of Human Rights in 1948. Since then, a set of international human rights treaties and other instruments have conferred legal structures on inherent human rights. The bulk of human rights protection has, therefore, emerged through a number of treaties and other instruments in international law. The organic nature of the concept of international human rights both shapes and is shaped by the contemporary international order, as has been shown. As Julie Cassidy has pointed out, the Declaration 'creates an expectation that certain international standards will be maintained and with the passage of time and the establishment of state practice has become recognised as laying down rules binding upon the States. In this way, it has provided evidence of, and helped crystallise, emerging principles of customary international law recognising individual human rights in international law'.[10]

Anthony D'Amato has argued that 'if human rights norms are part of international law, they take the form of universally-held entitlements'.[11] In other words, international human rights law is an organic reaction of international law against violations of internationally recognised human rights whose aim is to provide legal protection and effective remedy. International human rights law lays down duties and obligations that States are bound to respect. By assenting or becoming parties to international human rights instruments, States undertake and commit to duties and obligations under international law to respect, protect, and fulfil human rights. The obligation to respect human rights requires States to abstain from preventing or curtailing the enjoyment of such rights; the obligation to protect requires States to protect people and groups against violations of human rights; and the obligation to fulfil requires States to take positive courses of action to enable the enjoyment of basic human rights.[12]

Although human rights law has been developed chiefly through the use of covenants, treaties, and other instruments of international law, different perspectives on the position of human rights can be found in international law. There has been much debate over whether fundamental human rights have a higher status than other rights because they are regarded as essential to the protection of human life, welfare, and dignity and should therefore be accepted as fundamental and universal. In this sense, it must be noted that while any violation of recognised human rights necessitates legal enforcements with regards to effective reparation or redress, taking legal action against violations of fundamental human rights becomes highly important for the purpose of ending impunity and paying compensation or providing remedies.[13]

Chapter 1 highlighted the two fundamental interests in international law: States' interests and the interests of individuals' human rights. The contradiction between these interests occurs in the most obvious manner when fundamental human rights are violated by a State, or are side-lined through State immunity, Head of State immunity, and diplomatic immunity. *The Human Rights Challenge to Immunity in International Law* focuses on the human rights-based challenge to such immunities; it covers the subject of violations of those human rights that are recognised as *jus cogens* norms under international law and customary international law. Owing to the concept of *jus cogens* norms, fundamental human rights are endowed in international law with superiority in terms of their position in the hierarchy of rights; by virtue of these norms, they also are endowed with an internationally recognised character and a non-derogable nature. The peremptory character of *jus cogens* norms under international law is now examined to provide a foundation for characterising the prohibition of actions which violate fundamental human rights as *jus cogens* norms.

The Concept of Jus Cogens Norms

Applying a distinction established by Roman law, the principles of international law can be divided into two classes depending on whether their character is peremptory and non-derogable. Those without such characteristics (*jus dispositivum*) are 'laws from which States may deviate, that is, there may be situations where States, although violating an international obligation, may claim circumstances which preclude their wrongfulness'.[14] *Jus cogens* norms, by contrast, do not permit such deviation. Such norms are accepted as compelling and any violation of them is prohibited. They have a peremptory nature.

Jus cogens norms render void any non-peremptory principles or rules that come into conflict with them.[15] Hans Kelsen's approach to international law summarises the peremptory nature of *jus cogens* norms. He notes that:

> [the] power of the state to conclude treaties under general international law is in principle unlimited. States are competent to make treaties on whatever matter they please. But the content of the treaty must not conflict with a norm of general international law which has the character of *jus cogens*.[16]

The concept of *jus cogens* arose specifically as a limitation on international freedom of contract and was often cited by scholars before the Second World War.[17] Indeed, Judge Schücking, in his Separate Opinion to the 1934 *Oscar Chinn* case, employed the term *jus cogens*, the effect of which was that 'once States have agreed on certain rules of law, and have also given an undertaking that these rules may not be altered by some only of their number, any act adopted in contravention of that undertaking would be automatically void'.[18] This individual opinion of Judge Schücking appears to be the first reference to both the peremptory norms of general international law and hierarchically supreme status of those norms to be voiced in an international legal context.[19]

Alfred Verdross brought the concept of *jus cogens* into academic discourse, and his influence can be seen in the 1969 Vienna Convention on the Law of Treaties (hereafter referred to as the 1969 Vienna Convention). Verdross states that a *jus cogens* norm:

> consists of the general principle prohibiting states from concluding treaties *contra bonos mores*. This prohibition [...] is the consequence of the fact that every judicial order regulates the rational and moral coexistence of the members of a community. No juridical order can, therefore, admit treaties between juridical subjects, which are obviously in contradiction to the ethics of a certain community.[20]

Indeed, in 1966 the International Law Commission introduced the concept of the peremptory norm in Articles 50 and 61 of the final draft of the law of treaties.[21] This concept eventually came to the forefront of international law through the 1969 Vienna Convention. Article 53 of the Vienna Convention reads as follows:

> A treaty is void if, at the time of its conclusion, it conflicts with a peremptory norm of general international law. For the purposes of the present Convention, a peremptory norm of general international law is a norm accepted and recognized by the international community of States as a whole as a norm from which no derogation is permitted and which can be modified only by a subsequent norm of general international law having the same character.

Article 64 of the 1969 Vienna Convention reflects the prevailing nature of the concept of *jus cogens* by stating that: 'If a new peremptory norm of general international law emerges, any existing treaty which is in conflict with that norm becomes void and terminates'. In 2001, the International Law Commission also remarked that the concept of 'peremptory norms of general international law is recognised in international practice, in the jurisprudence of international and national courts and tribunals and in legal doctrine'.[22]

These provisions demonstrate that any treaty can be invalidated if its content is found to conflict with a peremptory norm of general international law, because a peremptory norm has a non-derogable nature and is recognised and accepted by the international community. On this point, Allain states that the 'incorporation of the notion of peremptory norms into the Vienna Convention acknowledged the fact that there were such principles which States could not simply legislate away, or agree amongst themselves to abrogate'.[23]

In its Report (2006), the International Law Commission under the guidance of Martti Koskenniemi articulated three types of conflict scenario in which a *jus cogens* norm may become a party to that conflict. This conflict might arise in the context of a regular treaty, a rule of customary international law and/or with another norm of equal rank to *jus cogens* norms. In the first scenario, any emergent or extant conflict of a treaty with *jus cogens* norms renders that treaty or a separable clause thereof invalid, regardless of whether the treaty is multilateral or bilateral. In the second scenario, the same logical track can be addressed to a conflict between customary law and *jus cogens* norms. This conflict renders the former invalid.[24] This scenario may be best voiced by Lord Millett in the case of *Pinochet No* 3 before the UK House of Lords: 'International law cannot be supposed to have established a crime having the character of a *jus cogens* and at the same time to have provided an immunity which is coextensive with the obligation it seeks to impose'.[25] In relation to the third scenario, the International Law Commission emphasises that no hierarchy can be established between *jus cogens* norms *inter se*.[26] It follows that *jus cogens* norms are at the top of the hierarchical structure.

Given that *jus cogens* norms are at the apex of the international legal hierarchy, they acquire supreme authority by standing for the values of the international community and by prevailing over State sovereignty. Article 53 of the 1969 Vienna Convention establishes a norm under general international law and obligates the entire international community of States to recognise that derogation from those norms is impermissible. That said, while this recognition precludes a State from vetoing the emergence of a *jus cogens* norm, it creates a high threshold for classifying such a norm and bases the identification directly in State consent.[27]

The foregoing analysis of the peremptory nature of *jus cogens* norms sheds light on the concept of fundamental human rights that take place in the sphere of *jus cogens* norms. However, before investigating those fundamental human rights, the next section examines the hierarchy among human rights in terms of the *jus cogens* concept.

Hierarchy Among Human Rights with Respect to Jus Cogens

Both State interests and human rights interests are fundamental in international law; however, a hierarchy would be required in order to adjudicate cases where there was a contradiction between the interests in question. *Jus cogens*, as explained above, is a set of principles or rules from which a State may not derogate; it follows, therefore, that the right to immunity may not be claimed when the State act in question transgresses those rules. Since the immunity of a State and its agents cannot be regarded as a peremptory norm when that immunity is invoked to exempt it from punishment for violations of law, a hierarchy may be established to protect fundamental human rights recognised as *jus cogens*.

This emerging contradiction gives rise to the issue of whether a hierarchy can be established among human rights, and if so, how the apex of human rights can be identified. In *Basic Rights*, Henry Shue argues that basic rights are the 'morality of depths. They specify the line beneath which no one is to be allowed to sink'.[28] For Shue, basic rights are a shield against loss of subsistence and loss of security. With these words Shue implies that there is a hierarchy among human rights. Furthermore, he argues that 'if a right is basic, [then] other, non-basic rights may be sacrificed, if necessary, in order to secure the basic right. But the protection of a basic right may not be sacrificed in order to secure the enjoyment of a non-basic right'.[29]

Accordingly, a limited series of fundamental rights, which are internationally accepted and recognised, non-derogable, and of superior character among the principles of international law, is found within a number of international treaties, legal documents, and law reports. These fundamental human rights may be interpreted as having a *jus cogens* character.

Fundamental human rights, which are attributed to *jus cogens* norms, are placed at the apex in this hierarchy. There is a quasi-intrinsic relationship between human rights and *jus cogens* norms. *Jus cogens* norms are mainly associated with human rights protections.[30] Considering international human rights as components of the ethical values that inform the law, Trindade evaluates the declaration of *jus cogens* in contemporary international law as the fulfilment of the minimum requirement of the international legal order that the juridical and ethical pillars of the international legal order be merged.[31] Human rights principles protect the interests of human beings, not the individual interests of a State; it follows that those interests that are protected by human rights principles neither are at the disposal of States nor can be disrupted by reciprocal non-compliance or retaliations.[32] In other words, human rights arguments are accepted as the foundation for the creation *jus cogens* norms in international law. Those norms institute the legal protection for human beings against any other norms that run the risk of violating those particular human rights.

Although *jus cogens* norms, because of their legal supremacy and prevalence over any incompatible norm, obviously cannot encompass every human right, in 1966, Judge Tanaka, in his Dissenting Opinion in the *South West Africa* case, argued for the quasi-intrinsic relationship between human rights and *jus cogens* as follows:

> If we can introduce in the international field a category of law, namely *jus cogens*, recently examined by the International Law Commission, a kind of imperative law which constitutes the contrast to the *jus dispositivum*, capable of being changed by way of agreement between States, surely the law concerning the protection of human rights may be considered to belong to the *jus cogens*.[33]

Alfred Verdross took a similar position when he stated that most *jus cogens* norms are the rules of general international law; they are invented for, and grounded on, humanitarian arguments. Most conventions and treaties under international law, such as the Genocide Convention, are created in the higher interest of human rights, not to protect and defend the interests of individual States.[34] In academic discourse, there has been a trend towards considering fundamental human rights as *jus cogens* norms; as a result, it follows that the great bulk of the contemporary human rights instructions is obviously identifiable as *jus cogens* norms.[35]

This book, for its part, considers this quasi-intrinsic relationship between human rights and *jus cogens* norms as a reflection of the organic nature of the context and domain of *jus cogens* norms rather than considering that all human rights are recognised as *jus cogens* norms.

Ultimately, the nature of *jus cogens* incorporates elements that are fundamentally important for the international community and those elements become more important than State consent, which confirms the validity of norms in international law.[36] Therefore, any transgression of *jus cogens* norms may be said to breach the principles of general international law, including State sovereignty, immunity, and the protection of human rights. It follows that the concept of peremptory norms *per se* may be regarded as protecting the State and its representatives rather than chipping away at its rights. *Jus cogens* norms, therefore, should be recognised as a fundamental and inevitable principle for the international community as a whole.

Differentiation of Jus Cogens Human Rights from Non-derogability

Although the 1969 Vienna Convention does not provide a set of *jus cogens* norms, Article 53 of that document outlines four prerequisites for establishing a norm which bears a peremptory character. They are: (1) the norm must belong to general international law; (2) it must be accepted and recognised by the international community; (3) it must have a non-derogable nature; and (4) the norm may be modified or altered only by a subsequent norm which bears the same nature.

As has been shown, non-derogabality is one of the recognised pillars on which to establish *jus cogens* norms under Article 53 of the 1969 Vienna Convention. Fundamental human rights, of which no derogation is permitted even in the event of a public emergency or in time of war, can be found in various international human rights documents.[37] Nevertheless, it should be noted that the domain of human rights recognised as *jus cogens* cannot be limited to some human rights which are nominated as non-derogable rights on the basis of human rights conventions, treaties, or covenants. Under the provisions of those human rights instruments, appointed non-derogable human rights may be deemed to be a reference point for the designation of the ambit of *jus cogens* norms in the field of human rights; however, the *jus cogens* norms in question cannot be framed or limited by those human rights instruments. In this sense, derogation under human rights instruments and derogation under the 1969 Vienna Convention convey quite different meanings. On the one hand, derogation under human rights instruments transpires within the system; in other words, this derogation does not affect the nature and continuity of the given human rights. On the other hand, derogation under Article 53 of the Vienna Convention is an attempt to invalidate a *jus cogens* norm among others.[38] At this point, General Comment 29 of the UN Human Rights

Committee emphasises that the scope of *jus cogens* in human rights is neither limited by nor entirely similar to a set of human rights designated as non-derogable under the International Covenant on Civil and Political Rights:

> The enumeration of non-derogable provisions in article 4 is related to, but not identical with, the question whether certain human rights obligations bear the nature of peremptory norms of international law. [...] [T]he category of peremptory norms extends beyond the list of non-derogable provisions as given in article 4, paragraph 2. State parties may in no circumstances invoke article 4 of the Covenant as justification for acting in violation of humanitarian law or peremptory norms of international law, for instance by taking hostages, by imposing collective punishments, through arbitrary deprivations of liberty or by deviating from fundamental principles of fair trial, including the presumption of innocence.[39]

In this book, the particular human rights in question are considered not only in relation to whether they bear a non-derogable nature or not, but also on the question of whether these human rights fall into the scope of *jus cogens* or *jus dispositivum*. To put it another way, the peremptory character of human rights transcends the non-derogable nature of human rights. In this respect, the concept of *jus cogens* norms is organic and therefore there is no fixed list of particular human rights that have a *jus cogens* character. In this regard, the Advisory Opinion on the *Juridical Condition and Rights of Undocumented Migrants* maintains that:

> There is no finite list of *jus cogens* norms, because, there appear to be no criteria that allow them to be identified. It is the courts that determine whether a norm can be considered *jus cogens*, for the purpose of invalidating a treaty. Such norms establish limits to the will of States; consequently, they create an international public order (*ordre public*), and thus become norms of enforceability *erga omnes*.[40]

The elucidation of the domain and the concept of the *jus cogens* norms in international law, while it is flourishing, is still far from being completed.[41] In fact, this process is organic and ongoing, as was noted in the case of *Suresh v Canada* before the Canadian Supreme Court, in which it was held that *jus cogens* norms 'develop over time and by general consensus of the international community'.[42]

The following section aims to identify those human rights that have been established as *jus cogens* under the law as a foundation for the discussion of the human rights-based challenge to immunities.

Human Rights Recognised as Jus Cogens

In its final draft of the Law of Treaties, the International Law Commission did not provide definite examples of rules that fall within the domain of *jus cogens* since 'there is no simple criterion by which to identify a general rule of international law as having the character of *jus cogens*'.[43] On this point, Lord McNair stated famously that 'it is easier to illustrate these rules than to define them'.[44] In this sense, it is better to identify particular human rights recognised as *jus cogens* by following the method adopted by the International Law Commission:

> The Commission considered the right course to be to provide in general terms that a treaty is void if it conflicts with a rule of *jus cogens* and to leave the full content of this rule to be worked out in State practice and in the jurisprudence of international tribunals.[45]

I will now draw from international and domestic case law, legal reports, other jurisprudential sources, and the work of internationally acknowledged scholars in order to clarify those human rights that are recognised as *jus cogens* into view. As stated earlier, this book views the relationship between *jus cogens* norms and human rights as a reflection of the organic nature of the sphere and framework of *jus cogens* norms rather than asserting that all human rights are accepted as *jus cogens* norms. Since the notion of *jus cogens* norms has an organic nature, an agreed and fixed list of human rights that have a *jus cogens* nature may not be feasible.

Such human rights can be found in judicial practice since the concept of *jus cogens* was first advanced by legal sources, international case law, and law reports. The *jus cogens* character of fundamental human rights has been reflected and upheld in legal practice. In this way, a set of human rights recognised as peremptory under general international law may be introduced.

According to the IACtHR, the prohibition of torture should be placed within the domain of *jus cogens*.[46] Additionally, the IACtHR, in several cases, stated that torture (in all its forms, including physical and psychological) and other inhuman, cruel, and degrading treatment or punishment together with extra-legal executions are regarded as violations of *jus cogens* norms.[47] Article 5 of the American Convention on Human Rights also recognises the prohibition of torture and cruel, inhuman or degrading punishment or treatment as non-derogable. Moreover, recognition of this prohibition has been approached as a peremptory norm in international case law.[48] The IACtHR, in a number of cases, stated that the prohibition against torture constitutes a form of peremptory norm and as such is strictly forbidden by international human rights law.[49]

Yet another principle that has attained the status of a *jus cogens* norm is the principle of *non-refoulement*[50] in the ambit of the International Law of Refugees.[51] This principle was enshrined in Article 33 of the 1951 Geneva Convention relating to the Status of Refugees. Furthermore, the *jus cogens* character of the principle of *non-refoulement* has been both stated by international case law and sustained by international scholars. The IACtHR, in one of its advisory opinions, asserted that the principle of *non-refoulement* is associated with the prohibition of torture. The Court added that since 'it is an obligation derived from the prohibition of torture, the principle of *non-refoulement* in this area is absolute and also becomes a peremptory norm of customary international law; in other words, of *jus cogens*'.[52] Additionally, Judge Pinto de Albuquerque, in his Concurring Opinion to a decision of the European Court of Human Rights (ECtHR) in the case of *Hirsi Jamaa and Others v. Italy*, remarked that the prohibition of *non-refoulement* is a rule of customary international law, binding on all States, and also it falls within the sphere of *jus cogens* norms since no derogation is allowed and finally no reservations to it are admitted.[53]

As discussed earlier, article 53 of the 1969 Vienna Convention outlines stringent criteria for recognising a norm as a peremptory norm of general international law. As Special Rapporteur James Crawford indicated, the number of recognised peremptory norms is, so far, relatively few; however, various international and national tribunals have endorsed and affirmed that the scope of *jus cogens* norms is not limited to the terms outlined in the law of treaties. Thus, there are extant and emerging prohibitions, including those of torture, racial discrimination, genocide, and slavery, which are recognised and accepted as peremptory norms of general international law.[54]

The concept of *jus cogens* has also emerged in the law governing the international responsibilities of States; therefore, it reaches the very foundations of the international legal order and general international law.[55] Indeed, Judge Trindade, in one of his separate opinions, stated that although Articles 53 and 64 of the 1969 Vienna Convention establish the function of *jus cogens*:

> [I]n the domain proper to the law of treaties, it is an ineluctable consequence of the existence itself of *imperative* norms of international law that these latter are not limited to the violations resulting from treaties, and that they encompass every and any violation, including those resulting from every and any action and any unilateral acts of the States. To the *objective* international responsibility of the States corresponds necessarily the notion of objective *illegality* (one of the elements underlying the concept of *jus cogens*).[56]

It is now widely recognised that *jus cogens* norms effectively bring forth obligations *erga omnes* which engender a general right of standing among whole States subject to the obligation to make a claim if those obligations are violated.[57] The resemblance between *jus cogens* norms and *erga omnes* obligations is not vague; indeed, James Crawford states that *erga omnes* obligations and *jus cogens* norms are virtually coextensive. Crawford also describes *jus cogens* norms and obligations *erga omnes* as *super-norms* in general international law, by which he means 'substantive rules of international law which are said to have some additional force or effect, over and above the effect that a *normal* rule of customary international law would have'.[58] Crawford goes on to argue that 'if a particular obligation can be set aside or displaced as between two States, it is hard to see how that obligation is owed to the international community as a whole'.[59] However, this resemblance does not imply that two concepts are interchangeable. This truth was clearly laid out by the International Law Commission:

> While peremptory norms of general international law focus on the scope and priority to be given to a certain number of fundamental obligations, the focus of obligations to the international community as a whole is essentially on the legal interest of all States in compliance—i.e. in terms of the present articles, in being entitled to invoke the responsibility of any State in breach. Consistently with the difference in their focus, it is appropriate to reflect the consequences of the two concepts in two distinct ways. First, serious breaches of obligations arising under peremptory norms of general international law can attract additional consequences, not only for the responsible State but for all other States. Secondly, all States are entitled to invoke responsibility for breaches of obligations to the international community as a whole.[60]

Although *jus cogens* norms always engender obligations *erga omnes*, not all of those obligations are engendered by *jus cogens* norms, nevertheless, the two conceptions are inextricably entwined.[61] Given that *jus cogens* norms generate obligations *erga omnes*, those norms endow them with a necessarily objective character that encompasses all those to whom obligations *erga omnes* are addressed.[62] Obligations *erga omnes* include fundamental values and interests. Obedience to those obligations binds all States and the entire international community.

An explanation of the concept and term of *erga omnes* was offered in the 1970 *Barcelona Traction* case by the ICJ. In this case, the Court stated that

> [A]n essential distinction should be drawn between the obligations of a State towards the international community as a whole, and those arising *vis-à-vis* another State [...] By their very nature the former are the concern of all States. In view of the importance of the rights involved, all States can be held to have a legal interest in their protection; they are obligations *erga omnes*.
>
> Such obligations derive, for example, in contemporary international law, from the outlawing of acts of aggression, and of genocide, as also from the principles and rules concerning the basic rights of the human person, including protection from slavery and racial discrimination.[63]

The ICJ has considered obligations *erga omnes* with regards to the fundamental nature of humanity. In the 1949 *Corfu Channel Case*, the Court stated that the obligations of States are not necessarily based on the nature of the convention; those obligations may be also based on 'certain general and well-recognized principles, namely: elementary considerations of humanity'.[64] The Court, in an advisory opinion on the 1996 *Legality of the Threat or Use of Nuclear Weapons*, recalling the elementary considerations mentioned in the 1949 *Corfu Channel Case*, referred to 'intransgressible principles of international customary law'.[65] In an advisory opinion from 2004, the Court reiterated the term intransgressible principles and stated that these principles 'incorporate obligations which are essentially of an *erga omnes* character'.[66] These statements of the ICJ and the logic through which the obligations *erga omnes* were established in the *Barcelona Traction* case demonstrate that the Court has endeavoured to underline the actual subsistence of particularly important norms of general international law.

The prohibitions enumerated in the 1970 *Barcelona Traction* case are obligations *erga omnes*. Indeed, those *erga omnes* obligations, which apply to the international community as a whole, have been endorsed by the 2001 International Law Commission's Articles on State Responsibility. As Jean Allain has observed, the notion of State Responsibility has moved away from the concept of international crimes towards drawing a distinction between obligations owed to an individual or injured State and those due to the international community as a whole.[67] In this regard, in 2001 the International Law Commission, under the direction of the Special Rapporteur James Crawford, adopted articles in relation to serious breaches of fundamental obligations to the international community under *jus cogens* norms and the specific, legal consequences of those breaches.[68]

Furthermore, Article 42(b) of the 2001 International Law Commission Articles on State Responsibility indicates that any transgression from these prohibitions entitles an injured State to invoke the principle of State Responsibility. The aforementioned statement of the ICJ, in *Barcelona Traction*, demonstrates that for 'the purposes of State Responsibility certain obligations are owed to the international community as a whole, and that by reason of "the importance of the rights involved" all States have a legal interest in their protection'.[69] Such references to the adoption by International Law Commission of articles regarding serious breaches of obligations *erga omnes* to the international community as a whole clearly indicate that the domain and concept of *jus cogens* have firmly moved beyond the law of treaties. On this point, it may be noted that *erga omnes* obligations are concerned with the enforceability of *jus cogens* norms, the transgression of which affects not only the individual State or States, but all members of the international community.[70]

In summary, regarding human rights, the domain of *jus cogens* norms should not be seen as a closed legal category, and therefore should not be limited to those norms currently recognised as *jus cogens*. This view is reflected in the judgement of the IACtHR in *Cantoral Benavides v Peru*:

> [C]ertain acts that were classified in the past as inhuman or degrading treatment, but not as torture, may be classified differently in the future, that is, as torture, since the growing demand for the protection of fundamental rights and freedoms must be accompanied by a more vigorous response in dealing with infractions of the basic values of democratic societies.[71]

This gradual expansion of the domain of *jus cogens* necessitates careful analysis of those human rights violations recognised as transgressions of peremptory norms of general international law.

Returning to the case of *Barcelona Traction*, the outlawed acts enumerated as obligations *erga omnes* also bear the character of *jus cogens*.[72] Evidence of this expansion of the sphere of human rights violations that are deemed to be violations of *jus cogens* norms can be found in international and domestic case law, law reports, other legal materials, and the works of internationally recognised scholars as well. For example, according to the Report of International Law Commission, the obligations of States to outlaw and protect individuals from slavery and the slave trade, by virtue of establishing obligation *erga omnes*, are recognised as *jus cogens* norms.[73] This perspective was also affirmed in the High Court of Australia by Kirby J in 2008 in *The Queen v Tang* case as follows:

> *In conformity with the jus cogens norms*, slavery is prohibited as a peremptory norm from which no derogation is permitted. This further reinforces the seriousness of slavery and hence the need to define it very carefully and precisely.[74]

The peremptory character of the prohibition of slavery has been supported by academic writers.[75] Jean Allain, for example, states that:

> [S]lavery has attained the level of a *jus cogens* norm [...] [This] means that when violations transpire, they carry with them what in domestic law might be termed strict liability. That is to say that no justification could preclude State Responsibility for a breach of an obligation tied to slavery. One further manifestation of slavery as a *super-norm* is recognised, this time in international human rights treaties where—and leading on from its *jus cogens* nature—slavery is deemed to be a non-derogable right, wherein the prohibition against slavery is exempt from being suspended in times of war or national emergency.[76]

In its Commentary on the Draft Articles on State Responsibility in 2001, the International Law Commission listed a number of prohibitions recognised as *jus cogens* norms, including slavery, genocide, and torture.[77]

Numerous decisions of the ICTY in the Trial Chambers recognised torture and genocide as transgressions of *jus cogens* norms.[78] The Tribunal, in the *Prosecutor v Anto Furundzija* case, further identified torture as both a *jus cogens* norm and an obligation *erga omnes*. The Tribunal stated that 'the prohibition of torture imposes upon States obligations *erga omnes*, that is, obligations owed towards all other members of the international community, each of which then has a correlative right'.[79] An important characteristic of the principle of prohibition of torture 'relates to the hierarchy of rules in the international normative order. Because of the importance of the values it protects, this principle has evolved into a peremptory norm or *jus cogens* [...]'.[80]

Furthermore, the Tribunal, in *Prosecutor v Milan Simic*, in the Trial Chamber II, recapitulated its position that the protection from torture is recognised in conventional and customary international law as a *jus cogens* norm. In the cases of *Prosecutor v. Radoslav Brdjanin* and *Prosecutor v. Milomir Stakic*, the Trial Chambers II also reiterated that the prohibition of genocide falls within the domain of *jus cogens* norms.[81]

The *Pinochet No 3* case before the UK House of Lords is the most significant case to reflect the superiority of *jus cogens* norms over the principle of immunity. In that case, the Lords held that the *jus cogens* character of torture 'justifies states in taking universal jurisdiction over torture wherever committed'.[82] The Lords also stated that the prohibition of torture has the character of *jus cogens* or obligation *erga omnes* under international law.[83] Furthermore, the Canadian Supreme Court, in the 2002 *Suresh v Canada* case, stated that the prohibition of torture becomes an emerging *jus cogens* norm of general international law from which derogation is simply impossible.[84] The Canadian Supreme Court also indicated that there are three convincing indicia that the prohibition of torture is a norm of *jus cogens*. The first of these is the great set of multilateral instruments[85] which uncomplicatedly outlaw torture. Second, no State has legalised torture in its domestic law and no State appears to be willing to admit that the act of torture becomes a method of its administrative practice. Third, as already noted, a set of international authorities have explicitly or implicitly manifested that the prohibition on torture is an established norm that falls within the species of *jus cogens*.[86]

Concerning the prohibition of genocide as an obligation *erga omnes*, the ICJ stated that 'the contracting States do not have any interests of their own; they merely have, one and all, a common interest, namely, the accomplishment of those high purposes which are the *raison d'être* of the convention [and in such a convention], one cannot speak of individual advantages or disadvantages to States, or of the maintenance of a perfect contractual balance between rights and duties'.[87] The ICJ, at the preliminary objections stage of the *Case Concerning Application of the Convention on the Prevention and Punishment of the Crime of Genocide*, also stated that the rights and obligations articulated in that Convention were rights and obligations *erga omnes*.[88] The Court, in a judgement in the 2007 *Genocide Convention Case*, provided that the norm prohibiting genocide is assuredly a *jus cogens* norm.[89]

There are also other violations of international human rights such as forced or compulsory labour, which highlight the tension between fundamental human rights and diplomatic immunity. In 2007, the International Labour Organisation Committee of Experts on the Application of Conventions and Recommendations stated that the 'prohibition of the use of forced or compulsory labour in all its forms is considered [...] as a peremptory norm of modern international law on human rights'.[90] It was then determined that the use of any form of forced or compulsory labour falling within the domain of the Forced Labour Convention 'could no longer be justified by invoking observance of the transitional provisions [Article 1, paragraph 2, and Articles 3–24], since this would contradict the spirit of the Convention'.[91] Although the adoption of the 2014 Protocol to the Forced Labour Convention, 1930, stated that 'the transitional period provided for in the Convention has expired, and the [transitional provisions] are no longer applicable',[92] the conventional definition of forced labour, as Jean Allain underscored, is 'of fundamental importance in contemporary debates, as they set the normative basis for understanding'[93] what this term means in law. The 1930 Forced Labour Convention set out that 'forced or compulsory labour shall mean all work or service which is exacted under menace of any penalty for its non-performance and for which the worker concerned does not offer himself voluntarily'.[94] As it can be observed from the legislative background of the 1930 Forced Labour Convention, contemporary debates in respect of forced labour centre on the issue of whether forced labour falls within the scope of peremptory norms of general international law (*jus cogens* norms).[95] The International Labour Organisation has reiterated the *jus cogens* nature of forced labour; for instance, the Report of the Commission of Inquiry considered forced labour as a peremptory norm and accordingly declared that 'there exists now in international law a peremptory norm prohibiting any recourse to forced labour and that the rights not to be compelled to perform forced or compulsory labour is one of the basic human rights'.[96] However, a number of exceptions to the application of the Forced Labour Convention are found in the Article 2(2) of the Convention.[97] The existence of these exceptions constitutes an impediment to approaching forced labour as a peremptory norm of general international law. In this context, Allain rightly remarks that if 'these exceptions to the concept of forced or compulsory labour were abandoned, this would allow for this norm to establish itself both in fact and in law as a true peremptory norm of international law which would be absolutely binding on States and from which no derogation would be permitted'.[98] Ultimately, considering the legislative history of the 1930 Forced Labour Convention, while it has been argued that forced or compulsory labour has attained the threshold of *jus cogens* norms, at the very least, as set out in Article 5 of the 1926 Slavery Convention, States had to take 'all necessary measures to prevent compulsory or forced labour from developing into conditions analogous to slavery'.[99]

The Restatement (Third) of the Foreign Relations Law of the United States should also be noted, as it lists a number of acts which, if practiced, encouraged or condoned by a State as a matter of State policy, violate the rules of general international law. These forbidden acts include genocide; slavery or slave trade; torture or other cruel, inhuman, or degrading treatment or punishment; systematic racial discrimination; or a consistent pattern of serious violations of internationally recognised human rights.[100] This proscriptive list of principles of customary international law can now be deemed as existing within the domain of *jus cogens* norms on the grounds that any international agreement or policy which constitutes a violation of any of the prohibited acts listed above would be null and void under international law.

States and their agents cannot, in any way, seek legal justification when they violate fundamental human rights as long as the protection of those rights has attained the normative value of *jus cogens*. Ultimately, this book, for its part, considers *jus cogens* norms to be a declaration to secure the absolute protection of fundamental rights for all human beings. Finally, regarding the language of this book, when the phrase violation(s) of (fundamental) human rights or (fundamental) human right(s) is used, it signifies or reads as *jus cogens* human rights.

Conclusion

Generally speaking, State and human rights interests are inalienable notions of international law. Any extant conflicts between those interests engender to establish a hierarchical interrelation between them. Since *jus cogens* norms are vested with peremptory nature and no derogation is allowed and legitimated from this norm, any non-peremptory rule or principle becomes null and void if it becomes incongruous with *jus cogens* norms. As discussed in this chapter, a quasi-intrinsic relationship between *jus cogens* norms and human rights requires us to distinguish those human rights which fall within the scope of peremptory norms of general international law. Therefore, this chapter elucidated those human rights by drawing from international and national case law, legal reports, and the work of worldwide acknowledged scholars. This chapter prised out a number of fundamental human rights that fall within the domain of *jus cogens* norms: prohibitions of torture and other inhuman, cruel, and degrading treatment or punishment; the principle of *non-refoulement*; prohibitions of genocide, racial discrimination, slave trade, and slavery; and prohibition of forced or compulsory labour.[101] It should be noted, once more, that since those human rights have an organic nature, the list of fundamental human rights recognised as *jus cogens* norms should not be subject to limitations.

Notes

1. Jack Donnelly, *Universal Human Rights in Theory and Practice*, 3rd ed. (Ithaca, NY: Cornell University Press, 2013), 10.
2. See Donnelly, *Universal Human Rights in Theory and Practice.*
3. The 1969 American Convention on Human Rights, the 1966 International Covenant on Civil and Political Rights, the 1950 European Convention for the Protection of Human Rights and Fundamental Freedoms, the 1993 Vienna Declaration and Programme of Action, and the 1984 Convention Against Torture are some of those human rights documents.
4. Anthony D'Amato, 'The Concept of Human Rights in International Law', *Columbia Law Review* 82, no. 6 (1982): 1110.
5. The Code of Hammurabi in Babylonia (Iraq, c. 2000 BCE) was the earliest and the most complete written legal code; its stated purpose was 'to cause justice to prevail in the land, to destroy the wicked and the evil, to prevent the strong from oppressing the weak [...] to enlighten the land and to further the welfare of the people'. King of Babylonia Hammurabi, *The Code of Hammurabi, King of Babylon, about 2250 B.C.: Autographed Text, Transliteration, Translation, Glossary, Index of Subjects, Lists of Proper Names, Signs, Numerals, Corrections, and Erasures, with Map, Frontispiece and Photograph of Text*, ed. Robert Francis Harper, 2nd ed. (Chicago: University Of Chicago Press, 1904), 3.

6. For further details see Brian D. Lepard, 'International Law and Human Rights', in *Handbook of Human Rights*, ed. Thomas Cushman (New York, NY: Routledge, 2014), 583–97.
7. Christian Reus-Smit, 'Human Rights and the Social Construction of Sovereignty', *Review of International Studies* 27, no. 04 (2001): 521.
8. Rhona K. M. Smith, 'Human Rights in International Law', in *Human Rights: Politics and Practice*, ed. Michael Goodhart, 2nd ed. (Oxford: Oxford University Press, 2013), 59.
9. UN, 'Charter of the United Nations', 1 UNTS XVI (1945) Article 1(3).
10. Julie Cassidy, 'Emergence of the Individual as an International Juristic Entity: Enforcement of International Human Rights', *Deakin Law Review* 9, no. 2 (2004): 555.
11. D'Amato, 'The Concept of Human Rights in International Law', 1112.
12. UN, *International Legal Protection of Human Rights in Armed Conflict*, HR/PUB/11/01 (New York and Geneva: United Nations Publication, 2011), 14.
13. Theo van Boven, 'Categories of Rights', in *International Human Rights Law*, ed. Daniel Moeckli, Sangeeta Shah, and Sandesh Sivakumaran, 2nd ed. (Oxford: Oxford University Press, 2014), 143–56.
14. Jean Allain, 'The Jus Cogens Nature of Non-Refoulement', *International Journal of Refugee Law* 13, no. 4 (2002): 534–35.
15. Lauri Hannikainen, *Peremptory Norms (Jus Cogens) in International Law: Historical Development, Criteria, Present Status* (Helsinki: Finnish Lawyers' Publishing Company, 1988), 716–23.
16. Hans Kelsen, *Principles of International Law* (Clark, NJ: The Lawbook Exchange, Ltd., 2003), 322–23.
17. For further details, see Dinah Shelton, 'Normative Hierarchy in International Law', *American Journal of International Law* 100, no. 2 (2006): 297–99.
18. *Oscar Chinn (United Kingdom v. Belgium), Judgment*, (Ser. A/B) No. 63 (Permanent Court of International Justice 12 December 1934) at 149.
19. Antonios Tzanakopoulos, 'The Permanent Court of International Justice and the "International Community"', in *Legacies of the Permanent Court of International Justice*, ed. Christian J. Tams and Malgosia Fitzmaurice (Leiden and Boston: Martinus Nijhoff Publishers, 2013), 352.
20. Alfred Verdross, 'Forbidden Treaties in International Law', *American Journal of International Law* 31, no. 4 (1937): 572.
21. Article 50 reads: 'A treaty is void if it conflicts with a peremptory norm of general international law from which no derogation is permitted and which can be modified only by a subsequent norm of general international law having the same character'. Article 61 reads: 'If a new peremptory norm of general international law of the kind referred to in Article

50 is established, any existing treaty which is in conflict with that norm becomes void and terminates'. International Law Commission, *Draft Articles on the Law of Treaties with Commentaries*, vol. II (New York: Yearbook of the International Law Commission, 1966), 247–61.

22. International Law Commission, *Draft Articles on Responsibility of States for Internationally Wrongful Acts, with Commentaries*, vol. II (New York: Yearbook of the International Law Commission, 2001), 112.
23. Allain, 'The Jus Cogens Nature of Non-Refoulement', 535.
24. Martti Koskenniemi, 'Fragmentation of International Law: Difficulties Arising from the Diversification and Expansion of International Law: Report of the Study Group of the International Law Commission' (Geneva: United Nations, 13 April 2006) at para 367.
25. *R v. Bow Street Metropolitan Stipendiary Magistrate and Others, ex parte Pinochet Ugarte (No. 3)*, 1 A.C. 147 (House of Lords 2000) at 278.
26. Koskenniemi, 'Fragmentation of International Law: Difficulties Arising from the Diversification and Expansion of International Law: Report of the Study Group of the International Law Commission' at para 367.
27. Shelton, 'Normative Hierarchy in International Law', 300.
28. Henry Shue, *Basic Rights: Subsistence, Affluence, and U.S. Foreign Policy*, 2nd ed. (Princeton, NJ: Princeton University Press, 1996), 18.
29. Shue, 18.
30. See further Christine Chinkin, 'Jus Cogens, Article 103 of the UN Charter and Other Hierarchical Techniques of Conflict Solution', *Finnish Yearbook of International Law* 17 (2006): 68. Andrea Bianchi reads the idea of inherent connection between human rights and *jus cogens* norms as a 'natural intellectual reflex'. Andrea Bianchi, 'Human Rights and the Magic of Jus Cogens', *European Journal of International Law* 19, no. 3 (2008): 495.
31. Antônio Augusto Cançado Trindade, *International Law for Humankind: Towards a New Jus Gentium*, 2nd ed. (Leiden and Boston: Martinus Nijhoff Publishers, 2013), 292.
32. See Alexander Orakhelashvili, *Peremptory Norms in International Law* (Oxford and New York: Oxford University Press, 2006), 53.
33. *South West Africa (Liberia v. South Africa), Second Phase, Judgment*, ICJ Reports 6 (1966) at 298.
34. Alfred Verdross, 'Jus Dispositivum and Jus Cogens in International Law', *American Journal of International Law* 60, no. 1 (1966): 55–63.
35. Lung-Chu Chen, *An Introduction to Contemporary International Law: A Policy-Oriented Perspective*, 3rd ed. (Oxford and New York: Oxford University Press, 2015), 256.
36. *Juridical Condition and Rights of Undocumented Migrants, Advisory Opinion*, OC-18/03 (IACtHR 17 September 2003) at 32.

37. See Organization of American States, 'American Convention on Human Rights', Treaty Series, No. 36 (1969) Article 27; UN General Assembly, 'International Covenant on Civil and Political Rights', UNTS 999 (1966) Article 4; Council of Europe, 'European Convention for the Protection of Human Rights and Fundamental Freedoms', ETS 005 (1950) Article 15.
38. See Orakhelashvili, *Peremptory Norms in International Law*, 58–59.
39. UN Human Rights Committee, 'CCPR General Comment No. 29: Article 4: Derogations during a State of Emergency', CCPR/C/21/Rev.1/Add.11, 31 August 2001 at para. 11.
40. *Juridical Condition and Rights of Undocumented Migrants, Advisory Opinion* at 80. *Erga omnes* is a Latin phrase that means towards all. This phrase is 'usually applied to obligations owed by a state to all other states or the international community at large, such as the duty not to engage in genocide or piracy, or to claim sovereignty over the high seas'. Aaron X. Fellmeth and Maurice Horwitz, *Guide to Latin in International Law* (New York, NY: Oxford University Press, 2009), 88.
41. Hannikainen, *Peremptory Norms (Jus Cogens) in International Law*, 723.
42. *Suresh v. Canada (Minister of Citizenship and Immigration)*, 1 S.C.R. 3, 2002 SCC 1 (Canada: Supreme Court 2002) at para 61.
43. International Law Commission, *Draft Articles on the Law of Treaties with Commentaries*, II:247–48.
44. Lord Arnold Duncan McNair, *The Law of Treaties* (Oxford: Clarendon Press, 1961), 215.
45. International Law Commission, *Draft Articles on the Law of Treaties with Commentaries*, II:248.
46. *Case of Goiburú et al. v. Paraguay, Judgment*, Serie C No. 153 (IACtHR 22 September 2006) at paras 84, 93, and 128.
47. *Fermín Ramírez v. Guatemala, Judgment*, Series C No. 126 (IACtHR 20 June 2005) at para 117; *Tibi v. Ecuador, Judgment*, Series C No. 114 (IACtHR 7 September 2004) at para 143; *Maritza Urrutia v. Guatemala, Judgment*, Series C No. 103 (IACtHR 27 November 2003) at para 92; *Cantoral Benavides v. Peru, Judgment*, Series C No. 69 (IACtHR 18 August 2000) at para 95.
48. *The Massacres of El Mozote and nearby places v. El Salvador, Judgment*, Series C No. 252 (IACtHR 25 October 2012) at para 147; *Barrios Family v. Venezuela, Judgment*, Series C No. 237 (IACtHR 24 November 2011) at para 50.
49. *Baldeón-García v. Perú, Judgment*, Series C No. 147 (IACtHR 6 April 2006) at para 117; *García-Asto and Ramírez-Rojas v. Peru, Judgment*, Series C No. 137 (IACtHR 25 November 2005) at para 222.

50. According to public international law, 'the principle that a nation state is prohibited from expelling a legitimate refugee to his or her country of origin'. Elizabeth A. Martin, *A Dictionary of Law*, 7th ed. (Oxford: Oxford University Press, 2009), 370.
51. See Allain, 'The Jus Cogens Nature of Non-Refoulement'.
52. *Rights and Guarantees of Children in the Context of Migration and/or in Need of International Protection, Advisory Opinion*, OC-21/14 (IACtHR 19 August 2014) at para 225.
53. *Hirsi Jamaa and Others v. Italy, Judgment*, Application no. 27765/09 (ECtHR 23 February 2012) at 67.
54. James Crawford, *The International Law Commission's Articles on State Responsibility: Introduction, Text and Commentaries* (Cambridge: Cambridge University Press, 2002), 188.
55. *Juridical Condition and Rights of Undocumented Migrants, Advisory Opinion* at para 99.
56. See Separate Opinion of Judge Trindade to the *Blake v. Guatemala, Judgment*, Series C No. 36 (IACtHR 24 January 1998) at para 25.
57. See Christian J. Tams, *Enforcing Obligations Erga Omnes in International Law* (Cambridge: Cambridge University Press, 2005); Trindade, *International Law for Humankind*, 312.
58. James Crawford, *Multilateral Rights and Obligations in International Law*, Collected Courses of the Hague Academy of International Law 319 (Leiden: Martinus Nijhoff Publishers, 2006), 452.
59. James Crawford, 'Third Report on State Responsibility', UN Doc. A/CN.4/507 and Add. 1–4, Yearbook of the International Law Commission Vol. II Part 1, 2000, 34.
60. Crawford, *The International Law Commission's Articles on State Responsibility: Introduction, Text and Commentaries*, 244–45.
61. For further analysis, see Trindade, *International Law for Humankind*, 312–26; Karl Zemanek, 'New Trends in the Enforcement of Erga Omnes Obligations', *Max Planck Yearbook of United Nations Law* 4 (2000): 6–8.
62. Trindade, *International Law for Humankind*, 326.
63. *Barcelona Traction, Light and Power Company, Limited (Belgium v. Spain), Second Phase, Judgment*, ICJ Reports 3 (1970) at 32.
64. *Corfu Channel case, Judgment of April 9th*, 1949, ICJ Reports 4 (1949) at 22.
65. *Legality of the Threat or Use of Nuclear Weapons, Advisory Opinion*, ICJ Reports 226 (1996) at 257.
66. *Legal Consequences of the Construction of a Wall in the Occupied Palestinian Territory, Advisory Opinion*, ICJ Reports 136 (2004) at 199.
67. Allain, 'The Jus Cogens Nature of Non-Refoulement', 536.

68. Crawford, *The International Law Commission's Articles on State Responsibility: Introduction, Text and Commentaries*, 242–53.
69. Crawford, 242.
70. Peter Malanczuk, 'Countermeasures and Self-Defence as Circumstances Precluding Wrongfulness in the International Law Commission's Draft Articles on State Responsibility', *Heidelberg Journal of International Law* 43 (1983): 742–47.
71. *Cantoral Benavides v. Peru, Judgment* at para 99.
72. Michael Byers, 'Conceptualising the Relationship between Jus Cogens and Erga Omnes Rules', *Nordic Journal of International Law* 66 (1997): 230.
73. International Law Commission, *Draft Articles on the Law of Treaties with Commentaries*, II:248.
74. *The Queen v Tang*, [2008] HCA 39 (High Court of Australia 2008) at 49–50 *[Emphasis Added].*
75. Jean Allain, *Slavery in International Law: Of Human Exploitation and Trafficking* (Leiden: Martinus Nijhoff Publishers, 2013); Hannikainen, *Peremptory Norms (Jus Cogens) in International Law*, 445–46.
76. Allain, *Slavery in International Law*, 110.
77. International Law Commission, *Draft Articles on Responsibility of States for Internationally Wrongful Acts, with Commentaries*, II:85.
78. *Prosecutor v. Radislav Krstic (IT-98-33-T), Trial Judgement* (ICTY 2 August 2001) at para 541; *Prosecutor v. Dragoljub Kunarac et al. (IT-96-23-T & IT-96-23/1-T), Trial Judgment* (ICTY 22 February 2001) at para 466; *Prosecutor v. Kupreskic et al. (IT-95-16-T), Trial Judgement* (ICTY 14 January 2000) at para 520; *Prosecutor v. Goran Jelisic (IT-95-10-T), Trial Judgement* (ICTY 14 December 1999) at para 60.
79. *Prosecutor v. Anto Furundzija (IT-95-17/1-T), Trial Judgement* (ICTY 10 December 1998) at para 151.
80. *Prosecutor v. Anto Furundzija (IT-95-17/1-T), Trial Judgement* at para 153.
81. *Prosecutor v. Milan Simic (IT-95-9/2-S), Sentencing Judgement* (ICTY 17 October 2002) at para 34.; *Prosecutor v. Radoslav Brdjanin (IT-99-36-T), Trial Judgement* (ICTY 1 September 2004) at para 680; *Prosecutor v. Milomir Stakic (IT-97-24-T), Trial Judgement* (ICTY 31 July 2003) at para 500.
82. *R v. Bow Street Metropolitan Stipendiary Magistrate and Others, ex parte Pinochet Ugarte (No. 3)*, 1 A.C. 147 at 198.
83. *R v. Bow Street Metropolitan Stipendiary Magistrate and Others, ex parte Pinochet Ugarte (No. 3)*, 1 A.C. 147 at 174.

84. *Suresh v. Canada (Minister of Citizenship and Immigration)*, 1 S.C.R. 3, 2002 SCC 1 at 4.
85. See *Suresh v. Canada (Minister of Citizenship and Immigration)*, 1 S.C.R. 3, 2002 SCC 1 at para 62.
86. For details of all three indicia mentioned above, see *Suresh v. Canada (Minister of Citizenship and Immigration)*, 1 S.C.R. 3, 2002 SCC 1 at paras 62, 63, and 64.
87. *Reservations to the Convention on Genocide, Advisory Opinion*, ICJ Reports 15 (1951) at 23.
88. *Application of the Convention on the Prevention and Punishment of the Crime of Genocide, Preliminary Objections, Judgment*, ICJ Reports 595 (1996) at 616.
89. *Application of the Convention on the Prevention and Punishment of the Crime of Genocide (Bosnia and Herzegovina v. Serbia and Montenegro), Judgment*, ICJ Reports 43 (2007) at 111.
90. International Labour Organization, 'Eradication of Forced Labour, General Survey Concerning the Forced Labour Convention, 1930 (No. 29), and the Abolition of Forced Labour Convention, 1957 (No. 105)', Report III (Part 1B) (Geneva: International Labour Office, 2007), xi.
91. Jean Allain, 'The Implications of Preparatory Works for the Debate Regarding Slavery, Servitude and Forced Labour', in *Research Handbook on Transnational Labour Law*, ed. Adelle Blackett and Anne Trebilcock (Cheltenham and Northampton: Edward Elgar Publishing, 2015), 524–25.
92. International Labour Organization, 'Protocol of 2014 to the Forced Labour Convention, 1930' (2014) Preamble.
93. Allain, 'The Implications of Preparatory Works for the Debate Regarding Slavery, Servitude and Forced Labour', 525.
94. International Labour Organization, 'Forced Labour Convention, 1930 (No. 29)' (1930) Article 2(1).
95. Allain, 'The Implications of Preparatory Works for the Debate Regarding Slavery, Servitude and Forced Labour', 532.
96. International Labour Organization, 'Forced Labour in Myanmar (Burma): Report of the Commission of Inquiry Appointed under Article 26 of the Constitution of the International Labour Organization to Examine the Observance by Myanmar of the Forced Labour Convention, 1930 (No. 29)', 2 July 1998 at para 203.
97. See generally for exceptions Jean Allain, *The Law and Slavery: Prohibiting Human Exploitation* (Leiden: BRILL, 2015), 371.
98. Allain, 'The Implications of Preparatory Works for the Debate Regarding Slavery, Servitude and Forced Labour', 534.

99. League of Nations, 'Convention to Suppress the Slave Trade and Slavery', 60 LNTS 253 (1926) Article 5.
100. American Law Institute, 'The Restatement (Third) of the Foreign Relations Law of the United States' (St. Paul, MN, 1987) § 702.
101. For discussions on whether the prohibition of forced labour is recognised as *jus cogens* norm or not, see the title of *Human Rights Recognised as Jus Cogens* of this chapter.

References

Allain, Jean. *Slavery in International Law: Of Human Exploitation and Trafficking*. Leiden: Martinus Nijhoff Publishers, 2013.

———. 'The Implications of Preparatory Works for the Debate Regarding Slavery, Servitude and Forced Labour'. In *Research Handbook on Transnational Labour Law*, edited by Adelle Blackett and Anne Trebilcock, 523–35. Cheltenham and Northampton: Edward Elgar Publishing, 2015a.

———. 'The Jus Cogens Nature of Non-Refoulement'. *International Journal of Refugee Law* 13, no. 4 (2002): 533–58.

———. *The Law and Slavery: Prohibiting Human Exploitation*. Leiden: BRILL, 2015b.

American Law Institute. 'The Restatement (Third) of the Foreign Relations Law of the United States'. St. Paul, MN, 1987.

Application of the Convention on the Prevention and Punishment of the Crime of Genocide (Bosnia and Herzegovina v. Serbia and Montenegro), Judgment, ICJ Reports 43 (2007).

——— *of Genocide, Preliminary Objections, Judgment*, ICJ Reports 595 (1996).

Baldeón-García v. Perú, Judgment, Series C No. 147 (IACtHR 6 April 2006).

Barcelona Traction, Light and Power Company, Limited (Belgium v. Spain), Second Phase, Judgment, ICJ Reports 3 (1970).

Barrios Family v. Venezuela, Judgment, Series C No. 237 (IACtHR 24 November 2011).

Bianchi, Andrea. 'Human Rights and the Magic of Jus Cogens'. *European Journal of International Law* 19, no. 3 (2008): 491–508.

Blake v. Guatemala, Judgment, Series C No. 36 (IACtHR 24 January 1998).

Boven, Theo van. 'Categories of Rights'. In *International Human Rights Law*, edited by Daniel Moeckli, Sangeeta Shah, and Sandesh Sivakumaran, 2nd ed., 143–56. Oxford: Oxford University Press, 2014.

Byers, Michael. 'Conceptualising the Relationship between Jus Cogens and Erga Omnes Rules'. *Nordic Journal of International Law* 66 (1997): 211–39.

Cantoral Benavides v. Peru, Judgment, Series C No. 69 (IACtHR 18 August 2000).

Case of Goiburú et al. v. Paraguay, Judgment, Serie C No. 153 (IACtHR 22 September 2006).

Cassidy, Julie. 'Emergence of the Individual as an International Juristic Entity: Enforcement of International Human Rights'. *Deakin Law Review* 9, no. 2 (2004): 533–72.

Chen, Lung-Chu. *An Introduction to Contemporary International Law: A Policy-Oriented Perspective*. 3rd ed. Oxford and New York: Oxford University Press, 2015.

Chinkin, Christine. 'Jus Cogens, Article 103 of the UN Charter and Other Hierarchical Techniques of Conflict Solution'. *Finnish Yearbook of International Law* 17 (2006): 63–82.

Corfu Channel case, Judgment of April 9th, 1949, ICJ Reports 4 (1949).

Council of Europe. European Convention for the Protection of Human Rights and Fundamental Freedoms, ETS 005 (1950).

Crawford, James. *Multilateral Rights and Obligations in International Law*. Collected Courses of the Hague Academy of International Law 319. Leiden: Martinus Nijhoff Publishers, 2006.

———. *The International Law Commission's Articles on State Responsibility: Introduction, Text and Commentaries*. Cambridge: Cambridge University Press, 2002.

———. 'Third Report on State Responsibility'. UN Doc. A/CN.4/507 and Add. 1–4. Yearbook of the International Law Commission Vol. II Part 1, 2000.

D'Amato, Anthony. 'The Concept of Human Rights in International Law'. *Columbia Law Review* 82, no. 6 (1982): 1110–59.

Donnelly, Jack. *Universal Human Rights in Theory and Practice*. 3rd ed. Ithaca, NY: Cornell University Press, 2013.

Fellmeth, Aaron X., and Maurice Horwitz. *Guide to Latin in International Law*. New York, NY: Oxford University Press, 2009.

Fermín Ramírez v. Guatemala, Judgment, Series C No. 126 (IACtHR 20 June 2005).

García-Asto and Ramírez-Rojas v. Peru, Judgment, Series C No. 137 (IACtHR 25 November 2005).

Hammurabi, King of Babylonia. *The Code of Hammurabi, King of Babylon, about 2250 B.C.: Autographed Text, Transliteration, Translation, Glossary, Index of Subjects, Lists of Proper Names, Signs, Numerals, Corrections, and Erasures, with Map, Frontispiece and Photograph of Text*. Edited by Robert Francis Harper. 2nd ed. Chicago: University of Chicago Press, 1904.

Hannikainen, Lauri. *Peremptory Norms (Jus Cogens) in International Law: Historical Development, Criteria, Present Status*. Helsinki: Finnish Lawyers' Publishing Company, 1988.

Hirsi Jamaa and Others v. Italy, Judgment, Application no. 27765/09 (ECtHR 23 February 2012).

International Labour Organization. 'Eradication of Forced Labour, General Survey Concerning the Forced Labour Convention, 1930 (No. 29), and the

Abolition of Forced Labour Convention, 1957 (No. 105)'. Report III (Part 1B). Geneva: International Labour Office, 2007.
———. 'Eradication of Forced Labour'. Forced Labour Convention, 1930 (No. 29) (1930a).
———. 'Eradication of Forced Labour'. Forced Labour in Myanmar (Burma): Report of the Commission of Inquiry Appointed under Article 26 of the Constitution of the International Labour Organization to Examine the Observance by Myanmar of the Forced Labour Convention, 1930b (No. 29)', 2 July 1998.
———. 'Eradication of Forced Labour'. Protocol of 2014 to the Forced Labour Convention, 1930 (2014).
International Law Commission. *Draft Articles on Responsibility of States for Internationally Wrongful Acts, with Commentaries*. Vol. II. New York: Yearbook of the International Law Commission, 2001.
———. *Draft Articles on the Law of Treaties with Commentaries*. Vol. II. New York: Yearbook of the International Law Commission, 1966.
Juridical Condition and Rights of Undocumented Migrants, Advisory Opinion, OC-18/03 (IACtHR 17 September 2003).
Kelsen, Hans. *Principles of International Law*. Clark, NJ: The Lawbook Exchange, Ltd., 2003.
Koskenniemi, Martti. 'Fragmentation of International Law: Difficulties Arising from the Diversification and Expansion of International Law: Report of the Study Group of the International Law Commission'. Geneva: United Nations, 13 April 2006.
League of Nations. Convention to Suppress the Slave Trade and Slavery, 60 LNTS 253 (1926).
Legal Consequences of the Construction of a Wall in the Occupied Palestinian Territory, Advisory Opinion, ICJ Reports 136 (2004).
Legality of the Threat or Use of Nuclear Weapons, Advisory Opinion, ICJ Reports 226 (1996).
Lepard, Brian D. 'International Law and Human Rights'. In *Handbook of Human Rights*, edited by Thomas Cushman, 583–97. New York, NY: Routledge, 2014.
Malanczuk, Peter. 'Countermeasures and Self-Defence as Circumstances Precluding Wrongfulness in the International Law Commission's Draft Articles on State Responsibility'. *Heidelberg Journal of International Law* 43 (1983): 705–812.
Maritza Urrutia v. Guatemala, Judgment, Series C No. 103 (IACtHR 27 November 2003).
Martin, Elizabeth A. *A Dictionary of Law*. 7th ed. Oxford: Oxford University Press, 2009.
McNair, Lord Arnold Duncan. *The Law of Treaties*. Oxford: Clarendon Press, 1961.

Orakhelashvili, Alexander. *Peremptory Norms in International Law*. Oxford and New York: Oxford University Press, 2006.

Organization of American States. American Convention on Human Rights, Treaty Series No. 36 (1969).

Oscar Chinn (United Kingdom v. Belgium), Judgment, (Ser. A/B) No. 63 (Permanent Court of International Justice 12 December 1934).

Prosecutor v. Anto Furundzija (IT-95-17/1-T), Trial Judgement (ICTY 10 December 1998).

Prosecutor v. Dragoljub Kunarac et al. (IT-96-23-T & IT-96-23/1-T), Trial Judgment (ICTY 22 February 2001).

Prosecutor v. Goran Jelisic (IT-95-10-T), Trial Judgement (ICTY 14 December 1999).

Prosecutor v. Kupreskic et al. (IT-95-16-T), Trial Judgement (ICTY 14 January 2000).

Prosecutor v. Milan Simic (IT-95-9/2-S), Sentencing Judgement (ICTY 17 October 2002).

Prosecutor v. Milomir Stakic (IT-97-24-T), Trial Judgement (ICTY 31 July 2003).

Prosecutor v. Radislav Krstic (IT-98-33-T), Trial Judgement (ICTY 2 August 2001).

Prosecutor v. Radoslav Brdjanin (IT-99-36-T), Trial Judgement (ICTY 1 September 2004).

R v. Bow Street Metropolitan Stipendiary Magistrate and Others, ex parte Pinochet Ugarte (No. 3), 1 A.C. 147 (House of Lords 2000).

Reservations to the Convention on Genocide, Advisory Opinion, ICJ Reports 15 (1951).

Reus-Smit, Christian. 'Human Rights and the Social Construction of Sovereignty'. *Review of International Studies* 27, no. 04 (2001): 519–38.

Rights and Guarantees of Children in the Context of Migration and/or in Need of International Protection, Advisory Opinion, OC-21/14 (IACtHR 19 August 2014).

Shelton, Dinah. 'Normative Hierarchy in International Law'. *American Journal of International Law* 100, no. 2 (2006): 291–323.

Shue, Henry. *Basic Rights: Subsistence, Affluence, and U.S. Foreign Policy*. 2nd ed. Princeton, NJ: Princeton University Press, 1996.

Smith, Rhona K. M. 'Human Rights in International Law'. In *Human Rights: Politics and Practice*, edited by Michael Goodhart, 2nd ed., 58–74. Oxford: Oxford University Press, 2013.

South West Africa (Liberia v. South Africa), Second Phase, Judgment, ICJ Reports 6 (1966).

Suresh v. Canada (Minister of Citizenship and Immigration), 1 S.C.R. 3, 2002 SCC 1 (Canada: Supreme Court 2002).

Tams, Christian J. *Enforcing Obligations Erga Omnes in International Law*. Cambridge: Cambridge University Press, 2005.

The Massacres of El Mozote and nearby places v. El Salvador, Judgment, Series C No. 252 (IACtHR 25 October 2012).
The Queen v Tang, [2008] HCA 39 (High Court of Australia 2008).
Tibi v. Ecuador, Judgment, Series C No. 114 (IACtHR 7 September 2004).
Trindade, Antônio Augusto Cançado. *International Law for Humankind: Towards a New Jus Gentium*. 2nd ed. Leiden and Boston: Martinus Nijhoff Publishers, 2013.
Tzanakopoulos, Antonios. 'The Permanent Court of International Justice and the "International Community"'. In *Legacies of the Permanent Court of International Justice*, edited by Christian J. Tams and Malgosia Fitzmaurice, 339–60. Leiden and Boston: Martinus Nijhoff Publishers, 2013.
UN. Charter of the United Nations, 1 UNTS XVI (1945).
———. *International Legal Protection of Human Rights in Armed Conflict*. HR/PUB/11/01. New York and Geneva: United Nations Publication, 2011.
UN General Assembly. International Covenant on Civil and Political Rights, UNTS 999 (1966).
UN Human Rights Committee. 'CCPR General Comment No. 29: Article 4: Derogations during a State of Emergency'. CCPR/C/21/Rev.1/Add.11, 31 August 2001.
Verdross, Alfred. 'Forbidden Treaties in International Law'. *American Journal of International Law* 31, no. 4 (1937): 571–77.
———. 'Jus Dispositivum and Jus Cogens in International Law'. *American Journal of International Law* 60, no. 1 (1966): 55–63.
Zemanek, Karl. 'New Trends in the Enforcement of Erga Omnes Obligations'. *Max Planck Yearbook of United Nations Law* 4 (2000): 1–52.

CHAPTER 4

State Immunity or State Impunity in Cases of Jus Cogens Violations

The issue of sovereign immunity dates back to the ancient credo that *the King can do no wrong*. Its origin is likely correlated to the concept of absolute sovereignty. Sovereignty has never vanished from international law, but its structure and meaning have been constantly evolving. The traditional concept of sovereignty has undergone 'ceaseless modification and re-negotiation in the face of material forces in world politics, institution-building inter-disciplinary struggle and theoretical contestation'.[1] If State immunity stems from State sovereignty, its denotation and effect must be connected with the current scope of State sovereignty. If *jus cogens* violations committed under international law are in question, the concept of State sovereignty and the principle of *par in parem non habet imperium* (equals do not have authority over one another)[2] cannot create any obstacles to external investigation. These *jus cogens* violations become a more complicated issue than the extent to which they are consistent with the law of one State. In the last instance, these *jus cogens* violations bear upon the whole international community.

Historically, the essential purpose of vesting immunity in the ruler was to maintain the absolute sovereign structure of the State and to defend the State's territory and domestic interests from foreign interventions. Before sovereign States came into being, proto-States had been recognised as exceptional institutions which had special privileges that prevented them from facing prosecution by other quasi-State entities.[3] Despite its very old

S. Özdan, *The Human Rights Challenge to Immunity in International Law*, https://doi.org/10.1007/978-3-030-92923-7_4

history and the legal or natural necessity for jurisdictional immunities, the law of State immunity has not settled under contemporary international law; in other words, the 'law of State immunity is not static'.[4]

State immunity remains primarily a restriction placed on the jurisdictional competence of domestic courts by international law; it follows that these domestic courts remain unable to be involved in certain pleas that are directed at a foreign State. In this sense, State immunity will be a bar against exercising jurisdiction in particular cases.

As State immunity is a rule of customary international law it may be deduced that it is only an exception to the domestic jurisdiction of the State and the principle of territorial sovereignty. Be that as it may, the extent of State immunity has been undeniably eroded since the Second World War, to the extent that international law has transformed from a State-centric approach towards a human-centric approach which protects the fundamental values related to international human rights. The changing and expanding problems at both the national and international level have forced the international community to probe the issue of State immunity. As a consequence, international law now incorporates and considers not only the interests embodied in the concept of State immunity, but also the protection of fundamental human rights. Under international law, there are obviously two interests that directly affect the State. International law must pursue the balance between bestowing immunity on the State and protecting human rights. As recent cases (e.g. *Jurisdictional Immunities of the State*[5]) demonstrate, however, this balance is mostly lost in favour of the State, and the granting of immunity remains a significant bar to justice and compensation for victims of violations of human rights. The granting of immunity to the State may cause impunity from jurisdiction in cases in which *jus cogens* human rights have been violated. Ultimately, the distinction between State immunity and State impunity must be made through an international legal order.

This chapter examines the principle of State immunity and its origins. It looks at the controversial exceptions to State immunity and subsequently analyses the tension between the violation of fundamental human rights and the preservation of State immunity by considering a landmark judgement by the ICJ (*Jurisdictional Immunities of the State*). At the heart of this chapter lies a significant argument: State immunity should not equate to State impunity when fundamental human rights norms are violated.

Bases of State Immunity

Considering the basis of jurisdictional immunities, State immunity cannot be grounded on only one principle or rule. Although State immunity can be based on a wide variety of factors, once immunity is established it is important to examine closely its specific basis to ensure it is justified in law.

A number of texts are important when analysing the sources from which State immunity is derived. Xiaodong Yang argues that immunity cannot be derived from the concept of sovereignty, nor does it originate from the principle of *par in parem non habet imperium*, for two reasons. The first is that it is extremely difficult, if not impossible, to claim that 'immunity stems from sovereignty, but not from independence, or equality, or dignity'.[6] As evidence, Yang refers to the following statement by Lord Wilberforce in *I Congresso del Partido*:

> To require a state to answer a claim based upon such [commercial or other private law] transactions does not involve a challenge to or inquiry into any act of sovereignty or governmental act of that state. It is, in accepted phrases, neither a threat to the dignity of that state, nor any interference with its sovereign functions.[7]

Yang also demonstrates that the principle of *par in parem non habet imperium* is indeed based on canon law and this principle was originally the basis for the relationship between successive rulers in different ages. Therefore, Yang asserts, the origin of this principle is not directly linked in any way to State immunity and international law. Yang believes that the developing body of case law and the decisions of international courts are crucial technical factors for the legal basis of immunity.[8]

Some scholars approach the sources of State immunity from another perspective, which concentrates overwhelmingly on the principle of sovereign equality. Jürgen Bröhmer emphasises that the sovereignty concept and the principle of State equality are the primary bases on which State immunity is established and developed.[9] In this sense, Shaw pointed out that the rule of State immunity, which occupies an important place in international relations and is essential to ensure enforcement of customary international law, derives in fact from the principle of the sovereign equality of States, although questions of State immunity emerge most frequently in domestic courts.[10]

In the contemporary international order, 'the institution of sovereign immunity constitutes a consequence of the sovereignty, independence and equality of nations, whilst its aim is to avoid the disturbance of international relations'.[11] The concept of State immunity is mainly interpreted as an important and inevitable privilege vested in foreign States by the forum State.[12] That being the case, Lee Caplan designates the departure point for State immunity which provides privilege to States under necessary conditions as 'the forum state's waiver of adjudicatory jurisdiction with the aim of promoting mutually beneficial interstate relations'.[13] It follows that the principle of sovereign equality does not compel the State to claim immunity.

However, the practical basis of State immunity should be considered as well as its theoretical basis. While the latter reflects the history of State immunity and includes no significant exceptions, the practical basis reflects the legal aspects of State immunity that are derived from various technical points in case law. Furthermore, the practical basis for immunity reflects some exceptional situations arising out of contemporary international problems. These problems cannot be explained or resolved without reference to the theoretical basis of State immunity.

In theory, State immunity derives from State sovereignty. State sovereignty becomes an important concept for the principle of *par in parem non habet imperium*, which in this context means one Sovereign cannot exercise his or her authority over another via its legal system. This principle informs the concept of sovereign equality, which Edwin DeWitt Dickinson states 'means nothing more nor less than that each state may exercise equally with others all rights that are based upon its existence as a state in the international society'.[14] The principle of *par in parem non habet imperium* is stated in the explanatory report of the Council of Europe with regard to State immunity: 'State immunity is a concept of international law, which has developed out of the principle *par in parem non habet imperium*, by virtue of which one State is not subject to the jurisdiction of another State'.[15]

In terms of its practical basis, State immunity can be understood on the basis of case law, customary international law, and treaty law. The current play of State immunity has been established in large part as a result of the findings of domestic courts in proceedings against foreign States. It is an established principle of customary international law that a State enjoys immunity from the jurisdiction of the foreign States' courts.

On this basis, State immunity has evolved in both domestic and international courts. In 1812 *The Schooner Exchange*[16] became the first reference point from a technical perspective for the practical basis of State immunity. *The Schooner Exchange* case also reflects the absolute aspect of State immunity, which will be discussed in further detail in this chapter. In international legislation, State immunity is based on two specific treaties, the regional 1972 European Convention on State Immunity and the 2004 UN Convention on Jurisdictional Immunities of States and their Property, as well as customary international law. These conventions were established to provide direction to domestic courts.[17] This is rather important as the principles and rules of State immunity have developed from 'within the States, not between them; that is, such rules are primarily the result of hundreds of cases decided by various domestic courts in their handling of claims brought against foreign States'.[18]

State Immunity Under International Law

In international law, State immunity refers to 'the legal rules and principles determining the conditions under which a foreign state may claim freedom from the jurisdiction of another state'.[19] The decisions of international and national courts in relation to State immunity are very important in crystallising issues of State immunity for the future. These decisions may raise some challenging points as well. Therefore, the law of State immunity should be clearly and deeply examined. In this sense, it should be noted that the 2004 UN Convention on Jurisdictional Immunities of States and their Property is central to the law on State immunity.[20] That said, international and national legislation on State immunity must be considered in reference to State practice.

State immunity is based on the common law principle that *the King can do no wrong*. Each State is vested with coercive powers and every State enjoys jurisdictional immunity on its own property from the proceedings of other States' courts; it follows that a State cannot be sued in the courts of foreign States unless the State gives its express consent. State immunity appears as the exclusive jurisdiction of the State and its own territory; therefore, a forum State needs express licence to exercise its national jurisdiction. The adjudications of State immunity manage and govern the scope of a State which claims to be free from the jurisdiction of a court in another State. A distinction between immunity and jurisdictional immunity should be made at this point. Immunity from execution is different from jurisdictional immunity, as immunity from execution restrains a national court's enforcement authority, while jurisdictional immunity limits the adjudicatory power of the national court.[21]

State immunity protects a foreign State from being sued or being a party to legal proceedings, and therefore 'prevents the subjection of an independent State to proceedings in another country relating to a dispute about its exercise of governmental power'.[22] Lord Browne-Wilkinson clarified the meaning of State immunity when he observed that it 'is a basic principle of international law that one sovereign state (the forum state) does not adjudicate on the conduct of a foreign state. The foreign state is entitled to procedural immunity from the processes of the forum state. This immunity extends to both criminal and civil liability'.[23]

State immunity rules have been evident in the legal practice of individual States since the nineteenth century. Municipal courts played a crucial role in establishing the rules of State immunity, and American courts became the first place (in point of time) where the doctrine of State immunity began to be mapped out. The judgement of Chief Justice Marshall in *The Schooner Exchange* has been recognised as the first judicial statement of the absolute immunity doctrine.[24] The general principle of foreign State immunity is accordingly based on the *Schooner Exchange* case in 1812, which became the *locus classicus* (an authoritative reference for a certain doctrine[25]) of the State immunity doctrine.[26]

In the *Schooner Exchange* case, the United States Supreme Court held that United States courts had no jurisdiction over a vessel which belongs to another nationality in United States ports. This decision was based on the State immunity principle.[27] While the *Schooner Exchange* may be the point of origin of State immunity, the process through which State immunity has developed and its current position in international law cannot be understood by reference to the *Schooner Exchange* alone, because the circumstances in the eighteenth century were substantially different from those of the present. Furthermore, in the *Schooner Exchange* case there was no legal basis for the vesting of State immunity, because there was no precedent set beforehand; in other words, there was no existing legal rule to apply.[28]

The historic decision of Chief Justice Marshall formulated State immunity as follows:

> This perfect equality and absolute independence of sovereigns, and this common interest impelling them to mutual intercourse, and an exchange of

> good offices with each other, have given rise to a class of cases in which every sovereign is understood to waive the exercise of a part of that complete exclusive territorial jurisdiction, which has been stated to be the attribute of every nation.[29]

State immunity is believed to have evolved in response to the requirements of both national and international systems. As part of the process which has transformed the concept and limitations of immunity, the protection it affords has transferred from the Prince to the State. Accordingly, the United States Court of Appeals observed in 1964 that the doctrine of State immunity

> originated in an era of personal sovereignty, when kings could theoretically do no wrong and when the exercise of authority by one sovereign over another indicated hostility or superiority. With the passing of that era, sovereign immunity has been retained by the courts chiefly to avoid possible embarrassment to those responsible for the conduct of the nation's foreign relations.[30]

Article 5 of the UN Convention on State Immunity states: 'A State enjoys immunity, in respect of itself and its property, from the jurisdiction of the courts of another State'.[31] The principle of State immunity thus acts as an obstacle to suing a foreign State in national courts. The principle of State immunity is a crucial concept for developing international law based on sovereign equality, because this principle applies to each State and therefore appears to be a neutral way of 'denying jurisdiction to States over the international administration of another State and diverting claims to settlement in the courts of that State'.[32]

Absolute and Restrictive Immunity

A review of the law of State immunity uncovers the existing conflict between two concepts of sovereign immunity: one which holds it to be absolute and another which holds it to be limited. According to the absolute theory, a sovereign cannot be sued in the courts of another sovereign; by contrast, the restrictive theory maintains that sovereign immunity is vested for sovereign or public acts (*jure imperii*) of the State, but not vested for non-sovereign or private acts (*jure gestionis*) of the State.

Until relatively recently, the concept of State sovereignty was considered as pertaining to a particular individual in a State rather than as an abstract demonstration of the State's power and existence. The Sovereign 'was a definable person, to whom allegiance was due'.[33] Thereby, the sovereign State could not be subjected to the judicial procedure of his country; and accordingly, the sovereign State could not be brought to the justice before a foreign court.

During the eighteenth and nineteenth centuries, the concept of absolute immunity clearly emerged in international law. Absolute sovereign immunity means that the State, government, or sovereign is 'completely immune from foreign jurisdiction in all cases regardless of circumstances'.[34] In the current international order, however, no form of State immunity is absolute, because of the many exceptions and derogations which apply. In fact, in 1963 the absolute doctrine of State immunity was criticised by the German Constitutional Court in the following terms:

> In the period up to the First World War the clearly preponderant State practice was to grant unlimited immunity to foreign States [...] Since then, however, State immunity has been involved in a process of contraction [and] its history has become the history of the struggle over the number, nature and extent of the exceptions.[35]

As a consequence, the language of modern international law avoids the term in all cases irrespective of circumstances to explain when the State can be immune from foreign jurisdiction.

Absolute Theory

Absolute sovereign immunity shields and ensures the immunity rights of the State before another State's court in respect of both private and public acts of the State. Absolute immunity also provides that a suit is unlikely to be brought against a sovereign State in a foreign court unless it gives consent and abdicates its sovereign rights. With regard to the functions of absolute immunity and considering the Westphalian concept of State sovereignty, in the nineteenth century, absolute sovereign immunity was a protective legal discourse ideally suited to sovereign States.[36]

As noted, the absolute theory of foreign sovereign immunity was first propounded in *The Schooner Exchange* case. The absolute theory was grounded on the restricted role which sovereign States played at that time.

The formulation of a general rule of sovereign immunity was originally founded on the absolute theory of State immunity whereby a foreign State or sovereign could not be prosecuted (i.e. brought before a foreign State's court) without consideration of the nature of the State's act (whether public or private). However, *The Schooner Exchange* case was decided in a period when the 'critical functions of governments [...] were geared essentially to political activities. Their concern was limited more or less exclusively to problems of internal administration or to the pursuit of diplomatic and military objectives'.[37] For this reason States were completely involved in governmental or political deeds, and therefore the doctrine of sovereign immunity was invoked on all occasions involving foreign States.[38] Chief Justice Marshall established a legal principle that a foreign sovereign bears absolute immunity rights:

> the jurisdiction of the nation within its own territory is necessarily exclusive and absolute. It is susceptible of no limitation not imposed by itself. Any restriction upon it deriving validity from an external source would imply a diminution of its sovereignty to the extent of the restriction [...] in that power which could impose such restriction. All exceptions, therefore, to the full and complete power of a nation within its own territories must be traced up to the consent of the nation itself. They can flow from no other sources.[39]

Immediately after this statement, Justice Marshall made reference to the doctrine of perfect equality and absolute independence[40] between States, according to which all States should grant State immunity to each other. In this sense, it 'has become an established rule that between two equals, one cannot exercise sovereign will or power over the other, *par in parem non habet imperium*'.[41] Vested immunity rights to States cannot be ignored unless a State consents to waive its sovereign immunity rights.

The absolute doctrine was implied in English law by Lord Atkin, in 1938 in *The Cristina* case as follows:

> The foundation for the application to set aside the writ and arrest of the ship is to be found in two propositions of international law engrafted into our domestic law which seems to me to be well established and to be beyond dispute. The first is that the courts of a country will not implead a foreign sovereign, that is, they will not by their process make him against his will a party to legal proceedings whether the proceedings involve process against his person or seek to recover from him specific property or damages. The second is that they will not by their process, whether the sovereign is a party

> to the proceedings or not, seize or detain property which is his or of which he is possession or control.[42]

Three essential points concerning the rule of absolute sovereign immunity arise from this statement: first, the connotation of the State as an entity symbolising a foreign sovereign which therefore cannot be directly impleaded; second, the connotation of 'State property, because under the rule a State may not be indirectly impleaded by proceedings taken against its property'[43]; and finally, the waiver doctrine, because sovereign immunity functions exclusively as an obstacle to the jurisdiction of a foreign court where proceedings are taken against the State's will, and consent to the jurisdiction of the foreign court withdraws sovereign immunity.[44] A fourth point might further be made: the character of the activity for which immunity is granted to a State is not included in Lord Atkin's statement.[45] This missing point is of course a characterisation of the State with respect to sovereign (public) acts and non-sovereign (private) acts; it is on this point that a distinction is made between absolute and restrictive sovereign immunity.[46]

Returning to the subject of Marshall's decision in *The Schooner Exchange*, while he laid the foundations for the doctrine of absolute State immunity, he enumerated three exceptions to the exercise of full sovereignty. First, he underscored the exception of the person of the sovereign entity from arrest and detention within a territory of a foreign sovereign entity. With respect to this exception, Justice Marshall clearly explained that a 'foreign sovereign is not understood as intending to subject himself to a jurisdiction incompatible with [the foreign sovereign's] dignity, and the dignity of his nation, and it is to avoid this subjection that the license has been obtained'.[47]

The second exception derives from the 'immunity which all civilised nations allow to foreign ministers'.[48] Justice Marshall actually signalled the vesting of sovereign immunity to high-ranking State officials. Although his statement literally included only foreign State ministers, it has been deemed the basis for bestowing foreign sovereign immunity on other high-ranking State officials such as Heads of State. Finally, Justice Marshall states that a 'third case in which a sovereign is understood to cede a portion of his territorial jurisdiction is where he allows the troops of a foreign prince to pass through his dominions'.[49] In other words, these three exceptional cases indicate that sovereign immunity rights became available both for visiting State officials who are tasked with international political and governmental acts and State officials bestowed with legal responsibilities abroad in the international arena in the name of their sovereign State. Vesting these immunities to the State itself and its high-ranking officials requires that every sovereign State must stick to the principle of sovereign equality; wherein, every State, regardless of the degree of power (both political and legal) they command in the international arena, must be vested in the equal juridical approach.[50]

It can be observed that *The Schooner Exchange*, as the first precedent, reveals the critical issue among States, crystallised into an absolute sovereign immunity from the territorial jurisdiction of a foreign State.[51] At the time of *The Schooner Exchange*, the sovereign immunity principle had been limited to issues between States such as governmental or political acts. However, increasingly interrelated business between sovereign States in the intervening years and developing disputes between trading countries expanded the range of situations in which sovereign immunity might apply. Consequently, a restrictive theory has been developed under international law. This theory reflects the variety of State acts and hence both produces more specific results and sets forth a clearer and more definitive characterisation of sovereign immunity than the discourse first propounded in *The Schooner Exchange*.

Rise of the Restrictive Theory

During the twentieth century, the changing structure of State sovereignty and corresponding changes in the position of the State in the international arena have chipped away at the absolute theory of sovereign immunity. Growing commercial and trading activities between sovereign States have become the focus of proceedings among States. Consequently, it became necessary to distinguish between the private acts and the public acts of a State in order to correctly interpret the circumstances under which sovereign immunity should be bestowed on a State in contemporary inter-State cases. On this point, Philip Jessup stated:

> The state has more and more assumed the control of various activities which were formerly left to private initiative. The state operation of railways, telegraphs, radio and numerous other enterprises, as well as state monopolies such as those of tobacco, salt, matches and other common articles of commerce, have necessarily brought the state into commercial relationships with private individuals and have accordingly resulted in numerous litigations

> which have been brought before the courts of many states. [Domestic] courts have been slow to break away from the traditional conceptions of state sovereignty, independence and equality, but gradually the demands of justice and the necessities of the situation have been reflected in a growing tendency in the jurisprudence of many countries to emphasise exceptions to state immunity rather than to emphasise the basic rule itself.[52]

Increasing dissatisfaction with the implementation of the absolute theory of sovereign immunity, especially in relation to States' commercial acts, led many States to adopt a more restrictive form of sovereign immunity. The restrictive method allows jurisdiction to be implemented over States' acts which are not deemed sovereign.

In the 1975 case, *The Philippine Admiral*, Lord Cross of Chelsea described the evolving structure of State immunity after the Second World War as follows:

> There is no doubt [...] that since the Second World War there has been both in the decisions of courts outside this country and in the views expressed by writers on international law a movement away from the absolute theory of sovereign immunity championed by Lord Atkin [...] in *The Cristina* towards a more restrictive theory. This restrictive theory seeks to draw a distinction between acts of a state which are done *jure imperii* and acts done by it *jure gestionis* and accords the foreign state no immunity either in actions *in personam* or in actions *in rem* in respect of transactions falling under the second head.[53]

In 1976, the Foreign Sovereign Immunities Act was passed by the United States Congress both to clarify and to codify the restrictive sovereign immunity theory in that country. The Act declares that subject 'to existing international agreements to which the United States is a party at the time of [adoption] of this Act a foreign state shall be immune from the jurisdiction of the courts of the United States and of the States [...]'.[54] The Act, then, set out excepted categories that preclude foreign States from having the defence of sovereign immunity. Section 1605 of the Foreign Sovereign Immunities Act states that:

> a foreign State shall not be immune from the jurisdiction of courts of the United States in any case

(1) in which *there is an implicit or explicit waiver of immunity by the foreign State*;
(2) in which the action is based upon a commercial activity carried on in the United States by the foreign state; or upon an act performed in the United States in connection with a commercial activity of the foreign state elsewhere; or upon an act outside the territory of the United States in connection with a commercial activity of the foreign state elsewhere and that act causes a direct effect in the United States;
(3) in which rights in property taken in violation of international law are in issue [...];
(4) in which rights in property in the United States [are] acquired by succession or gifts [...];
(5) not otherwise encompassed in paragraph (2) above, in which money damages are sought against a foreign state for personal injury or death [...] occurring in the United States and caused by the tortious act or omission of that foreign state or any official or employee of that foreign state [...];
(6) in which the action is brought, either to enforce an agreement made by the foreign state with or for the benefit of a private party to submit to arbitration [...];
(7) in which money damages are sought against a foreign state for personal injury or death that was caused by an act of torture, extra-judicial killing, aircraft sabotage, hostage taking, or the provision of material support or resources for such an act if such act or provision of material support of resources is engaged in by an official, employee, or agent of such foreign state while acting within the scope of his or her office, employment, or agency;
(8) in which a suit in admiralty is brought to enforce a maritime lien against a vessel or cargo of the foreign state, which maritime lien is based upon a commercial activity of the foreign state.[55]

Considering the restrictive theory of sovereign immunity in the case of the United States, the general legal principle put forward by *The Schooner Exchange* remains; namely, foreign States can benefit from sovereign immunity when governmental or political acts are at stake. However, according to the Foreign Sovereign Immunities Act, the foreign State has a legal right to be vested with sovereign immunity unless it is involved in exceptional activities as set out in Sections 1605 and 1605A of the Act. In fact, imposing some limitations on granting State immunity to all States was considered when international commerce and inter-State economic activities began spreading through and affecting the world order. In this way a restrictive immunity doctrine has come to be widely accepted, with the exception of a few States (the former Soviet Union and China being the most notable).[56]

The restrictive theory of sovereign immunity makes a distinction between the private and public acts of a sovereign State. Through this distinction, sovereign immunity is considered for a foreign State defendant only where its public acts are at stake and since commercial activities are administered by private law, commercial transactions of a State fall outside of State sovereign authority.[57] This interpretation is mirrored in the UN Convention on Jurisdictional Immunities of States and Their Property as follows: 'A state enjoys immunity in respect of itself and its property, from the jurisdiction of the courts of another state subject to the provisions of the present Convention'.[58] Under the doctrine of restrictive foreign sovereign immunity, governmental 'acts with regard to which immunity would be granted are termed acts *jure imperii* [...] while those relating to private or trade activity are termed acts *jure gestionis*'.[59]

The restrictive approach to sovereign immunity makes a distinction between *acts jure imperii* and *acts jure gestionis*, and was highlighted by the Federal Republic of Germany in the *Distomo Massacre* case. The factual context of the *Distomo Massacre* case can be summarised as follows: On 10 June 1944, German armed forces committed a massacre in the Greek village of Distomo resulting in the deaths of many civilians. On 25 September 1997, a Greek Court of First Instance of Livadia delivered a judgement against Germany and awarded damages to relatives of the victims of the Distomo massacre. In 2000, though the Hellenic Supreme Court confirmed that judgement, it was not possible to uphold these two judgements because the Greek Minister for Justice had not granted the required authorisation to hold a judgement against a foreign State. The plaintiffs in the *Distomo Massacre* case later brought proceedings against Germany and Greece before the ECtHR. In 2002, the plaintiffs' application was found inadmissible by invoking the principle of State immunity. Greek plaintiffs then sought to enforce the judgements of the Greek courts in Italy and the Italian court held that the 1997 Greek judgement was enforceable in Italy.[60] The Court of Cassation in the *Distomo Massacre* case stated that:

> It is now accepted by the international legal community that the immunity of foreign States does not cover all their actions (absolute immunity) but merely those actions which constitute an exercise of sovereign power in rela-

> tion to third parties (*acta jure imperii*). It is not upheld for those acts which the foreign State carries out as a fiscus within the framework of its relations under private law (*acta jure gestionis*) [...] the criterion for making this distinction is the nature of the act of the foreign State, meaning whether the act itself involves the exercise of sovereign power.[61]

As Fairman notes: 'All the rights which a state has abroad may be reduced to one: the right to respect in the exercise of its *imperium* within the limits recognised by international law'.[62] The absolute theory of State immunity, which is based on the maxim *par in parem non habet imperium*, becomes practicable only for inter-State relations; and ultimately, the restrictive theory erodes the premise of State immunity instituted in *The Schooner Exchange*.

Controversial Exceptions

Although the distinction between *acta jure imperii* and *acta jure gestionis* is now largely accepted, some further, controversial, exceptions are found in international law. Within the scope of this book, two exceptional situations are relevant, namely, the territorial tort exception and the contravention of peremptory norms (*jus cogens*). Beyond the restrictive doctrine of State immunity, these exceptions present considerable challenges in relation to international immunity under international law.

The territorial tort exception concerns the actions of a foreign State in a forum State. Specifically, if an act by a foreign State occurs in the territory of a forum State and engenders physical injury, death, or damage to property, the territorial tort exception should apply. According to this exception, a State cannot claim immunity from jurisdiction before a foreign State's court. Article 12 of the UN Convention on Jurisdictional Immunities of States and Their Property and Article 11 of the 1972 European Convention on State Immunity established the tort exception as follows:

> Unless otherwise agreed between the States concerned, a State cannot invoke immunity from jurisdiction before a court of another State which is otherwise competent in a proceeding which relates to pecuniary compensation for death or injury to the person, or damage to or loss of tangible property, caused by an act or omission which is alleged to be attributable to the State, if the act or omission occurred in whole or in part in the

> territory of that other State and if the author of the act or omission was present in that territory at the time of the act or omission.[63]

Although the territorial tort exception is codified under both the UN Convention and the European Convention on State Immunity, its extent and availability are still controversial, because many States assert that it breaches the rule that States can benefit from jurisdictional immunity for their sovereign acts. However, it is clear from the aforementioned instruments and from the Foreign Sovereign Immunities Act that the territorial tort exception is exercised in the forum State, and that even the State's act from which the injury or death results is recognised as an inherently sovereign act.[64]

As for *jus cogens* norms, those are a well-established principle of the international community which are meant to trump all incompatible and inconsistent lesser rules, acts, or norms, regardless of their nature. Furthermore, as established in Article 53 of the 1969 Vienna Convention on the Law of Treaties, no derogation is permissible for such *jus cogens* norms. Therefore, it can be stated that bestowing immunity on the State does not, in and of itself, establish a violation of peremptory norms unless this bestowal gives rise to a situation which breaches *jus cogens* norms.[65] In fact, there is a strong doctrinal perspective that the peremptory norms trump the jurisdictional immunity of the State before a national court; and, in this case, that the main purpose of the peremptory norms is to disrupt and deny any means by which impunity might be enjoyed by a State that violates certain human rights recognised as *jus cogens* norms.[66] On this basis, the abolition of impunity in cases of violations of *jus cogens* human rights becomes the basis of this book.

The International Law Commission has characterised the prohibition of aggression, genocide, slavery, racial discrimination, and torture as the *jus cogens* norms.[67] The controversial question here is whether jurisdictional immunities apply to the State in cases of violations of those specific human rights. Also of importance is the issue of whether or not State immunity equates to State impunity when those human rights are violated by the State. This issue will be addressed in the following pages through analysis of the 2012 *Jurisdictional Immunities of the State* and particularly the dissenting opinion of Judge Antônio Cançado Trindade. It must be noted that dissenting opinions are not legally binding but are morally authoritative; for this reason, they may serve as advisory opinions in the future and the minority argument may, in the future, become the majority argument.

Tension Between State Immunity and Violations of Jus Cogens Norms

In accordance with the normative hierarchy in international law, *jus cogens* norms triumph over non-peremptory norms. In this sense, human rights recognised as *jus cogens* norms in theory preponderate the rule of State immunity. The jurisdictional immunity of the State should hence be waived when the State violates *jus cogens* human rights. It is extensively asserted that States and its high-ranking officials cannot avoid criminal suits before foreign courts when they violate jus cogens norms by pleading State immunity. In compliance with the hierarchy of international law norms, the rule of State immunity has a status below jus cogens norms, and accordingly should be cast aside.[68] Increasing human rights violations spark off tension between bestowing State immunity and protecting human rights. Indeed, *Jurisdictional Immunities of the State*, by challenging the rule of State immunity, makes an important contribution to international law. It manifests a contentious issue on whether States enjoy jurisdictional immunity when violations of *jus cogens* human rights are at stake. This case further brings the discussion over whether State immunity amounts to State impunity even when violations of *jus cogens* norms are alleged. In this respect, it should be noted that the Dissenting Opinions of Judge Trindade, *inter alia*, enlighten us on the differentiation between State immunity and impunity.

The main question of debate here is whether sovereign acts of the State involving violations of jus cogens norms on the grounds that jurisdictional immunity may be asserted by States in order to **escape from** foreign justice. As previously stated, international law has evolved towards a human-based approach; however, the absolute character of jus cogens human rights has not yet been uniformly accepted as a fundamental tenet of international law and therefore lacks the power to diminish, let alone nullify, the rule of State immunity.[69] For example, according to the majority opinion in *Jurisdictional Immunities of the State*, States that violate international human rights law are not exempt from invoking jurisdictional immunity before a foreign court.[70]

I will now elucidate aforementioned debate over whether State immunity equates to impunity through the *Jurisdictional Immunities of the State* case. This case was brought before the ICJ by Germany, which asserted that its State immunity was breached before Italian domestic courts. Civil claims against Germany were brought by Italy before the Italian courts to seek compensation for injuries caused by transgressions committed by the German Reich during the Second World War. Germany, in response to this, argued that Italy, by allowing civil claims, failed to respect the jurisdictional immunity which Germany enjoys under international law. Further, Germany claimed that Italy had violated Germany's immunity 'by taking measures of constraint against Villa Vigoni, German State property situated in Italian territory'.[71]

For the sake of declining State immunity of Germany, Italy raised two main claims which essentially put forward that Germany should not be entitled to jurisdictional immunity. Before the ICJ, Italy firstly claimed that under customary international law, Germany should not be entitled to immunity with reference to acts engendering death, personal injury, or damage to property on the forum State's territory even though the acts in question fall within the scope of *jure imperii* or *jure gestionis*.[72] The Court considered whether the principle of State immunity protects Germany with regard to torts perpetuated by its armed forces on another State's territory. In a thorough analysis of both European Convention on State Immunity and UN Convention on Jurisdictional Immunities, the Court found no sound footing for this claim. Namely, the Court concluded that the holding of Italian courts to decline immunity to Germany cannot be justified by virtue of the territorial tort principle.[73] Ultimately, the Court dismissed the first claim of the Italian side.

Secondly, Italy claimed that the acts in question were unquestionably violations of *jus cogens* norms and should override the principle of State immunity. Here the Court addressed the contradiction between *jus cogens* norms and the principle of State immunity. Italy canalised this claim in three strands. In the first strand, Italy claimed that the State immunity principle should be set aside when grave violations of international human rights law and humanitarian law are at stake. Even when the grave nature of the acts was recognised and accepted, the Court could find almost no State practice or domestic decisions which champion the claim that a State is deprived of its right to jurisdictional immunity in grave violations of international law.[74] On the contrary, the Court could find number of cases that support the argument that State immunity cannot be chipped away in such cases.[75] The Court therefore dismissed this claim and declared that 'States generally proceed on the basis that there is a right to immunity under international law, together with a corresponding obligation on the part of other States to respect and give effect to that immunity'.[76]

The second strand of Italy's claim is based on the superiority relationship between *jus cogens* norms and the rule of State immunity. Italy claimed that, since jus cogens norms prevail over any inconsistent principle of international law, State immunity cannot be vested in Germany in respect of its violations in question. However, the Court disagreed that there was a contradiction between *jus cogens* norms and the rule of State immunity.[77] Thereupon, the Court highlighted that these two principles of international law (*jus cogens* norms and State immunity) deal with different matters. The State immunity principle bears a procedural nature, and it is confined to determining whether a State can be brought before another State's domestic courts.[78] The Court underscored that recognising State immunity is not tantamount to recognising the transgression of a *jus cogens* norm as lawful. *Jus cogens* norms have a substantive nature and State immunity is recognised as a procedural matter. Hence, one does not hinge on the other. The Court held that the rule of State immunity cannot be derogated under customary international law for sovereign deeds which create a breach of *jus cogens* norms.[79] Here, the Court adopted Hazel Fox's logic that:

> State immunity is a procedural rule going to the jurisdiction of a national court. It does not go to substantive law; it does not contradict a prohibition contained in a *jus cogens* norm but merely diverts any breach of it to a different method of settlement. Arguably then, there is no substantive content in the procedural plea of State immunity upon which a *jus cogens* mandate can bite.[80]

As I previously discussed with respect to the Court's approach and justification, jus cogens norms enjoy a peremptory nature and as maintained by international law, such norms should supersede all other legal rules regardless of their preliminary character. It follows that, in cases of breaches of *jus cogens* norms, the distinction between the procedural character of the State immunity rule and the substantive nature of *jus cogens* imperatives turns out to be 'artificial and misguided'.[81] The distinction in question is vague and hinges on an incoherent conceptual basis, and this scenario ultimately may induce impunity.[82]

In the final strand, Italy claimed that its domestic courts were justified in declining State immunity of Germany since all other attempts to secure compensation for the victims had failed.[83] The Court declined Italy's contention and could find no grounds in existing international law that 'makes the entitlement of a State immunity dependent upon the existence of effective alternative means of securing redress'.[84] The Court therefore turned down Italy's argument that State immunity could be removed from Germany. Further, the Court noted that the State immunity principle is not at variance with the legal obligation to make reparation. Accordingly, the Court, by considering previous State practices, believed it was difficult to find that requiring the payment of full compensation to each victim was not supported by legal foundation under international law.[85]

Overall, no argument put forward by Italy could find any justification before the Court. It follows that the Court requires that domestic courts should clarify questions of immunity at the outset of the proceedings before deliberation of the merits.[86] The Court therefore held that Italy breached its legal duty to respect Germany's State immunity for sovereign acts in respect of allowing the judicial proceeding against Germany before its domestic courts. That is to say, Germany enjoyed State immunity before Italian courts for deeds perpetrated by its armed forces since their acts fall within the scope of *acta jure imperii*.

Picking Holes in the ICJ Judgement

The Court, in its judgement, adopted an orthodox method to State immunity. For each rejection of the Italian arguments, the Court based its holdings on existing international law and State practices. The Court accepted that granting State immunity to Germany did not mean that Germany had not perpetuated gross violations of international human rights. However, the main distinction between State immunity and State impunity should not be overlooked here for the sake of prevention of grave violations of international human rights. This distinction must also be revealed to highlight the superior nature of *jus cogens* norms.

Closing all avenues for the Italian arguments brings a problem with regards to the superiority of *jus cogens* norms. As Italy argued, international law cannot, on one hand, constitute number of substantive principles and norms, which cannot be derogated from and whose transgression cannot be tolerated and justified. On the other hand, bestowing immunity on perpetrators of violations of such norms in cases in which it is clear that State immunity is considerable is tantamount to impunity.[87] It must be noted that granting immunity in cases of violations of *jus cogens* norms turns the substantive *jus cogens* norm into an ostensible norm.[88]

When immunity creates an obstacle for claiming compensation in respect of *jus cogens* violations, this situation becomes substantially more than merely raising a procedural drawback; it is fundamentally a refusal of the normative basis of the substantive norm, and constitutes a breach.[89] Indeed, International Law Commission in 2001 underlined that no State can acknowledge as legitimate a situation caused by violations of a State obligation arising from a *jus cogens* norm.[90] In other words, such obligations of a State cannot be nullified by jurisdictional immunity.

It is recognised that *jus cogens* norms are not at variance with the rule of State immunity and yet the non-derogable character of *jus cogens* norms requires that acts including violations of such norms should not pave the way for impunity. Therefore, allowing for the granting of State immunity in cases of *jus cogens* norms violations may likely produce absolute impunity. In this sense, certain dissenting opinions to the ICJ judgements argue that immunity does not equate to impunity when violations of *jus cogens* norms are at stake. As I noted elsewhere, although dissenting opinions generally do not affect the final holdings of the Court, 'they should be considered valuable reference points when evaluating future conflicts between jurisdictional immunities and the violations of certain human rights'.[91]

The contradiction between the rule of State immunity and protection of human rights recognised as *jus cogens* norms can be observed in the civil lawsuit of *Al-Adsani v the United Kingdom* in which the ECtHR held that there was no transgression of Article 3 and Article 6(1) of European Convention on Human Rights which respectively states that: 'No one shall be subjected to torture or to inhuman or degrading treatment or punishment'. As for the latter, the Court found that there was no violation of Article 6(1) which guarantees the right to access to justice regarding the alleged acts of torture for which the State had claimed its immunity from jurisdiction. Accordingly, it may be strongly articulated that claiming State immunity does not pose an obstacle for the protection of *jus cogens* norms in the eyes of the Court.

This case arose from the allegation that Sulaiman Al-Adsani, a dual British/Kuwaiti national, was exposed to torture at the behest of the Sheik of Kuwait in 1991.[92] In 1992, Al-Adsani filed civil suits in the United

Kingdom to seek compensation against the State of Kuwait with regard to physical and mental damage caused by torture and life threats.[93] However, as I stated before, the Court held that Article 3 of the Convention was not enforceable, and the State was not liable to pay compensation to a person who was allegedly exposed to torture in another country. Although this case included allegations of torture which outlawed under *jus cogens* norms, it was justified for bestowing immunity to the defendant State.[94]

Since the non-derogable nature of *jus cogens* norms under general international law is well established, the joint dissenting opinion in the Al-Adsani case laid stress on the non-derogable nature as follows:

> *Jus cogens* rule [...] overrides any other rule which does not have the same status. In the event of a conflict between a *jus cogens* rule and any other rule of international law, the former prevails. The consequence of such prevalence is that the conflicting rule is null and void, or, in any event, does not produce legal effects which are in contradiction with the content of the peremptory rule.[95]

The non-derogable nature of *jus cogens* norms does not tolerate impunity for violations of human rights that fall within the domain of these norms. Under international law, it is well established that the prohibition of torture is accepted as a *jus cogens* imperative and should take precedence over the rule of State immunity when a conflict exists between them. Indeed, the joint dissenting opinion in Al-Adsani case rightly underscored this issue:

> Kuwait cannot validly hide behind the rules on State immunity to avoid proceedings for a serious claim of torture made before a foreign jurisdiction; and the courts of that jurisdiction (the United Kingdom) cannot accept a plea of immunity, or invoke it *ex officio*,[96] to refuse an applicant adjudication of a torture case.[97]

When a State act challenges *jus cogens* norms, jurisdictional immunity of a State should not be an impediment to prosecution; the procedural drawback of that immunity should be indeed impeded. It follows that clear differentiation between State immunity and State impunity is needed. For this task, precise delimitation for the rule of State immunity is required. It is well established under international law that State enjoys its immunity before foreign jurisdiction, but State immunity should be challenged in the case of violations of *jus cogens* norms. Hence, impunity will be unlikely vested in a State. In this sense, Judge Trindade, in his dissenting opinion to the *Jurisdictional Immunities of the State*, stated that 'State-planned and State-perpetrated crimes, engaging State responsibility, removed any bar to jurisdiction, at national and international levels, so as to avoid impunity'.[98]

In their final holdings of *Jurisdictional Immunities of the State* and *Al-Adsani v the United Kingdom* cases, it could be observed that the rule of State immunity predominated over the violations of *jus cogens* norms. Although these holdings provide absolute State immunity, it must be noted that while State immunity bears procedural matter, State impunity becomes a substantive matter. Thereby, they have unambivalently different readings. In other words, whether a State should be excused for its international obligation in respect of human rights transgressions becomes one issue, while whether the State should be held answerable for its acts before a foreign national court is decidedly another.[99]

Although State immunity and State impunity are different matters, impunity emerges as a prospective result of immunity, rather than immunity itself.[100] In this regard, Judge Trindade, in his dissenting opinion to *Jurisdictional Immunities of the State*, raised ground-breaking judgement for our age and accordingly stated that

> [i]t is not warranted, in my view, to invoke the factual origin of a dispute simply to try to argue that [...] *jus cogens* did not exist then, or [fundamental] rights inherent to the human person were not yet recognized, and at the same time hide oneself behind the shield of State immunity. That makes no sense to me at all, and leads to impunity and manifest injustice. That goes against international law. That is inacceptable in the past. It goes against the *recta ratio*,[101] which lies in the foundations of the law of nations, today as in the past.[102]

In 1997, a Greek court sought to abolish Germany's sovereign immunity in relation to breaches of *jus cogens* norms of humanitarian law arising from deeds committed by the Nazi troops in the period of the occupation of Greece. The Greek court established that hierarchy between norms and found that the granting State immunity for acts contrary to *jus cogens* norms would be tantamount to complicity of the domestic court to the encouragement of violation condemned by the international public order.[103]

While the principle of State immunity is a major obstacle to the pursuit of justice for violations of fundamental human rights, it can be observed that the scope and limitations of State immunity have not been well-established in respect of the protection of fundamental human rights under customary international law. Abdulqawi Yusuf, in his Dissenting Opinion to *Jurisdictional Immunities of the State*, reads this tangled issue as follows:

> State immunity is, as a matter of fact, as full of holes as Swiss cheese. Thus, to the extent that customary norms of international law are to be found in the practice and *opinio juris* of States, such practice clearly attests to the fact that the scope and extent of State immunity, particularly in the area of violations of human rights [...], which is currently characterised by conflicting decisions of national courts in its interpretation and application, remains an uncertain and unsettled area of international custom, whose contours are ill-defined.[104]

Ultimately, transgressions of *jus cogens* norms should never be justified as sovereign acts since such transgressions are at odds with the international legal order. As Judge Trindade, in his dissenting opinion, rightly and spartanly stated, these transgressions of *jus cogens* norms 'cannot simply be removed or thrown into oblivion by reliance on State immunity'.[105] Warranting justice and ensuring compensation for victims of such violations straightforwardly hinge on recognising the distinction between State impunity and State immunity. International legal order is subject to a test on whether impunity is vested in States in case of violations of *jus cogens* norms. This test would simply enlighten the victims of those violations on seeking for the justice and reparation.

Conclusion

This chapter has argued that although the rule of State immunity is well recognised under international law, this rule cannot be used as an obstacle against the realisation of human rights which fall within the domain of *jus cogens* norms. Criticising the holdings of the ICJ in the *Jurisdictional Immunities of the State* would be tenable and rational so that the determined dissenting opinions articulated may likely be uttered and implemented efficiently in the future. Since I have already emphasised the importance of dissenting opinions, I will conclude this chapter with

Trindade: violations of *jus cogens* human rights 'perpetrated by States are not acts *jure gestionis*, nor acts *jure imperii*; they are crimes, ***delicta imperii***,[106] for which there is no immunity'.[107]

Notes

1. Gerry Simpson, *Great Powers and Outlaw States: Unequal Sovereigns in the International Legal Order* (Cambridge: Cambridge University Press, 2004), 11.
2. 'In public international law, the principle that one sovereign power cannot exercise jurisdiction over another sovereign power'. Elizabeth A. Martin, *A Dictionary of Law*, 7th ed. (Oxford: Oxford University Press, 2009), 393.
3. Ilias Bantekas and Susan Nash, *International Criminal Law*, 3rd ed. (Oxon: Routledge-Cavendish, 2007), 96.
4. Hazel Fox QC and Philippa Webb, *The Law of State Immunity*, 3rd ed. (Oxford: Oxford University Press, 2013), 3.
5. *Jurisdictional Immunities of the State (Germany v. Italy: Greece Intervening), Judgment*, ICJ Reports 99 (2012).
6. Xiaodong Yang, *State Immunity in International Law* (Cambridge: Cambridge University Press, 2012), 48.
7. *I Congreso del Partido*, 1 A.C. 244 (House of Lords 1983) at 262.
8. Yang, *State Immunity in International Law*, 58.
9. Jürgen Bröhmer, *State Immunity and the Violation of Human Rights* (The Hague, Boston and London: Martinus Nijhoff Publishers, 1997), 14.
10. Malcolm N. Shaw, *International Law*, 7th ed. (Cambridge: Cambridge University Press, 2014), 509.
11. *Prefecture of Voiotia v. Federal Republic of Germany (Distomo Massacre Case)*, 129 ILR 513 (Greece—Court of Cassation 2000) at 516.
12. Hazel Fox, 'In Defence of State Immunity: Why the UN: Convention on State Immunity Is Important', *International and Comparative Law Quarterly* 55, no. 02 (2006): 403.
13. Lee M. Caplan, 'State Immunity, Human Rights, and Jus Cogens: A Critique of the Normative Hierarchy Theory', *American Journal of International Law* 97, no. 4 (2003): 755.
14. Edwin DeWitt Dickinson, *The Equality of States in International Law* (Cambridge: Harvard University Press, 1920), 106.
15. Council of Europe, 'European Convention on State Immunity, Explanatory Report', ETS 074 (1972), 5.

16. *The Schooner Exchange v. McFaddon & Others*, 11 U.S. (7 Cranch) 116 (Supreme Court of the United States 1812).
17. Eileen Denza, 'The 2005 UN Convention on State Immunity in Perspective', *International and Comparative Law Quarterly* 55, no. 2 (2006): 395–98.
18. Yang, *State Immunity in International Law*, 26.
19. Peter Malanczuk, *Akehurst's Modern Introduction to International Law*, 7th ed. (London: Routledge, 1997), 118.
20. This UN Convention was adopted on 2 December 2004 but has not yet come into force.
21. See Ernest K. Bankas, *The State Immunity Controversy in International Law: Private Suits Against Sovereign States in Domestic Courts* (Berlin: Springer, 2005), 308; Malanczuk, *Akehurst's Modern Introduction to International Law*, 129.
22. Fox QC and Webb, *The Law of State Immunity*, 11.
23. *R v. Bow Street Metropolitan Stipendiary Magistrate and Others, ex parte Pinochet Ugarte (No. 3)*, 1 A.C. 147 (House of Lords 2000) at 201.
24. Gamal Moursi Badr, *State Immunity: An Analytical and Prognostic View* (Dordrecht: Martinus Nijhoff Publishers, 1984), 9–10.
25. James T. Bretzke, *Consecrated Phrases A Latin Theological Dictionary: Latin Expressions Commonly Found in Theological Writings*, 3rd ed. (Collegeville, MN: Liturgical Press, 2013), 132.
26. Yang, *State Immunity in International Law*, 44.
27. The date of this case is relevant, because it happened during the War of 1812 between the USA and the British Empire. France was an ally of the United States.
28. Yang, *State Immunity in International Law*, 45.
29. *The Schooner Exchange v. McFaddon & Others*, 11 U.S. (7 Cranch) 116 at 137.
30. *Victory Transport Incorporated v. Comisaria General de Abastecimientos y Transportes*, 336 F.2d 354 (US Court of Appeals Second Circuit 1964) at 357.
31. UN General Assembly, 'United Nations Convention on Jurisdictional Immunities of States and Their Property', A/RES/59/38 (2004) Article 5.
32. Fox, 'In Defence of State Immunity', 405.
33. Shaw, *International Law*, 507.
34. Shaw, 509.
35. *Claim Against the Empire of Iran*, 45 ILR 57 (German Constitutional Court 1963) at 61.
36. Absolute immunity 'was granted in an age when the distinction between sovereign and non-sovereign activities was less manifest, given that State

functions were at that time confined to the traditional spheres of, say, legislation, administration, national defence, and the conduct of State-to-State political relations and that […] it was possible and natural to regard "State" activities as synonymous with "sovereign" activities'. Yang, *State Immunity in International Law*, 8.

37. Theodore R. Giuttari, *The American Law of Sovereign Immunity: An Analysis of Legal Interpretation* (New York: Praeger Publishers, 1970), 3.
38. Adam C. Belsky, Mark Merva, and Naomi Roht-Arriaza, 'Implied Waiver under the FSIA: A Proposed Exception to Immunity for Violations of Peremptory Norms of International Law', *California Law Review* 77, no. 2 (1989): 379.
39. *The Schooner Exchange v. McFaddon & Others*, 11 U.S. (7 Cranch) 116 at 136.
40. *The Schooner Exchange v. McFaddon & Others*, 11 U.S. (7 Cranch) 116 at 137.
41. Sompong Sucharitkul, *Immunities of Foreign States before National Authorities*, Collected Courses of the Hague Academy of International Law 149 (Leiden, 1976), 117.
42. *The Cristina*, A.C. 485 (House of Lords 1938) at 490-491.
43. Fox QC and Webb, *The Law of State Immunity*, 137.
44. Fox QC and Webb, 137.
45. Fox QC and Webb, 137.
46. Fox QC and Webb, 137.
47. *The Schooner Exchange v. McFaddon & Others*, 11 U.S. (7 Cranch) 116 at 137.
48. *The Schooner Exchange v. McFaddon & Others*, 11 U.S. (7 Cranch) 116 at 138.
49. *The Schooner Exchange v. McFaddon & Others*, 11 U.S. (7 Cranch) 116 at 139.
50. Bankas, *The State Immunity Controversy in International Law*, 19.
51. Thora A. Johnson, 'A Violation of Jus Cogens Norms as an Implicit Waiver of Immunity Under the Federal Sovereign Immunities Act', *Maryland Journal of International Law* 19, no. 2 (1995): 259–91.
52. Philip C Jessup, 'Competence of Courts in Regard to Foreign States', *The American Journal of International Law* 26, no. 1: Supplement Codification of International Law (1932): 473–74.
53. *The Philippine Admiral*, A.C. 373 (Privy Council 1977) at 397.
54. Foreign Sovereign Immunities Act, 28 U.S.C. §§ 1602-1611 (1976) § 1604.
55. Foreign Sovereign Immunities Act §§ 1605 and 1605A *[Emphasis Added]*.
56. See the Singapore State Immunity Act (1979); the South African Foreign States Immunities Act (1981); the Pakistan State Immunity Ordinance

(1981); the Canadian State Immunity Act (1982); the Australian Foreign States Immunities Act (1985); and the United Nations Convention on Jurisdictional immunities of States and Their Property (2004) article 5, which does not apply to criminal proceedings because it is not in force yet; see Shaw, *International Law*, 513–14. For the China exception see Joanne Foakes, 'State Immunity: Recent Developments and Prospects', *Chatham House Briefing Paper*, December 2013, 4.

57. Legislative acts, internal administrative acts, diplomatic activities, acts concerning the armed forces, public loans that are deemed political, and public acts enjoy sovereign immunity under the restrictive theory of sovereign immunity. Shaw, *International Law*, 514.
58. UN General Assembly, United Nations Convention on Jurisdictional Immunities of States and Their Property Article 5.
59. Shaw, *International Law*, 509–10.
60. *Jurisdictional Immunities of the State (Germany v. Italy: Greece Intervening), Judgment*, ICJ Reports at 115–16; *Prefecture of Voiotia v. Federal Republic of Germany (Distomo Massacre Case)*, 129 ILR 513.
61. *Prefecture of Voiotia v. Federal Republic of Germany (Distomo Massacre Case)*, 129 ILR 513 at 516.
62. Charles Fairman, 'Some Disputed Applications of the Principle of State Immunity', *American Journal of International Law* 22, no. 3 (1928): 571.
63. UN General Assembly, United Nations Convention on Jurisdictional Immunities of States and Their Property Article 12; European Convention takes very similar approach to the UN Convention. See Council of Europe, 'European Convention on State Immunity', ETS 074 (1972) Article 11.
64. Rosanne van Alebeek, *The Immunity of States and Their Officials in International Criminal Law and International Human Rights Law* (Oxford: Oxford University Press, 2008), 68–69.
65. Christian Tomuschat, 'Reconceptualizing the Debate on Jus Cogens and Obligations Erga Omnes: Concluding Observations', in *The Fundamental Rules of the International Legal Order: Jus Cogens and Obligations Erga Omnes*, ed. Christian Tomuschat and Jean Marc Thouvenin (Leiden: Martinus Nijhoff Publishers, 2006), 433.
66. See Alexander Orakhelashvili, 'State Immunity and Hierarchy of Norms: Why the House of Lords Got It Wrong', *European Journal of International Law* 18, no. 5 (2007): 964.
67. International Law Commission, 'Draft Articles on Responsibility of States for Internationally Wrongful Acts, with Commentaries', in *Yearbook of the International Law Commission*, vol. II, part 2 (New York: United Nations, 2001), 85.

68. Alebeek, *The Immunity of States and Their Officials in International Criminal Law and International Human Rights Law*, 316.
69. Selman Özdan, 'State Immunity or State Impunity in Cases of Violations of Human Rights Recognised as Jus Cogens Norms', *The International Journal of Human Rights* 23, no. 9 (2019): 1525.
70. *Jurisdictional Immunities of the State (Germany v. Italy: Greece Intervening), Judgment*, ICJ Reports.
71. *Jurisdictional Immunities of the State (Germany v. Italy: Greece Intervening), Judgment*, ICJ Reports at para 37.
72. *Jurisdictional Immunities of the State (Germany v. Italy: Greece Intervening), Judgment*, ICJ Reports at para 62.
73. *Jurisdictional Immunities of the State (Germany v. Italy: Greece Intervening), Judgment*, ICJ Reports at paras 62-79.
74. *See Jurisdictional Immunities of the State (Germany v. Italy: Greece Intervening), Judgment*, ICJ Reports at para 83.
75. *Jurisdictional Immunities of the State (Germany v. Italy: Greece Intervening), Judgment*, ICJ Reports at paras 84-90.
76. *Jurisdictional Immunities of the State (Germany v. Italy: Greece Intervening), Judgment*, ICJ Reports at para 56.
77. *Jurisdictional Immunities of the State (Germany v. Italy: Greece Intervening), Judgment*, ICJ Reports at paras 92-93.
78. *Jurisdictional Immunities of the State (Germany v. Italy: Greece Intervening), Judgment*, ICJ Reports at para 93.
79. *Jurisdictional Immunities of the State (Germany v. Italy: Greece Intervening), Judgment*, ICJ Reports at paras 92-94-97.
80. Hazel Fox, *The Law of State Immunity* (Oxford: Oxford University Press, 2002), 525.
81. Özdan, 'State Immunity or State Impunity in Cases of Violations of Human Rights Recognised as Jus Cogens Norms', 1529.
82. Özdan, 1529.
83. *Jurisdictional Immunities of the State (Germany v. Italy: Greece Intervening), Judgment*, ICJ Reports at para 98.
84. *Jurisdictional Immunities of the State (Germany v. Italy: Greece Intervening), Judgment*, ICJ Reports at para 101.
85. *Jurisdictional Immunities of the State (Germany v. Italy: Greece Intervening), Judgment*, ICJ Reports at para 94.
86. *Jurisdictional Immunities of the State (Germany v. Italy: Greece Intervening), Judgment*, ICJ Reports at para 106.
87. Judge Antônio Augusto Cançado Trindade, *The Construction of a Humanized International Law: A Collection of Individual Opinions (1991-2013)* (Leiden: Brill Nijhoff and Hotei Publishing, 2015), 1500.

88. Alexander Orakhelashvili, 'Immunities of State Officials, International Crimes, and Foreign Domestic Courts: A Reply to Dapo Akande and Sangeeta Shah', *European Journal of International Law* 22, no. 3 (2011): 852.
89. Orakhelashvili, 852.
90. International Law Commission, 'Draft Articles on Responsibility of States for Internationally Wrongful Acts, with Commentaries', 112–14.
91. Özdan, 'State Immunity or State Impunity in Cases of Violations of Human Rights Recognised as Jus Cogens Norms', 1531.
92. *Al-Adsani v. The United Kingdom, Judgment*, Application No 35763/97 (ECtHR 21 November 2001) at paras 9-13.
93. *Al-Adsani v. The United Kingdom, Judgment* at para 14.
94. *Al-Adsani v. The United Kingdom, Judgment* at para 66.
95. See the Joint Dissenting Opinion to the *Al-Adsani v. The United Kingdom, Judgment* at 29–30.
96. The term *ex officio* refers to 'some right an individual has because of the office she or he occupies'. Bretzke, *Consecrated Phrases A Latin Theological Dictionary: Latin Expressions Commonly Found in Theological Writings*, 76.
97. See the Joint Dissenting Opinion to the *Al-Adsani v. The United Kingdom, Judgment* at 30.
98. See the Dissenting Opinion of Judge Trindade to the *Jurisdictional Immunities of the State (Germany v. Italy: Greece Intervening), Judgment*, ICJ Reports at 197.
99. Xiaodong Yang, 'State Immunity in the European Court of Human Rights: Reaffirmations and Misconceptions', *British Yearbook of International Law* 74, no. 1 (2004): 343.
100. Yang, 345.
101. *Recta ratio*, in Latin, refers to right reason. Bretzke, *Consecrated Phrases A Latin Theological Dictionary: Latin Expressions Commonly Found in Theological Writings*, 206–7.
102. See the Dissenting Opinion of Judge Trindade to the *Jurisdictional Immunities of the State (Germany v. Italy: Greece Intervening), Judgment*, ICJ Reports at 186.
103. See Helmut Philipp Aust, *Complicity and the Law of State Responsibility* (Cambridge: Cambridge University Press, 2011), 37; *Multi-member Court of Levadia, Judgment*, 137/1997 (1997).
104. See the Dissenting Opinion of Judge Yusuf to the *Jurisdictional Immunities of the State (Germany v. Italy: Greece Intervening), Judgment*, ICJ Reports at 298.
105. See the Dissenting Opinion of Judge Trindade to the *Jurisdictional Immunities of the State (Germany v. Italy: Greece Intervening), Judgment*, ICJ Reports at 288.

106. *Delicta imperii* refers to 'wrong of the sovereign'. 'A crime under international law committed by a sovereign State'. Aaron X. Fellmeth and Maurice Horwitz, *Guide to Latin in International Law*, 2nd ed. (New York, NY: Oxford University Press, 2021).
107. See the Dissenting Opinion of Judge Trindade to the *Jurisdictional Immunities of the State (Germany v. Italy: Greece Intervening), Judgment*, ICJ Reports at 288.

References

Al-Adsani v. The United Kingdom, Judgment, Application No 35763/97 (ECtHR 21 November 2001).

Alebeek, Rosanne van. *The Immunity of States and Their Officials in International Criminal Law and International Human Rights Law*. Oxford: Oxford University Press, 2008.

Aust, Helmut Philipp. *Complicity and the Law of State Responsibility*. Cambridge: Cambridge University Press, 2011.

Badr, Gamal Moursi. *State Immunity: An Analytical and Prognostic View*. Dordrecht: Martinus Nijhoff Publishers, 1984.

Bankas, Ernest K. *The State Immunity Controversy in International Law: Private Suits Against Sovereign States in Domestic Courts*. Berlin: Springer, 2005.

Bantekas, Ilias, and Susan Nash. *International Criminal Law*. 3rd ed. Oxon: Routledge-Cavendish, 2007.

Belsky, Adam C., Mark Merva, and Naomi Roht-Arriaza. 'Implied Waiver under the FSIA: A Proposed Exception to Immunity for Violations of Peremptory Norms of International Law'. *California Law Review* 77, no. 2 (1989): 365–415.

Bretzke, James T. *Consecrated Phrases a Latin Theological Dictionary: Latin Expressions Commonly Found in Theological Writings*. 3rd ed. Collegeville, MN: Liturgical Press, 2013.

Bröhmer, Jürgen. *State Immunity and the Violation of Human Rights*. The Hague, Boston and London: Martinus Nijhoff Publishers, 1997.

Caplan, Lee M. 'State Immunity, Human Rights, and Jus Cogens: A Critique of the Normative Hierarchy Theory'. *American Journal of International Law* 97, no. 4 (2003): 741–81.

Claim Against the Empire of Iran, 45 ILR 57 (German Constitutional Court 1963).

Council of Europe. European Convention on State Immunity, ETS 074 (1972a).

———. European Convention on State Immunity. European Convention on State Immunity, Explanatory Report, ETS 074 (1972b).

Denza, Eileen. 'The 2005 UN Convention on State Immunity in Perspective'. *International and Comparative Law Quarterly* 55, no. 2 (2006): 395–98.

Dickinson, Edwin DeWitt. *The Equality of States in International Law*. Cambridge: Harvard University Press, 1920.

Fairman, Charles. 'Some Disputed Applications of the Principle of State Immunity'. *American Journal of International Law* 22, no. 3 (1928): 566–89.

Fellmeth, Aaron X., and Maurice Horwitz. *Guide to Latin in International Law*. 2nd ed. New York, NY: Oxford University Press, 2021.

Foakes, Joanne. 'State Immunity: Recent Developments and Prospects'. *Chatham House Briefing Paper*, December 2013.

Foreign Sovereign Immunities Act, 28 U.S.C. §§ 1602–1611 (1976).

Fox, Hazel. 'In Defence of State Immunity: Why the UN: Convention on State Immunity Is Important'. *International and Comparative Law Quarterly* 55, no. 02 (2006): 399–406.

———. *The Law of State Immunity*. Oxford: Oxford University Press, 2002.

Fox QC, Hazel, and Philippa Webb. *The Law of State Immunity*. 3rd ed. Oxford: Oxford University Press, 2013.

Giuttari, Theodore R. *The American Law of Sovereign Immunity: An Analysis of Legal Interpretation*. New York: Praeger Publishers, 1970.

I Congreso del Partido, 1 A.C. 244 (House of Lords 1983).

International Law Commission. 'Draft Articles on Responsibility of States for Internationally Wrongful Acts, with Commentaries'. In *Yearbook of the International Law Commission*, Vol. II, part 2. New York: United Nations, 2001.

Jessup, Philip C. 'Competence of Courts in Regard to Foreign States'. *The American Journal of International Law* 26, no. 1: Supplement Codification of International Law (1932): 451–738.

Johnson, Thora A. 'A Violation of Jus Cogens Norms as an Implicit Waiver of Immunity Under the Federal Sovereign Immunities Act'. *Maryland Journal of International Law* 19, no. 2 (1995): 259–91.

Jurisdictional Immunities of the State (Germany v. Italy: Greece Intervening), Judgment, ICJ Reports 99 (2012).

Malanczuk, Peter. *Akehurst's Modern Introduction to International Law*. 7th ed. London: Routledge, 1997.

Martin, Elizabeth A. *A Dictionary of Law*. 7th ed. Oxford: Oxford University Press, 2009.

Multi-member Court of Levadia, Judgment, 137/1997 (1997).

Orakhelashvili, Alexander. 'Immunities of State Officials, International Crimes, and Foreign Domestic Courts: A Reply to Dapo Akande and Sangeeta Shah'. *European Journal of International Law* 22, no. 3 (2011): 849–55.

———. 'State Immunity and Hierarchy of Norms: Why the House of Lords Got It Wrong'. *European Journal of International Law* 18, no. 5 (2007): 955–70.

Özdan, Selman. 'State Immunity or State Impunity in Cases of Violations of Human Rights Recognised as Jus Cogens Norms'. *The International Journal of Human Rights* 23, no. 9 (2019): 1521–45.

Prefecture of Voiotia v. Federal Republic of Germany (Distomo Massacre Case), 129 ILR 513 (Greece—Court of Cassation 2000).

R v. Bow Street Metropolitan Stipendiary Magistrate and Others, ex parte Pinochet Ugarte (No. 3), 1 A.C. 147 (House of Lords 2000).

Shaw, Malcolm N. *International Law*. 7th ed. Cambridge: Cambridge University Press, 2014.

Simpson, Gerry. *Great Powers and Outlaw States: Unequal Sovereigns in the International Legal Order*. Cambridge: Cambridge University Press, 2004.

Sucharitkul, Sompong. *Immunities of Foreign States before National Authorities*. Collected Courses of the Hague Academy of International Law 149. Leiden, 1976.

The Cristina, A.C. 485 (House of Lords 1938).

The Philippine Admiral, A.C. 373 (Privy Council 1977).

The Schooner Exchange v. McFaddon & Others, 11 U.S. (7 Cranch) 116 (Supreme Court of the United States 1812).

Tomuschat, Christian. 'Reconceptualizing the Debate on Jus Cogens and Obligations Erga Omnes: Concluding Observations'. In *The Fundamental Rules of the International Legal Order: Jus Cogens and Obligations Erga Omnes*, edited by Christian Tomuschat and Jean Marc Thouvenin, 425–36. Leiden: Martinus Nijhoff Publishers, 2006.

Trindade, Judge Antônio Augusto Cançado. *The Construction of a Humanized International Law: A Collection of Individual Opinions (1991–2013)*. Leiden: Brill Nijhoff and Hotei Publishing, 2015.

UN General Assembly. United Nations Convention on Jurisdictional Immunities of States and Their Property, A/RES/59/38 (2004).

Victory Transport Incorporated v. Comisaria General de Abastecimientos y Transportes, 336 F.2d 354 (US Court of Appeals Second Circuit 1964).

Yang, Xiaodong. *State Immunity in International Law*. Cambridge: Cambridge University Press, 2012.

———. 'State Immunity in the European Court of Human Rights: Reaffirmations and Misconceptions'. *British Yearbook of International Law* 74, no. 1 (2004): 333–408.

CHAPTER 5

A Critique of the Demise of Heads of State Immunity in the Age of Human Rights

State officials have traditionally been immune from the jurisdiction of foreign States' courts when they would otherwise be required to account for the deeds they are accused of committing. However, this authoritative principle of international law becomes contentious in cases involving the violation of fundamental human rights, most strongly represented by the growth of international human rights law and the establishment of international tribunals and courts determined to end impunity for violations of fundamental human rights, irrespective of the perpetrators' official position.[1] Increasing concern for international human rights and greater international support for abolishing impunity for violators of fundamental human rights have led the international community to question the boundaries of Head of State immunity.

There were great expectations that international law would evolve in favour of international human rights after the Second World War, and these expectations undoubtedly continue. However, it would be a fantasy to imagine that international law always works in favour of human rights, even while there is a definite trend within the international community to seek to enhance and support international human rights. Head of State immunity appears to be a considerable impediment to realising the

A shorter version of this chapter was previously published, with minor differences, in *The Age of Human Rights Journal*, 2018, 11: 108–127. It is reprinted with permission.

S. Özdan, *The Human Rights Challenge to Immunity in International Law*, https://doi.org/10.1007/978-3-030-92923-7_5

expectation that international law can be used to challenge resistance to respect for human rights and to ending impunity.

This chapter examines the principle of Head of State immunity. It explains the various types of Head of State immunity and considers the developments under customary international law in respect of the rules regarding such immunity. This chapter subsequently discusses and analyses immunity and impunity for Heads of State when violations of fundamental human rights are perpetrated. To engage with this discussion, this chapter concentrates on the *Pinochet* Judgment for customary international law and the judgement of the ICJ in *Arrest Warrant of 11 April 2000 (Democratic Republic of the Congo v Belgium)* so as to criticise the issue of immunity in question. Finally, this chapter considers the question of whether Head of State immunity, in effect, means Head of State impunity in cases involving the violation of fundamental human rights. Here, the central aim of this chapter is to argue that Head of State immunity leads to *de facto* impunity in the case of violations of fundamental human rights.

Identification of Head of State

On the authority of international law, Heads of State are regarded as being able to act *ipso facto* as representatives of the State in respect of international relations.[2] In fact, Head of State immunity is based on the concept of sovereignty and State immunity stems from the sovereign rights of States. In other words, the position of Heads of State in international law is derived from the international rights and duties of their States, and not as a consequence of their own individual entitlement. In accordance with international law, a Head of State is endowed with *jus repraesentationis omnimodae*: the right to represent the State on an international level in every respect and the competence to speak internationally on behalf of the State. In other words, as the highest delegated persons of the State, it is understood that Heads of State represent their State in international relations. A Head of State's deeds or transgressions when acting in an official capacity on behalf of the State are attributable to the State itself. If the Head of State fails to respect his or her State's international commitments, the State shoulders international responsibility for the acts of that individual.[3] Head of State immunity applies to Heads of State as well as Heads of Government and foreign ministers since international relations are now conducted and performed by those authorities.[4]

In *Armed Activities on the Territory of the Congo—Democratic Republic of the Congo v Rwanda*, the ICJ observed that it is a well-established rule of international law that the Heads of State 'are deemed to represent the State merely by virtue of exercising their functions, including for the performance, on behalf of the said State, of unilateral acts having the force of international commitments'.[5] In addition to this statement, the ICJ in the *Arrest Warrant* Judgment explained that a Head of State 'responsible for the conduct of his or her State's relations with all other States, [...] is recognised under international law as representative of the State solely by virtue of his or her office. He or she does not have to present letters of credence'.[6]

The Convention on Special Missions, which was adopted by the General Assembly of the UN on 8 December 1969, also declared that the Heads of State and 'other persons of high rank, when they take part in a special mission of the sending State, shall enjoy in the receiving State or in a third State [...] the facilities, privileges and immunities accorded by international law'.[7]

Question of Head of State Immunity: Pinochet, Taylor, and Habré

This recognition of a Head of State as the principal commissioned officer of his or her State provides the justification for official immunities before the domestic courts of other States.[8] The concept of Head of State immunity was explicitly and conceptually located in the 1987 *In re Grand Jury Proceedings*, in which the United States Court of Appeals for the Fourth Circuit stated that Head of State immunity 'is a doctrine of customary international law. Generally speaking, the doctrine maintains that a head of state is immune from the jurisdiction of a foreign state's courts, at least as to authorised official acts taken while the ruler is in power'.[9]

In international law, a number of prominent decisions have bearing on the tension between vesting immunity in the Head of State and the protection of fundamental human rights. The suit against the former president of Chile Augusto Pinochet by the United Kingdom House of Lords in 1998 and 1999 was a landmark in international law as Pinochet could not claim immunity for acts of torture for which he was responsible.

In analysing Head of State immunity in the context of human rights violations, the *Arrest Warrant of 11 April 2000 (Democratic Republic of the Congo v Belgium)* case is also important, particularly in relation to the question of whether or not Head of State immunity equates to Head of State impunity in such cases. Heads of State sometimes enjoy considerable leeway to escape from proceedings in respect of human rights violations. In this sense, the concept of immunity is sometimes 'wrongfully utilised to signify that a person benefits from impunity or is not prosecuted, for reasons other than the technical legal bar of immunity'.[10]

International law regarding Head of State immunity has undergone a considerable and interesting evolution during the twentieth and twenty-first centuries. However, to date, no agreement, covenant, or treaty has been adopted to clarify or make alterations to the law of Head of State immunity; instead, the law is rooted in international customary law. Developments in the law with regard to Head of State immunity under international customary law are a particular concern to the future of international human rights. The question of whether or not international human rights create any exception to the customary international law of immunity *ratione materiae* remains open.[11] However, the issue of Head of State immunity in the *Pinochet* decision cannot be easily ignored, which is why it will be evaluated and considered for the future of Head of State immunity.

In 1973, Augusto Pinochet, the chief commander of the army in Chile, led the military *coup d'état* which overturned the elected government of President Salvador Guillermo Allende Gossens. Subsequently, the ruling military *junta* appointed Pinochet President of Chile. During the Pinochet administration, 'hundreds of thousands of people were detained for political reasons, and several thousand disappeared or were killed. Pinochet stepped down as President in 1990, but he remained head of the army until March 1998, when he was appointed Senator for Life'.[12]

Proceedings were instituted against Pinochet before the Spanish domestic court for human rights violations he allegedly committed during his presidency. On 17 October 1998, Pinochet was arrested in the United Kingdom while receiving medical treatment in London. The Spanish magistrate, Baltasar Garzon, requested Pinochet's extradition on the basis of a European Arrest Warrant from the United Kingdom so that he could stand trial for torture and other crimes against humanity; however, the United Kingdom's Home Secretary, Jack Straw, decided that Pinochet should not be extradited to Spain, leaving him free to return to Chile. Criminal proceedings were initiated in England to determine whether he was entitled to Head of State immunity to avoid arrest and extradition, as

Pinochet had claimed he was. The Divisional Court acknowledged Pinochet's claim and held that Pinochet was entitled to claim immunity *ratione materiae* even for human rights violations.[13] The lawyers requested an appeal before the House of Lords and decisions of *Pinochet No 1*,[14] *Pinochet No 2*,[15] and *Pinochet No 3*[16] were held by the United Kingdom Law Lords.

On 25 November 1998, the United Kingdom House of Lords held that a former Head of State cannot enjoy immunity for violations of fundamental human rights, amounting to peremptory norms of general international law, committed while in office. Former General Pinochet, therefore, had no immunity from United Kingdom jurisdiction with regard to his alleged crimes under international law, and hence he had no immunity from extradition.[17] In *Pinochet No 1*, Lord Slynn and Lord Lloyd held that:

> A claim to immunity by a head of state or a former head of state applied only to acts performed by him in the exercise of his functions as head of state. Although that referred to any of his functions as a head of state and not just those acts which had an international character, acts of torture and hostage-taking could not be regarded in any circumstances as a function of a head of state. It was a principle of international law, as shown by the Conventions against the Taking of Hostages and Torture, that hostage-taking and torture were not acceptable conduct on the part of anyone, including a head of state. It followed that since the acts of torture and hostage-taking with which the applicant was charged were offences under United Kingdom statute law, in respect of which the United Kingdom had taken extra-territorial jurisdiction, the applicant could not claim immunity from the criminal processes, including extradition, of the United Kingdom.[18]

Concerning *Pinochet No 1*, most of the Lords highlighted the fact that international law had evolved significantly since the Second World War. The most important aspect of this development was the identification of certain violations of human rights which deserve punishment and prosecution under international law. No act that may be seen as infringing on *jus cogens* can be regarded as a sovereign act with regard to issues of immunity. In *Pinochet No 1*, for example, Lord Nicholls of Birkenhead observed that 'it hardly needs saying that torture of his own subjects or of aliens would not be regarded by international law as a function of a head of state'. Lord Nicholls delivered a corresponding Opinion, which read in part:

> International law recognises, of course, that the functions of a head of state may include activities which are wrongful, even illegal, by the law of his own state or by the laws of other states. But international law has made plain that certain types of conduct, including torture and hostage-taking, are not acceptable conduct on the part of anyone. This applies as much to heads of state or even more so, as it does to everyone else; the contrary conclusion would make a mockery of international law.[19]

Lord Steyn, in a similar vein, stated that 'it seems to me difficult to maintain that the commission of such high crimes may amount to acts performed in the exercise of the functions of a head of state'.[20] By a majority decision (Lords Nicholls, Steyn, and Hoffmann), the appeal was allowed owing to the fact that torture cannot be deemed as an official act of a Head of State. Accordingly, the Lords held that the decision of the Divisional Court was wrong.[21]

After *Pinochet No 1*, the House of Lords uncovered a link between Lord Hoffmann, who had written the majority opinion that ruled to allow Pinochet's extradition, and Amnesty International Charity Limited. Pinochet brought a petition to set aside an order made by the United Kingdom House of Lords on 25 November 1998, claiming that this link suggested that Lord Hoffmann was biased against him. The case was, therefore, reheard, with the result that the judgement of *Pinochet No 1* was set aside by *Pinochet No 2* and the entire case, as well as the original issue of immunity, was reheard before the House of Lords again as *Pinochet No 3*.[22]

On 24 March 1999, at the final House of Lords hearing, the Appellate Committee decided that a former Head of State cannot enjoy immunity to perpetrate acts of torture or conspiracy, where such acts are manifestly included in the scope of violations of fundamental human rights and were perpetrated after 8 December 1998, the date on which the 1984 UN Convention against Torture was ratified by the United Kingdom.[23]

The decision of the House of Lords in *Pinochet No 3* rendered on 24 March 1999 confirmed that a former Head of State cannot benefit from immunity in cases of extradition or criminal proceedings instituted in the United Kingdom in regard to the international crime of torture. In reaching this conclusion, most of the Lords in *Pinochet No 3* relied exclusively on the UN Convention Against Torture, from which they determined that Head of State immunity should be abrogated in cases involving that particular violation of *jus cogens* norm. According to these Lords, Head of

State immunity is clearly incompatible with the Convention Against Torture, because torture is a constituent component of the violation of fundamental human rights recognised as *jus cogens* norms.[24]

The opinion of Lord Millett in *Pinochet No 3* has importance for future cases that highlight the contradiction between the protection of international human rights and the preservation of immunity for Heads of State. More comprehensively, Lord Millett endorsed the judgement that international human rights law is integral to the project of preventing human rights violations and, as such, should always triumph over Head of State immunity in cases involving such violations. Lord Millett, in *Pinochet No 3*, emphasised that the 'very official or governmental character of the acts which is necessary to found a claim to immunity *ratione materiae*, and which still operates as a bar to the civil jurisdiction of national courts, was now to be the essential element which made the acts an international crime'.[25]

Since the Second World War, international law has progressed at a staggering rate, and the emphasis on the protection of fundamental human rights is regarded as an essential factor in this development. Today, and in the future, any person who perpetrates injustice or violations against civil societies 'must expect to be called to account if fundamental human rights are to be properly protected. In this context, the exalted rank of the accused can afford no defence'.[26]

The opinions of the House of Lords in the *Pinochet No 3* case indicate that for all intents and purposes, violations of fundamental human rights should not be reckoned as sovereign official acts. The contradiction between granting immunities to Heads of State and the prohibition of human rights violations remains a complicated issue in international law. In fact, violations of fundamental human rights 'cannot be regarded as official acts because they are neither normal State functions nor functions that a State alone (in contrast to an individual) can perform'.[27] An order by a Head of State, which gives rise to violations of fundamental human rights, should be interpreted as a private act and cannot, therefore, be read as a pretext to enjoy immunity.[28] It follows that under no circumstances can violations of fundamental human rights be categorised as sovereign acts of a Head of State. On the whole, the frequent reference to *jus cogens* norms and obligations *erga omnes* 'attests to the fact that the emerging notion of an international public order based on the primacy of certain values and common interests is making its way into the legal culture and common practice of municipal courts'.[29]

It is surely beyond doubt that international law has made progress thanks to the resolution of the House of Lords regarding Augusto Pinochet. By limiting immunity, the House of Lords' rulings 'turned the world upside down and ushered in a new era of accountability for egregious violations of human rights'.[30] Although the perspective of the majority of Lords in the *Pinochet* Judgment constitutes a significant contribution to the effort to abolish impunity for the perpetrators of fundamental human rights violations, it must be recalled that this development relates to a former Head of State. That is to say, a former Head of State can in no way enjoy his or her right to immunity if violations of fundamental human rights are at stake.

The conviction of Charles Ghankay Taylor might be referred to here for the sake of considering an appearance of a former president before an international court. This conviction is important because he is the 'first former African president to have been indicted, fully tried, and then convicted by an international penal tribunal'.[31] Charles Taylor was also the 'first former head of state since Nuremberg to be indicted and subsequently tried and convicted for war crimes' by an international criminal tribunal.[32]

Charles Taylor was elected as president of Liberia in 1997 and was Head of State until 2003. During Taylor's indictment in 2003, he was still president of Liberia. On 7 March 2003, the Special Court for Sierra Leone (SCSL) issued a sealed indictment against Charles Taylor, and this indictment was unsealed when Taylor visited Ghana on 4 June 2003. On 31 May 2004, the Appeals Chamber rejected a motion brought on account of Charles Taylor which challenged this indictment by raising the claim of sovereign immunity and extraterritoriality. On 29 March 2006, Taylor was sent to the SCSL and then was transferred to The Hague on 30 June 2006. Charles Taylor was found guilty of war crimes (outrages upon personal dignity, violence to health, life and mental or physical well-being of persons—murder or cruel treatment—and pillage).[33] Under Article 6(1) of the Statute of the SCSL, the accused was found individually criminally responsible for aiding and abetting, and planning the commissions of the transgressions.[34] The Trial Chamber issued a decision that Charles Taylor be sentenced to 50 years prison sentence on 30 May 2012.[35]

The conviction of Hissene Habre can also be adduced as a landmark case here. Hissene Habre was the former president of Chad from 1982 until he was discharged in 1990 by Idriss Deby.[36] As an ousted leader, Habre went into exile in Senegal, where Habre has kept a low profile.[37]

Habre was indicted for transgressions of fundamental human rights, including war crimes and torture by the four investigating judges of the Extraordinary African Chambers on 2 July 2013. After a nineteen months' investigation, the judges found enough evidence for Hissene Habre to face charges of war crimes based on his command responsibility, and of torture as a member of a joint criminal enterprise. Habre was specifically charged with transgressions including torture and war crimes of murder, torture, illegitimate transfer and unlawful confinement, and violence to physical well-being and life.[38] Habre was convicted of war crimes (and torture) by the Extraordinary African Chambers in the court system of Senegal and ultimately sentenced to life in prison on 30 May 2016.[39] During Hissene Habre's tenure as the president of Chad, his term was marked by 'large scale, systematic violations, including those involving murder of an estimated 40,000 people, widespread sexual violence [...] enforced disappearance, and torture'.[40] John Kerry, in his press statement, considered this ruling to be a landmark in the international struggle against impunity for atrocities.[41]

The conviction of Hissene Habre and the trial of Habre before the Extraordinary African Chambers can be deemed a significant and encouraging example of abolishing tolerance for impunity in Africa, for holding perpetrators of violations of fundamental human rights accountable, and bringing them to justice in order to prevent exemption from punishment. Ultimately, the protection of fundamental human rights that are deemed *jus cogens* norms should always triumph over the assertion of immunity for a former Head of State whenever these principles conflict. Since the *jus cogens* norms are absolutely inderogable under international law, sovereign immunities can no longer be conceived as *jus cogens*. Specifically, sovereign immunities can be abrogated under the required conditions by international law. For example, a former Head of State can on no account enjoy her/his immunity if she/he perpetrates violations of *jus cogens* human rights. That is to say, any derogation from the enjoyment of Head of State immunity becomes an adequate reason to accept it outside of *jus cogens* norms.[42]

Developments of Head of State Immunity in International Legal System

In simple terms, the principle of immunity has been instituted to protect a State and its senior officials from being sued before its courts and particularly foreign courts, so that they can carry out their activities abroad without impediment. Since immunity from prosecution and execution is based upon the sovereign equality principle of States, this principle does not prevent senior State officials from being indicted before an international court as long as this court is vested in jurisdiction over serving or former Heads of State.[43]

Prior to 1919, there was little discussion of immunity for Heads of State before international tribunals or courts, as the issue had been all but taboo with regard to any waiver of such immunity. However, the Versailles Treaty, which is generally accepted as the first indictment of a former Head of State before an international tribunal, is seen by many as breaking this taboo. On this point, Article 227 of the Treaty reads as follows:

> The Allied and Associated Powers publicly arraign William II of Hohenzollern [The Kaiser], formerly German Emperor, for a supreme offence against international morality and the sanctity of treaties. A special tribunal will be constituted to try the accused, thereby assuring him the guarantees essential to the rights of defence. It will be composed of five judges, one appointed by each of the following powers: namely, the United States of America, Great Britain, France, Italy and Japan. In its decision the tribunal will be guided by the highest motives of international policy, with a view to vindicating the solemn obligations of international undertakings and the validity of international morality. It will be its duty to fix the punishment which it considers should be imposed. The Allied and Associated Powers will address a request to the Government of the Netherlands for the surrender to them of the ex-Emperor in order that he may be put on trial.[44]

However, the Kaiser was never tried. Before Armistice Day, the Kaiser fled to the Netherlands and asylum was granted to him by the Dutch government who refused to hand him over for trial.[45] After the Treaty of Versailles, the issue of immunity for Heads of State was challenged through the Statutes of the Nuremberg and Tokyo international military tribunals. Article 7 of the Charter of the Nuremberg Tribunal declared that the 'official position of defendants, whether heads of state or responsible officials in Government Departments, shall not be considered as freeing them from responsibility or mitigating punishment'.[46] A number of significant developments in international law have taken place whose outcome has been to restrict Head of State immunity in the interest of securing and maintaining fundamental human rights. The Nuremberg Principles include the assertion that the 'fact that a person who committed an act which constitutes a crime under international law acted as Head of State or responsible Government official does not relieve him from responsibility under international law'.[47] In a similar vein, Article 6 of the Statute of the Tokyo Tribunal declared that:

> Neither the official position, at any time, of an accused, nor the fact that an accused acted pursuant to order of his government or of a superior shall, of itself, be sufficient to free such accused from responsibility for any crime with which he is charged.[48]

In respect of both statements by international military tribunals, international law unequivocally protects State officials and provides immunity; however, in particular circumstances immunity for Heads of State cannot be invoked if his or her deeds constitute a violation of fundamental human rights. If violations of those human rights are at stake, the official position of a Head of State should not serve as a shield to avoid punishment. Immunity should apply only to sovereign acts; therefore, Heads of State should not enjoy functional immunity in relation to violations of fundamental human rights. Functional immunity provides protection for sovereign acts; however, acts which cause fundamental human rights violations should not be deemed as sovereign acts.[49]

Concerning individual criminal responsibility, it is clear that the statutes of the ICTY and the International Criminal Tribunal for Rwanda are considered important developments in terms of clarifying the position of Head of State immunity in relation to international crimes that give rise to fundamental human rights violations. Both statutes emphasise that Heads of State should not benefit from immunity. Article 7(2) of the Statute of the ICTY provides that the 'official position of any accused person, whether as Head of State or Government or as a responsible Government official, shall not relieve such person of criminal responsibility nor mitigate punishment'.[50] Article 6(2) of the Statute of the International Criminal Tribunal for Rwanda reiterates this statement. In so doing, this provision acknowledges that perpetrators of human rights violations, regardless of their official position, cannot hide behind the shield of immunity; and that

Heads of State enjoy no impunity. Furthermore, in 1997, the Appeal Chamber of the Yugoslavia Tribunal highlighted that:

> The general rule under discussion is well established in international law and is based on the sovereign equality of States (*par in parem non habet imperium*). The few exceptions relate to one particular consequence of the rule. These exceptions arise from the norms of international criminal law prohibiting war crimes, crimes against humanity and genocide. Under these norms, those responsible for such crimes cannot invoke immunity from national or international jurisdiction even if they perpetrated such crimes while acting in their official capacity.[51]

Likewise, Article 27 of the Rome Statute embodies provisions which indicate that the Statute applies to all individuals regardless of their official position within a State:

> This Statute shall apply equally to all persons without any distinction based on official capacity. In particular, official capacity as a Head of State or Government, a member of a Government or parliament, an elected representative or a government official shall in no case exempt a person from criminal responsibility under this Statute, nor shall it, in and of itself, constitute a ground for reduction of sentence.
>
> Immunities or special procedural rules which may attach to the official capacity of a person, whether under national or international law, shall not bar the Court from exercising its jurisdiction over such a person.[52]

The essential purpose of the incorporation of these provisions into the Rome Statute and *ad hoc* tribunals is to ensure individual criminal responsibility for all persons, and particularly Heads of State, who perpetrate violations of fundamental human rights which constitute international crimes. Furthermore, by ensuring individual criminal responsibility, those provisions prevent certain persons from using their official position as a shield against prosecution for those human rights violations.

Article 98(1) of the Statute of the International Criminal Court goes beyond States party to the Statute. Article 98(1), which is concerned with cooperation with respect to the waiver of immunity and consent to surrender, reads as follows:

> The Court may not proceed with a request for surrender or assistance which would require the requested State to act inconsistently with its obligations

> under international law with respect to the State or diplomatic immunity of a person or property of a third State, unless the Court can first obtain the cooperation of that third State for the waiver of the immunity.[53]

Articles 27 and 98(1) of the Rome Statute might be seen as contradictory in that the former rejects immunities while the latter endorses immunities. However, article 98(1) addresses a particular situation in which a State party to the Statute is required to surrender a person who is jurisdictionally untouchable by virtue of the immunities granted by a third State. In this sense, this case can be described as an equation with three knowns, a State Party, the Statute, and a person endowed with immunities, although it would appear that the equation always produces a tangled outcome for the State to whom the request is made. Specifically, the State Party to the Statute either must breach its obligation to meet the requirements of the Court or must breach its commitment to abide by immunities of a State that is not party to the Statute. The interaction between Articles 27 and 98(1) of the Statute thereby establishes a system wherein the State parties to the Statute consent to surrender all immunity rights in relation to the Court's requirements regarding their own State officials or representatives, while still abiding by the immunities of States that are not yet party to the Statute.[54]

Ultimately, Article 98(1) of the Statute implies three situations where the immunities bestowed on a person by a State that is not a party to the Statute can be trumped. First, if a State that is not a party to the Statute agrees to relinquish the immunity, the person can be prosecuted. Second, if the State official is no longer in office, the official's personal immunity ends (although functional immunity can still be enjoyed), thus enabling the official to be prosecuted for committed violations of human rights. Third, if the UN Security Council requests full participation under Chapter VII, the State which is not a party to the Statute automatically is deprived of its immunity rights, and must surrender the accused.[55]

The Problem of Head of State Immunity in Relation to Violations of Jus Cogens Norms

Strictly speaking, in respect of international law, the decision of the House of Lords with regard to Augusto Pinochet can be seen as one of the most important cases of the twentieth century. Although it might have been ruled on narrow grounds, this important decision appears to have marked the end of immunity in cases involving violations of fundamental human rights by a former Head of State, even when those violations were committed while the Head of State was in office.[56]

That said, the perspective of the ICJ for Mr Yerodia raises the issue of immunity or impunity for Heads of State when violations of fundamental human rights are perpetrated. In the *Arrest Warrant* case, Belgium argued that immunities accorded to incumbent Foreign Affairs Ministers cannot, under any circumstances, provide the minister with protection where he or she is suspected of having perpetrated violations of fundamental human rights. Subsequently, Belgium touched upon the question of whether a person's high-level status within a State constitutes an impediment to prosecution. On this point, Belgium claimed that the official position of a person should not be an obstacle to applying jurisdiction. On 11 April 2000, an international arrest warrant was issued by a Belgian investigating judge of the Brussels Tribunal of First Instance against Abdulaye Yerodia Ndombasi, the Minister for Foreign Affairs of the Democratic Republic of the Congo, in respect of alleged crimes against humanity and violations of international humanitarian law. Mr Yerodia was accused of having made some speeches that incited racial hatred and occasioned the massacre of Tutsi civilians in 1998. Mr Yerodia was charged by the Belgian judge with grave breaches of the International Geneva Conventions of 1949 and of their Additional Protocols I and II of 1977. The arrest warrant for Mr Yerodia was transferred to the Democratic Republic of the Congo and concurrently circulated at the international level via Interpol. Ultimately, Belgian authorities brought a suit against Mr Yerodia based on the Belgian Law of 16 June 1993, concerning the punishment of grave breaches of the Geneva Conventions and their Additional Protocols, which provides a basis for universal jurisdiction in regard to such violations.[57] Article 5(3) of the Belgian Law also provides that the immunity enjoyed by a person who acts in an official capacity does not create any obstacle to the application of the law.[58]

On 17 October 2000, the Democratic Republic of the Congo filed an application with the ICJ instituting proceedings against the Belgian Kingdom in relation to the case involving this international arrest warrant.[59] In making the Application, the Democratic Republic of the Congo relied on two legal grounds. First, the Democratic Republic of the Congo asserted that Belgium had violated its obligation to respect the immunity of the Minister of Foreign Affairs of a sovereign State. Second, the Democratic Republic of the Congo alleged that Belgium had breached the principle that a State cannot exercise its authority over another State's territory and the principle of sovereign equality of States. On this point, the Democratic Republic of the Congo claimed that the 'universal jurisdiction that the Belgian State attributes to itself under Article 7[60] of the law in question' does not comply with the principle of sovereign equality.[61] The heart and soul of the argument of the Democratic Republic of the Congo concerned the violation of customary international rule in relation to the absolute immunity and inviolability of incumbent foreign ministers from criminal jurisdiction. Arguing that Belgium had infringed the sovereign equality principle of States, the Democratic Republic of the Congo requested that the ICJ require Belgium to declare its international arrest warrant null and void.[62] The Democratic Republic of the Congo insisted that Belgium had no jurisdiction under international law to issue and circulate an international arrest warrant, and that by doing so it had breached the rights of the Democratic Republic of the Congo to perform and conduct its foreign affairs through its foreign minister.[63]

Belgium pointed to the decision rendered on 24 March 1999 by the House of Lords in the United Kingdom in relation to the former Head of State of Chile, General Augusto Pinochet Duarte, which recognised and accepted an exception to the principle of immunity in respect of violations of fundamental human rights under international law.

According to Belgium, the holding in the *Pinochet No 3* case advanced the development of international law by acknowledging an important exception to the principle of immunity for Heads of State or Government.[64] Belgium accordingly referred to a statement by Lord Millett that international law 'cannot be supposed to have established a crime having the character of a *jus cogens* and at the same time to have provided an immunity which is co-extensive with the obligation it seeks to impose'.[65] Belgium also cited the words of Lord Phillips of Worth Matravers that 'no established rule of international law requires state immunity *ratione materiae* to be accorded in respect of prosecution for an international crime'.[66]

The Democratic Republic of the Congo, following Belgium's argument concerning the *Pinochet* decision, emphasised that according to international law as it currently stands, there was no basis for any exception to the principle of Head of State immunity from criminal jurisdiction for a standing Minister of Foreign Affairs where she or he is accused of having perpetrated fundamental human rights violations under international law. The Democratic Republic of the Congo, by cross-referencing the *Pinochet* decision, emphasised Lord Browne-Wilkinson's statement that this 'immunity enjoyed by a head of state in power and an ambassador in post is a complete immunity attached to the person of the head of state or ambassador and rendering him immune from all actions or prosecutions whether or not they relate to matters done for the benefit of the state'.[67] Here, the focus is on whether the accused is an incumbent or a former Head of State rather than the gravity of their alleged crimes. The Democratic Republic of the Congo argued that the immunity 'accorded to Ministers for Foreign Affairs when in office covers all their acts, including any committed before they took office, and that it is irrelevant whether the acts done whilst in office may be characterized or not as official acts'.[68]

The ICJ examined the decision of the House of Lords in the *Pinochet* case but found that there was no applicable exception to the rule of Head of State immunity from criminal jurisdiction; moreover, it found that current Ministers of Foreign Affairs are particularly inviolable where they are suspected of having perpetrated violations of fundamental human rights. Accordingly, the Court rejected the Belgian argument in relation to the *Pinochet* decision by the House of Lords.[69]

Belgium's approach in the *Democratic Republic of the Congo v Belgium* case can be regarded as an important step towards the objective of abolishing impunity for perpetrators of fundamental human rights violations. On this point, Belgium pointed out that:

> [W]hile Ministers for Foreign Affairs in office generally enjoy an immunity from jurisdiction before the courts of a foreign State, such immunity applies only to acts carried out in the course of their official functions, and cannot protect such persons in respect of private acts or when acting otherwise than in the performance of their official functions.[70]

The ICJ stated that it is bound 'to find that, given the nature and purpose of the warrant, its mere issue violated the immunity which Mr Yerodia enjoyed as the [Democratic Republic of] the Congo's incumbent Minister for Foreign Affairs'.[71] The Court therefore decided that the warrant issue led to a violation of Belgium's obligation towards the Democratic Republic of the Congo, in that Belgium failed to respect Head of State immunity. According to the Court, Belgium also breached the immunity from criminal jurisdiction under international law.[72] It follows that the principle of immunity for an incumbent Head of State is still prevalent and alive, even in respect of violations of fundamental human rights prohibited under international law. In respect of the distinction between immunity and impunity bestowed on Heads of State, the ICJ underscored that the immunity from jurisdiction enjoyed by Heads of State in power does not mean that they can benefit from impunity with reference to any violations they may have perpetrated, regardless of their seriousness. 'Immunity from criminal jurisdiction and individual criminal responsibility are quite separate concepts. While jurisdictional immunity is procedural in nature, criminal responsibility is a question of substantive law'.[73] The Court added that while jurisdictional immunity may become an obstacle to prosecution for definite offences or for a definite period, 'it cannot exonerate the person to whom it applies from all criminal responsibility'.[74]

The Court implied that the immunities provided by international law for a current or former Head of State do not constitute an impediment to criminal prosecution in particular circumstances. Subsequently, the Court observed four exceptional situations to Head of State immunity under international law. Although the judgement of the ICJ implied that the immunity from jurisdiction enjoyed by Heads of State does not equate to impunity for international crimes, the exceptions to Head of State immunity outlined by the Court are insufficient to abolish impunity.

First, the Court stated that a Head of State does not enjoy immunity under international law from criminal proceedings in his/her own country's courts. Second, the Court held that Heads of State should be deprived of jurisdictional immunity before a foreign State's court if the State which they represent waives their immunity rights.[75]

Regarding the aforementioned two exceptional situations, prosecution requires 'a willingness of the State which appointed the person as a Foreign Minister to investigate and prosecute allegations against him domestically or to lift immunity in order to allow another State to do the same'.[76] Be that as it may, where domestic authorised bodies do not consent to open an investigation or start a prosecution, the committed violations of human rights will go unpunished. Such an outcome raises the issue of impunity.

The third exception the Court identified was that after a person's official position as a Minister for Foreign Affairs ends, he or she can no longer benefit from the immunities granted by international law in foreign States. 'Provided that it has jurisdiction under international law, a court of one State may try a former Minister for Foreign Affairs of another State in respect of acts committed prior or subsequent to his or her period of office, as well as in respect of acts committed during that period of office in a private capacity'.[77]

The last exception identified by the Court was that neither former nor incumbent Heads of State enjoy immunity when that immunity has been limited by a treaty establishing an international court. Afterwards, the ICJ listed the International Criminal Court (ICC) as one such tribunal which may overturn the immunity of a Head of State provided that it has jurisdiction under international law.[78] The jurisdiction of the Court arises from the authority vested by the contracting States in the Statute of the Court or via the UN Security Council. As Michael Tunks noted, 'no other country has jurisdiction over a third party's head of state, and, consequently, no two states may agree by treaty to waive the immunity of a third party's head of state without that other nation's consent'.[79] It follows that the alleged jurisdiction of the court's statute over a Head of State whose home State does not assent to the statute is not sufficient to rectify customary international law and protect fundamental human rights from Head of State impunity.

It would be untenable to claim that in the absence of the ICC, a Head of State who is suspected of having committed violations of human rights would be justiciable solely before his or her own State's courts.

Ending Impunity for Heads of State

With respect to the *jus cogens* nature of fundamental human rights, the decision by the ICJ offers no clear or plain solution to the tension between Head of State immunity and protection of fundamental human rights. The judgement undermined the argument that the principle of protection of fundamental human rights becomes hierarchically superior to immunity norms; if it were, immunity would be obtainable neither by States nor by current or former Heads of State.[80]

In the *Democratic Republic of the Congo v Belgium* case, Judge *ad hoc* Van den Wyngaert, in her Dissenting Opinion, claimed that there were no grounds in positive international law for bestowing full immunity on incumbent Heads of State against foreign criminal jurisdiction. She emphasised that neither State practice nor *opinio juris* constitutes an international custom that affects the Court's decision.[81] It follows that there is no treaty or legal opinion that supports the proposition of the Court. International law does not provide immunity to incumbent Heads of State from criminal proceedings when they perpetrate violations of fundamental human rights. In this sense, Belgium's act might seem to be at odds with international comity; however, that act did not breach an international legal obligation. Judge Wyngaert then stated that:

> [T]he Court's conclusion is reached without regard to the general tendency toward the restriction of immunity of the State officials (including even Heads of State), not only in the field of private and commercial law where the *par in parem* principle has become more and more restricted and deprived of its mystique, but also in the field of criminal law, when there are allegations of serious international crimes.[82]

It must be noted that the international arrest warrant was issued by Belgium in respect of accusations of war crimes which the ICJ failed to mention. It is important to ask what is required under international law and what international law permits States, as members of international society, to do when their officials are accused of violations of fundamental human rights. Two particular interests are reflected in contemporary international law: first, the demand for international accountability for having allegedly committed violations of fundamental human rights and second, the sovereign equality principle of States which is regarded as a prerequisite for immunities.[83] Redressing the balance between these two particular interests is important for resolving the contradiction between Head of State immunity and protection of fundamental human rights. The Court, instead of redressing the balance, considered a very narrow question on the immunities of incumbent Ministers of Foreign Affairs. By doing so, the Court 'has missed an excellent opportunity to contribute to the development of modern international criminal law'.[84]

The ICJ, in the *Arrest Warrant* case, recognised that a former and incumbent Foreign Affairs Minister 'might be subject to criminal proceedings before certain international criminal courts where they have jurisdiction'.[85] The Court specifically cited the ICC as an example.

This issue was indeed raised before the ICC in respect of an arrest warrant for the incumbent president of the Sudan, Omar Hassan Ahmad Al-Bashir. When, on 4 March 2009 and 12 July 2010, Pre-Trial Chamber I of the ICC issued two warrants of arrest for Omar Al-Bashir for crimes against humanity and war crimes, his arrest was required in accordance with the Rome Statute.[86] Omar Al-Bashir was suspected of being criminally responsible as an indirect violator, or co-perpetrator, for the liable person in respect of the crime of genocide.[87] Since the arrest warrants were issued, President Al-Bashir has travelled to several countries, including the

Republic of Kenya, Djibouti, Malawi, the Republic of Chad, South Africa. Although those countries are State parties to the Rome Statute and hence were obligated to arrest him, he has never been arrested.

On 15 February 2013, Pre-Trial Chamber II of the Court 'requested the Registry to send *Notes Verbales* to the Republic of Chad and the State of Libya, enquiring about said visit, and reminding the former of its obligations with respect to the arrest and surrender of Omar Al-Bashir to the Court'.[88] Al-Bashir travelled to Chad to attend a summit and departed from Chad; however, the Chadian Government took no measure to arrest him. The international community called on Chad to abide by the obligations decided upon by the Court regarding the arrest warrant for Al-Bashir and the Government of Chad was required to provide information to the Chamber about Al-Bashir's alleged journey. On 26 March 2013, Pre-Trial Chamber II issued that Chad had failed to cooperate with the ICC and indicated the non-compliance of Chad to the obligations of the Security Council.[89] Al-Bashir also attended the African Union summit scheduled from 7 to 15 June 2015 in South Africa. On 13 June 2015, Pre-Trial Chamber II asserted that the Republic of South Africa had an obligation to arrest and surrender Al-Bashir. South Africa failed to arrest him. On 15 October 2015, upon South Africa's request, Pre-Trial Chamber II extended the deadline to submit a report regarding the failure of the South African Government to arrest Al-Bashir.[90]

In respect of the jurisdiction, the Pre-Trial Chamber declared that the official position of Al-Bashir as Head of State did not free him from appearing before the ICC. The Chamber proposed four considerations in reaching this decision. First, the Chamber emphasised that one of the crucial goals of the Rome Statute is to end impunity for perpetrators of violations of international crimes which amount to human rights violations. Second, the Chamber noted that Article 27 of the Statute must be applied to achieve this goal. This provision makes immunity non-applicable and enforces the criminal responsibility of all persons regardless of their official capacity in a State. Third, as required by Article 21 of the Rome Statute, other sources of law can be applied only if there is a gap in the Rome Statute that cannot be filled by interpreting the Vienna Convention on the Law of the Treaties with respect to internationally accepted human rights norms. Fourth, the UN Security Council has accepted that the investigation into the situation in Sudan and any prosecution generated therefrom will be compatible with the Statutory framework of the ICJ.[91] On this point, Dapo Akande stated that 'the nature of the Charter as a sort of constitutional document, and [...] obligations under the Charter ought to be regarded as taking priority over the customary international law'.[92]

Sudan is not a state party to the Rome Statute; however, the UN Security Council, in referring the case in Darfur to the ICC, made reference to Article 13(b) of the Statute. Subsequently, the Council required that Sudan should co-operate with the Court.[93] Under Chapter VII of the UN Charter, the Security Council possesses full authority to take measures in order to contribute to the maintenance of international peace and to maintain and restore international security. By becoming a member of the UN, the Sudanese Government gives implicit consent to the Security Council for the abolition of Head of State immunity, because Article 25 of the Charter requires Member States to accept and execute the decisions of the Council. It follows that immunity for Al-Bashir before the courts of foreign States has been implicitly abolished. It must be noted that abolishing immunity in relation to the accusations in the Al-Bashir case conforms with the Security Council's objective, which is to avoid absolute impunity for perpetrators of fundamental human rights violations that pose a threat to international security and peace.[94]

Finally, the Appeals Chamber of the ICC delivered an anticipated judgement regarding the applicability of Head of State immunity and a State's failure to abide by its international obligations as a party State to the Rome Statute and arrest Al-Bashir. On 21 February 2017, on the basis of the news of Al-Bashir's expected attendance to the 28th Arab League Summit in Jordan on 29 March 2017, the Registry sent a *note verbal* to Jordan inviting it to provide information about his visit and 'renewing the request to cooperate with the Court in the arrest and surrender of Omar Al-Bashir, in the event that he enters Jordanian territory'.[95] On 11 December 2017, the Pre-Trial Chamber II ruled that 'Jordan failed to comply with its obligations under the Statute by not executing the Court's request for the arrest of Omar Al-Bashir and his surrender to the Court while he was on Jordanian territory'.[96] On 18 December 2017, Jordan requested leave to appeal and the Pre-Trial Chamber granted its request on 21 February 2018.[97] The Appeals Chamber, in its decision, 'unanimously confirmed' the Pre-Trial Chamber II judgement of December 2017 and unanimously found that 'Jordan's failure to comply with the Court's request prevented the Court from exercising an important function and power'.[98]

The Appeals Chamber temperately examined whether Head of State immunity is viable in the case of Al-Bashir and ultimately found that there is 'neither State practice nor *opinio juris* that would support the existence of Head of State immunity under customary international law *vis-à-vis* an international court'. The Chamber further stated that '[t]o the contrary, such immunity has never been recognised in international law as a bar to the jurisdiction of an international court'.[99] Furthermore, it found that

> The absence of a rule of customary international law recognising Head of State immunity vis-à-vis international court is relevant not only to the question of whether an international court may issue a warrant for the arrest of a Head of State and conduct proceedings against him or her, but also for the horizontal relationship between States when a State is requested by an international court to arrest and surrender the Head of State of another State. No immunities under customary international law operate in such a situation to bar an international court in its exercise of its own jurisdiction.[100]

The judgement of the Appeals Chamber becomes important and would definitely be referred in future cases because this judgement will significantly ensnarl it for a State to claim that there is a legal barrier to the arrest of incumbent Heads of State indicted by the ICC in the event of another indictment of this genre.[101]

International law does not prohibit investigation of alleged violations of human rights; in fact, international law supports such inquiries, even if the accused perpetrator committed the crime as a State agent in a foreign State.[102] This is evident in the history of international law, in which there are very significant codifications of the principle of individual accountability for violations of fundamental human rights. For example, the 1950 Nuremberg Principles highlighted that 'any person who commits an act which constitutes a crime under international law is responsible therefor and liable to punishment'.[103] Likewise, Article 4 of the Convention on the Prevention and Punishment of the Crime of Genocide reads as follows: 'Persons committing genocide or any of the other acts enumerated in Article 3 shall be punished, whether they are constitutionally responsible rulers, public officials or private individuals'.[104]

Prioritising the immunities for Heads of State in cases involving violations of fundamental human rights produces a tension between the immunity principle and the protection of those human rights. That is to say, the prohibitions against certain violations of human rights are deemed as *jus cogens* in nature, and since *jus cogens* norms are in no case trumped by any other norm, the hierarchy should be established by considering the superiority of *jus cogens* norms. It follows that the protection of fundamental human rights should take priority under international law. On this point, it must be noted that where violations of fundamental human rights 'are concerned, immunity cannot block investigations or prosecutions [of] such [violations], regardless of whether such proceedings are brought before national or before international courts'.[105] To protect and improve the fundamental values and interests of human beings, the effective prohibition of certain violations of human rights has been recognised by the international community as having a *jus cogens* character. If, therefore, this hierarchically superior norm becomes at variance with the principles guiding Head of State immunity, it should be trumped by those provisions which are designed to defend and maintain fundamental human rights.

Conclusion

The maintenance of peaceful relations among States requires that Heads of State be granted appropriate immunities from jurisdiction before the courts of foreign States. For the sake of maintaining an environment in which Heads of State can carry out their international duties while visiting foreign countries, Head of State immunity should certainly afford protection from criminal responsibility. However, when Heads of State are suspected of having committed violations of fundamental human rights, they should not be exempt from punishment; in other words, immunity should not amount to impunity.

Head of State immunities are considered to be an essential element of international relations and international law. However, they are not *jus cogens* in nature. The protection of fundamental human rights should override these procedural immunities. Head of State immunity from jurisdiction should on no account be applicable to human rights violations under international law which meet the threshold of a *jus cogens* norm, neither before domestic courts nor before international courts. Heads of State should not be allowed to enjoy immunities when violations of such human rights have been committed. Political concerns should not allow States to uphold the immunity of their own high-ranking officials when jus cogens norms have been breached. Where they do, as Lauterpacht rightly noted, the 'dignity of a foreign state may suffer more from an appeal to immunity than from a denial of it'.[106]

Notes

1. Hazel Fox QC and Philippa Webb, *The Law of State Immunity*, 3rd ed. (Oxford: Oxford University Press, 2013), 537.
2. *Application of the Convention on the Prevention and Punishment of the Crime of Genocide, Preliminary Objections, Judgment*, ICJ Reports 595 (1996) at 622.
3. See Arthur Watts, 'Heads of State', in *Max Planck Encyclopedia of Public International Law* (Oxford University Press, October 2010).
4. Joanne Foakes, *Immunity for International Crimes? Developments in the Law on Prosecuting Heads of State in Foreign Courts*, International Law Programme IL BP 2011/02 (London: The Royal Institute of International Affairs, 2011).
5. *Armed Activities on the Territory of the Congo (New Application: 2002) (Democratic Republic of the Congo v. Rwanda), Jurisdiction and Admissibility, Judgment*, ICJ Reports 6 (2006) at 27.
6. *Arrest Warrant of 11 April 2000 (Democratic Republic of the Congo v. Belgium), Judgment*, ICJ Reports 3 (2002) at 22.
7. UN General Assembly, 'Convention on Special Missions 1969', UNTS 1400 (1969) Article 21(2).
8. Fox QC and Webb, *The Law of State Immunity*, 541.
9. *In re Grand Jury Proceedings*, 817 F.2d 1108 (US Court of Appeals, Fourth Circuit 1987) at 1111.
10. Brigitte Stern, 'Immunities for Heads of State: Where Do We Stand?', in *Justice for Crimes Against Humanity*, ed. Mark Lattimer and Philippe Sands (Oxford and Portland, OR: Hart Publishing, 2003), 81.
11. The exception for international human rights refers to rejections of immunity *ratione materiae* for claimed violations of *jus cogens* norms; therefore, any act that gives rise to the violation of these norms cannot be identified as a sovereign act for which the actor may claim immunity. See Ingrid Wuerth, 'Pinochet's Legacy Reassessed', *The American Journal of International Law* 106, no. 4 (2012): 731–68.
12. Curtis A. Bradley and Jack L. Goldsmith, 'Pinochet and International Human Rights Litigation', *Michigan Law Review* 97 (1999): 2133.
13. *R v Bow Street Metropolitan Stipendiary Magistrate and Others, ex parte Pinochet Ugarte (No. 1)*, 4 AII ER 897 (House of Lords 1998).
14. *R v Bow Street Metropolitan Stipendiary Magistrate and Others, ex parte Pinochet Ugarte (No. 1)*, 4 AII ER 897.
15. *R v. Bow Street Metropolitan Stipendiary Magistrate and Others, ex parte Pinochet Ugarte (No. 2)*, 2 W.L.R. 272 (House of Lords 1999).
16. *R v. Bow Street Metropolitan Stipendiary Magistrate and Others, ex parte Pinochet Ugarte (No. 3)*, 1 A.C. 147 (House of Lords 2000).

17. *See R v Bow Street Metropolitan Stipendiary Magistrate and Others, ex parte Pinochet Ugarte (No. 1)*, 4 AII ER 897.
18. *R v Bow Street Metropolitan Stipendiary Magistrate and Others, ex parte Pinochet Ugarte (No. 1)*, 4 AII ER 897 at 898.
19. *R v Bow Street Metropolitan Stipendiary Magistrate and Others, ex parte Pinochet Ugarte (No. 1)*, 4 AII ER 897 at 939–40.
20. *R v Bow Street Metropolitan Stipendiary Magistrate and Others, ex parte Pinochet Ugarte (No. 1)*, 4 AII ER 897 at 945.
21. *R v Bow Street Metropolitan Stipendiary Magistrate and Others, ex parte Pinochet Ugarte (No. 1)*, 4 AII ER 897 at 947.
22. See Colin Warbrick, Dominic McGoldrick, and Hazel Fox, 'The Pinochet Case No. 3', *International and Comparative Law Quarterly* 48, no. 3 (1999): 689.
23. See *R v Bow Street Metropolitan Stipendiary Magistrate and Others, ex parte Pinochet Ugarte (No. 1)*, 4 AII ER 897.
24. See the opinions of Lord Browne-Wilkinson, Lord Goff of Chieveley, Lord Hope of Craighead, Lord Hutton, and Lord Saville of Newdigate for a particular concern on the UN Convention against Torture in case of enjoying immunity for Heads of State in the *R v. Bow Street Metropolitan Stipendiary Magistrate and Others, ex parte Pinochet Ugarte (No. 3)*, 1 A.C. 147.
25. *R v. Bow Street Metropolitan Stipendiary Magistrate and Others, ex parte Pinochet Ugarte (No. 3)*, 1 A.C. 147 at 273.
26. *R v. Bow Street Metropolitan Stipendiary Magistrate and Others, ex parte Pinochet Ugarte (No. 3)*, 1 A.C. 147 at 279.
27. See the Joint Separate Opinion of Judges Higgins, Kooijmans, and Buergenthal to the *Arrest Warrant of 11 April 2000 (Democratic Republic of the Congo v. Belgium), Judgment*, ICJ Reports at 88.
28. See Fox QC and Webb, *The Law of State Immunity*, 554.
29. Andrea Bianchi, 'Immunity versus Human Rights: The Pinochet Case', *European Journal of International Law* 10, no. 2 (1999): 248.
30. Wuerth, 'Pinochet's Legacy Reassessed', 731.
31. Charles Chernor Jalloh, 'Prosecutor v. Taylor', *The American Journal of International Law* 108, no. 1 (2014): 58.
32. SCSL. 'The Prosecutor vs. Charles Ghankay Taylor'. Accessed 10 August 2021. http://www.rscsl.org/Taylor.html., 'The Prosecutor vs. Charles Ghankay Taylor'.
33. *The Prosecutor v. Charles Ghankay Taylor*, SCSL-03-01-A 10766 (SCSL. 'The Prosecutor vs. Charles Ghankay Taylor'. Accessed 10 August 2021. http://www.rscsl.org/Taylor.html. 2013) at 10776.

34. UN Security Council, 'Statute of the SCSL. 'The Prosecutor vs. Charles Ghankay Taylor'. Accessed 10 August 2021. http://www.rscsl.org/Taylor.html.' (2002) Article 6(1).
35. *The Prosecutor v. Charles Ghankay Taylor*, SCSL-03-01-A at 10778.
36. Human Rights Watch, 'Q&A: The Case of Hissène Habré before the Extraordinary African Chambers in Senegal', 3 May 2016.
37. BBC News, 'Profile: Chad's Hissene Habre', 30 May 2016.
38. Human Rights Watch, 'Q&A: The Case of Hissène Habré before the Extraordinary African Chambers in Senegal'.
39. Human Rights Watch, 'Chad's Ex-Dictator Convicted of Atrocities', 30 May 2016.
40. John Kerry, 'Conviction of Hissene Habre for War Crimes, Crimes Against Humanity, and Torture' (U.S. Department of State, 30 May 2016).
41. Kerry.
42. See Stern, 'Immunities for Heads of State: Where Do We Stand?'
43. Stern.
44. 'Peace Treaty of Versailles' (1919) Article 227.
45. See Gary D. Solis, *The Law of Armed Conflict: International Humanitarian Law in War* (Cambridge: Cambridge University Press, 2010), 74.
46. UN, 'Charter of the International Military Tribunal' (1945) Article 7.
47. International Law Commission, 'Principles of International Law Recognized in the Charter of the Nuremberg Tribunal and in the Judgment of the Tribunal', in *Yearbook of the International Law Commission*, vol. II (New York: United Nations, 1950) Principle 3.
48. 'International Military Tribunal for the Far East Charter' (1946) Article 6.
49. International Law Commission, 'Second Report on Immunity of State Officials from Foreign Criminal Jurisdiction: By Roman Anatolevich Kolodkin, Special Rapporteur' (UN General Assembly, 10 June 2010), at paras 28, 29, 30 and 31.
50. UN Security Council, 'Statute of the International Criminal Tribunal for the Former Yugoslavia' (1993) Article 7(2).
51. *Prosecutor v. Tihomir Blaskic, Judgement on The Request of The Republic of Croatia for Review of The Decision of Trial Chamber II of 18 July 1997* (ICTY Appeals Chamber 29 October 1997) at para 41.
52. UN General Assembly, 'Rome Statute of the International Criminal Court' (1998) Article 27(1),(2).
53. UN General Assembly Article 98(1).
54. See Paola Gaeta, 'Official Capacity and Immunities', in *The Rome Statute of the International Criminal Court: A Commentary*, ed. Antonio

Cassese, Paola Gaeta, and John R. W. D. Jones, vol. I (Oxford: Oxford University Press, 2002), 975–1002.

55. Robert Cryer et al., *An Introduction to International Criminal Law and Procedure*, 2nd ed. (Cambridge: Cambridge University Press, 2010), 556.
56. Michael Tunks, 'Diplomats or Defendants? Defining the Future of Head-of-State Immunity', *Duke Law Journal* 52, no. 3 (2002): 659.
57. See *Arrest Warrant of 11 April 2000 (Democratic Republic of the Congo v. Belgium), Judgment*, ICJ Reports.
58. 'Belgium: Act of 1999 Concerning the Punishment of Grave Breaches of International Humanitarian Law' (1999).
59. *Arrest Warrant of 11 April 2000 (Democratic Republic of the Congo v. Belgium), Judgment*, ICJ Reports at 6.
60. Article 7 of the Act of 1999 Concerning the Punishment of Grave Breaches of International Humanitarian Law is about competence, applicable procedure, and the execution of sentences. It states that the 'Belgian courts shall be competent to deal with breaches provided for in the present Act, irrespective of where such breaches have been committed'. Belgium: Act of 1999 Concerning the Punishment of Grave Breaches of International Humanitarian Law.
61. *Arrest Warrant of 11 April 2000 (Democratic Republic of the Congo v. Belgium), Judgment*, ICJ Reports at 10.
62. *Arrest Warrant of 11 April 2000 (Democratic Republic of the Congo v. Belgium), Judgment*, ICJ Reports at 26.
63. Arrest Warrant of 11 April 2000 (Democratic Republic of the Congo v. Belgium), Judgment, ICJ Reports.
64. *Arrest Warrant of 11 April 2000 (Democratic Republic of the Congo v. Belgium), Judgment*, ICJ Reports at 23.
65. *R v. Bow Street Metropolitan Stipendiary Magistrate and Others, ex parte Pinochet Ugarte (No. 3)*, 1 A.C. 147 at 278.
66. *R v. Bow Street Metropolitan Stipendiary Magistrate and Others, ex parte Pinochet Ugarte (No. 3)*, 1 A.C. 147 at 289.
67. *R v. Bow Street Metropolitan Stipendiary Magistrate and Others, ex parte Pinochet Ugarte (No. 3)*, 1 A.C. 147 at 201–2.
68. *Arrest Warrant of 11 April 2000 (Democratic Republic of the Congo v. Belgium), Judgment*, ICJ Reports at 20.
69. *Arrest Warrant of 11 April 2000 (Democratic Republic of the Congo v. Belgium), Judgment*, ICJ Reports at 24–25.
70. *Arrest Warrant of 11 April 2000 (Democratic Republic of the Congo v. Belgium), Judgment*, ICJ Reports at 20.
71. *Arrest Warrant of 11 April 2000 (Democratic Republic of the Congo v. Belgium), Judgment*, ICJ Reports at 29.

72. *Arrest Warrant of 11 April 2000 (Democratic Republic of the Congo v. Belgium), Judgment*, ICJ Reports at 29.
73. *Arrest Warrant of 11 April 2000 (Democratic Republic of the Congo v. Belgium), Judgment*, ICJ Reports at 25.
74. *Arrest Warrant of 11 April 2000 (Democratic Republic of the Congo v. Belgium), Judgment*, ICJ Reports at 25.
75. *Arrest Warrant of 11 April 2000 (Democratic Republic of the Congo v. Belgium), Judgment*, ICJ Reports at 25–26.
76. See the Dissenting Opinion of Judge Van den Wyngaert to the *Arrest Warrant of 11 April 2000 (Democratic Republic of the Congo v. Belgium), Judgment*, ICJ Reports at 159.
77. *Arrest Warrant of 11 April 2000 (Democratic Republic of the Congo v. Belgium), Judgment*, ICJ Reports at 25.
78. *Arrest Warrant of 11 April 2000 (Democratic Republic of the Congo v. Belgium), Judgment*, ICJ Reports at 25–26.
79. Tunks, 'Diplomats or Defendants?', 665.
80. See Wuerth, 'Pinochet's Legacy Reassessed', 741.
81. See the Dissenting Opinion of Judge Van den Wyngaert to the *Arrest Warrant of 11 April 2000 (Democratic Republic of the Congo v. Belgium), Judgment*, ICJ Reports at 139–142–51.
82. See the Dissenting Opinion of Judge Van den Wyngaert to the *Arrest Warrant of 11 April 2000 (Democratic Republic of the Congo v. Belgium), Judgment*, ICJ Reports at 151.
83. See the Dissenting Opinion of Judge Van den Wyngaert to the *Arrest Warrant of 11 April 2000 (Democratic Republic of the Congo v. Belgium), Judgment*, ICJ Reports at 140–41.
84. See the Dissenting Opinion of Judge Van den Wyngaert to the *Arrest Warrant of 11 April 2000 (Democratic Republic of the Congo v. Belgium), Judgment*, ICJ Reports at 141.
85. Fox QC and Webb, *The Law of State Immunity*, 558.
86. *The Prosecutor v Al Bashir, First Arrest Warrant* ICC-02/05-01/09 (ICC Pre-Trial Chamber I 4 March 2009); *The Prosecutor v Al Bashir, Second Arrest Warrant* ICC-02/05-01/09-95 (ICC Pre-Trial Chamber I 12 July 2010); UN General Assembly, Rome Statute of the International Criminal Court Article 58(1)(b).
87. See *The Prosecutor v Al Bashir, Second Arrest Warrant* ICC-02/05-01/09-95.
88. *The Prosecutor v Omar Al Bashir* ICC-02/05-01/09-151 (ICC Pre-Trial Chamber II 26 March 2013) at para 8.
89. See *The Prosecutor v Omar Al Bashir* ICC-02/05-01/09-151.
90. See *The Prosecutor v Omar Al Bashir* ICC-02/05-01/09-242 (ICC Pre-Trial Chamber II 12 June 2015).

91. See *The Prosecutor v Al Bashir, First Arrest Warrant* ICC-02/05-01/09 at paras. 41, 42, 43, 44 and 45.
92. Dapo Akande, 'The Legal Nature of Security Council Referrals to the ICC and Its Impact on Al Bashir's Immunities', *Journal of International Criminal Justice* 7, no. 2 (2009): 348.
93. Jessica Needham, 'Protection or Prosecution for Omar Al Bashir? The Changing State of Immunity in International Criminal Law', *Auckland University Law Review* 17 (2011): 247.
94. See generally Sophie Papillon, 'Has the United Nations Security Council Implicitly Removed Al Bashir's Immunity?', *International Criminal Law Review* 10, no. 2 (2010): 275–88. There is another perspective that claims that the implicit removal of immunity by the Security Council would be at odds with customary international law and treaty principles which provide immunity for serving Heads of State. Be that as it may, Article 103 of the UN Charter reports that in 'the event of a conflict between the obligations of the Member of the United Nations under the present Charter and their obligations under any other international agreement, their obligations under the present Charter shall prevail'. For a critique of the implicit removal of immunity by the Council see Paola Gaeta, 'Does President Al Bashir Enjoy Immunity from Arrest?', *Journal of International Criminal Justice* 7, no. 2 (2009): 315–32.
95. *The Prosecutor v Omar Al Bashir, Decision Under Article 87(7) of the Rome Statute on the Non-compliance by Jordan with the Request by the Court for the Arrest and Surrender of Omar Al-Bashir*, ICC-02/05-01/09 (ICC Pre-Trial Chamber II 11 December 2017) at para 5.
96. *The Prosecutor v Omar Al Bashir, Decision Under Article 87(7) of the Rome Statute on the Non-compliance by Jordan with the Request by the Court for the Arrest and Surrender of Omar Al-Bashir*, ICC-02/05-01/09 at 21.
97. *The Prosecutor v Omar Al Bashir Judgment in the Jordan Referral re Al-Bashir Appeal* ICC-02/05-01/09 OA2 (ICC Appeals Chamber 6 May 2019) at para 17.
98. *The Prosecutor v Omar Al Bashir Judgment in the Jordan Referral re Al-Bashir Appeal* ICC-02/05-01/09 OA2 at para 2.
99. *The Prosecutor v Omar Al Bashir Judgment in the Jordan Referral re Al-Bashir Appeal* ICC-02/05-01/09 OA2 at 5.
100. *The Prosecutor v Omar Al Bashir Judgment in the Jordan Referral re Al-Bashir Appeal* ICC-02/05-01/09 OA2 at 5.
101. Angela Mudukuti, 'Prosecutor v. Omar Hassan Ahmad Al-Bashir, Judgment in the Jordan Referral Re Al-Bashir Appeal', *American Journal of International Law* 114, no. 1 (2020): 107.

102. See the Dissenting Opinion of Judge Van den Wyngaert to the *Arrest Warrant of 11 April 2000 (Democratic Republic of the Congo v. Belgium), Judgment,* ICJ Reports.
103. International Law Commission, 'Principles of International Law Recognized in the Charter of the Nuremberg Tribunal and in the Judgment of the Tribunal' Principle 1.
104. UN General Assembly, 'Convention on the Prevention and Punishment of the Crime of Genocide', UNTS 78 (1948) Article 4. The acts listed in Article 3 are genocide, conspiracy to commit genocide, direct and public incitement to commit genocide, attempt to commit genocide, and complicity in genocide.
105. See the Dissenting Opinion of Judge Van den Wyngaert to the *Arrest Warrant of 11 April 2000 (Democratic Republic of the Congo v. Belgium), Judgment,* ICJ Reports at 158.
106. H. Lauterpacht, 'The Problem of Jurisdictional Immunities of Foreign States', *British Yearbook of International Law* 28 (1951): 232.

References

Akande, Dapo. 'The Legal Nature of Security Council Referrals to the ICC and Its Impact on Al Bashir's Immunities'. *Journal of International Criminal Justice* 7, no. 2 (2009): 333–52.

Application of the Convention on the Prevention and Punishment of the Crime owef Genocide, Preliminary Objections, Judgment, ICJ Reports 595 (1996).

Armed Activities on the Territory of the Congo (New Application: 2002) (Democratic Republic of the Congo v. Rwanda), Jurisdiction and Admissibility, Judgment, ICJ Reports 6 (2006).

Arrest Warrant of 11 April 2000 (Democratic Republic of the Congo v. Belgium), Judgment, ICJ Reports 3 (2002).

BBC News. 'Profile: Chad's Hissene Habre', 30 May 2016. Accessed 10 August 2021. http://www.bbc.com/news/world-africa-18927845.

Belgium: Act of 1999 Concerning the Punishment of Grave Breaches of International Humanitarian Law (1999).

Bianchi, Andrea. 'Immunity versus Human Rights: The Pinochet Case'. *European Journal of International Law* 10, no. 2 (1999): 237–77.

Bradley, Curtis A., and Jack L. Goldsmith. 'Pinochet and International Human Rights Litigation'. *Michigan Law Review* 97 (1999): 2129–84.

Cryer, Robert, Hakan Friman, Darryl Robinson, and Elizabeth Wilmshurst. *An Introduction to International Criminal Law and Procedure.* 2nd ed. Cambridge: Cambridge University Press, 2010.

Foakes, Joanne. *Immunity for International Crimes? Developments in the Law on Prosecuting Heads of State in Foreign Courts.* International Law Programme IL BP 2011/02. London: The Royal Institute of International Affairs, 2011.

Fox QC, Hazel, and Philippa Webb. *The Law of State Immunity.* 3rd ed. Oxford: Oxford University Press, 2013.

Gaeta, Paola. 'Does President Al Bashir Enjoy Immunity from Arrest?' *Journal of International Criminal Justice* 7, no. 2 (2009): 315–32.

———. 'Official Capacity and Immunities'. In *The Rome Statute of the International Criminal Court: A Commentary*, edited by Antonio Cassese, Paola Gaeta, and John R. W. D. Jones, I:975–1002. Oxford: Oxford University Press, 2002.

Human Rights Watch. 'Chad's Ex-Dictator Convicted of Atrocities', 30 May 2016. Accessed 10 August 2021. https://www.hrw.org/news/2016/05/30/chads-ex-dictator-convicted-atrocities.

———. 'Q&A: The Case of Hissène Habré before the Extraordinary African Chambers in Senegal', 3 May 2016. Accessed 10 August 2021. https://www.hrw.org/news/2016/05/03/qa-case-hissene-habre-extraordinary-african-chambers-senegal.

In re Grand Jury Proceedings, 817 F.2d 1108 (US Court of Appeals, Fourth Circuit 1987).

International Law Commission. 'Principles of International Law Recognized in the Charter of the Nuremberg Tribunal and in the Judgment of the Tribunal'. In *Yearbook of the International Law Commission*, Vol. II. New York: United Nations, 1950.

———. 'Second Report on Immunity of State Officials from Foreign Criminal Jurisdiction: By Roman Anatolevich Kolodkin, Special Rapporteur'. UN General Assembly, 10 June 2010.

International Military Tribunal for the Far East Charter (1946).

Jalloh, Charles Chernor. 'Prosecutor v. Taylor'. *The American Journal of International Law* 108, no. 1 (2014): 58–66.

Kerry, John. 'Conviction of Hissene Habre for War Crimes, Crimes Against Humanity, and Torture'. U.S. Department of State, 30 May 2016.

Lauterpacht, H. 'The Problem of Jurisdictional Immunities of Foreign States'. *British Yearbook of International Law* 28 (1951): 220–72.

Mudukuti, Angela. 'Prosecutor v. Omar Hassan Ahmad Al-Bashir, Judgment in the Jordan Referral Re Al-Bashir Appeal'. *American Journal of International Law* 114, no. 1 (2020): 103–9.

Needham, Jessica. 'Protection or Prosecution for Omar Al Bashir? The Changing State of Immunity in International Criminal Law'. *Auckland University Law Review* 17 (2011): 219–48.

Papillon, Sophie. 'Has the United Nations Security Council Implicitly Removed Al Bashir's Immunity?' *International Criminal Law Review* 10, no. 2 (2010): 275–88.

Peace Treaty of Versailles (1919).
Prosecutor v. Tihomir Blaskic, Judgement on The Request of The Republic of Croatia for Review of The Decision of Trial Chamber II of 18 July 1997 (ICTY Appeals Chamber 29 October 1997).
R v Bow Street Metropolitan Stipendiary Magistrate and Others, ex parte Pinochet Ugarte (No. 1), 4 AII ER 897 (House of Lords 1998).
R v. Bow Street Metropolitan Stipendiary Magistrate and Others, ex parte Pinochet Ugarte (No. 2), 2 W.L.R. 272 (House of Lords 1999).
R v. Bow Street Metropolitan Stipendiary Magistrate and Others, ex parte Pinochet Ugarte (No. 3), 1 A.C. 147 (House of Lords 2000).
SCSL. 'The Prosecutor vs. Charles Ghankay Taylor'. Accessed 10 August 2021. http://www.rscsl.org/Taylor.html.
Solis, Gary D. *The Law of Armed Conflict: International Humanitarian Law in War*. Cambridge: Cambridge University Press, 2010.
Stern, Brigitte. 'Immunities for Heads of State: Where Do We Stand?' In *Justice for Crimes Against Humanity*, edited by Mark Lattimer and Philippe Sands, 73–106. Oxford and Portland, OR: Hart Publishing, 2003.
The Prosecutor v Al Bashir, First Arrest Warrant ICC-02/05-01/09 (ICC Pre-Trial Chamber I 4 March 2009).
The Prosecutor v Al Bashir, Second Arrest Warrant ICC-02/05-01/09-95 (ICC Pre-Trial Chamber I 12 July 2010).
The Prosecutor v. Charles Ghankay Taylor, SCSL-03-01-A 10766 (SCSL. 'The Prosecutor vs. Charles Ghankay Taylor'. Accessed 10 August 2021. http://www.rscsl.org/Taylor.html. 2013).
The Prosecutor v Omar Al Bashir, Decision Under Article 87(7) of the Rome Statute on the Non-compliance by Jordan with the Request by the Court for the Arrest and Surrender of Omar Al-Bashir, ICC-02/05-01/09 (ICC Pre-Trial Chamber II 11 December 2017).
The Prosecutor v Omar Al Bashir ICC-02/05-01/09-151 (ICC Pre-Trial Chamber II 26 March 2013).
The Prosecutor v Omar Al Bashir ICC-02/05-01/09-242 (ICC Pre-Trial Chamber II 12 June 2015).
The Prosecutor v Omar Al Bashir Judgment in the Jordan Referral re Al-Bashir Appeal ICC-02/05-01/09 OA2 (ICC Appeals Chamber 6 May 2019).
Tunks, Michael. 'Diplomats or Defendants? Defining the Future of Head-of-State Immunity'. *Duke Law Journal* 52, no. 3 (2002): 651–82.
UN. Charter of the International Military Tribunal (1945).
UN General Assembly. Convention on Special Missions 1969, UNTS 1400 (1969).
———. Convention on the Prevention and Punishment of the Crime of Genocide, UNTS 78 (1948).
———. Rome Statute of the International Criminal Court (1998).

UN Security Council. Statute of the International Criminal Tribunal for the Former Yugoslavia (1993).

———. Statute of the SCSL. 'The Prosecutor vs. Charles Ghankay Taylor'. Accessed 10 August 2021. http://www.rscsl.org/Taylor.html. (2002).

Warbrick, Colin, Dominic McGoldrick, and Hazel Fox. 'The Pinochet Case No. 3'. *International and Comparative Law Quarterly* 48, no. 3 (1999): 687–702.

Watts, Arthur. 'Heads of State'. In *Max Planck Encyclopedia of Public International Law*. Oxford University Press, October 2010. Accessed 10 August 2021. https://opil.ouplaw.com/view/10.1093/law:epil/9780199231690/law-9780199231690-e1418?rskey=DYWrpH&result=23&q=immunity&prd=EPIL.

Wuerth, Ingrid. 'Pinochet's Legacy Reassessed'. *The American Journal of International Law* 106, no. 4 (2012): 731–68.

CHAPTER 6

Human Rights Versus Diplomatic Immunity

Diplomatic immunity is regarded as one of the most interesting elements in contemporary international law and is a vital requirement for contemporary international relations. It maintains smooth diplomatic relations among States by bestowing immunities and privileges on diplomatic agents. Any misinterpretation of the extent of diplomatic privileges and immunities by diplomatic agents could well violate the principles of international law. It should be noted that a host (receiving) State may tolerate some abuses of diplomatic immunity unless such misconduct leads to violations of fundamental human rights. Said tolerance is shown by the international community and the host State towards diplomatic agents in order to maintain smooth diplomatic and international relations and also to allow for effective performance of diplomatic functions.

Granting diplomatic immunity and protecting fundamental human rights are important rules of international law, but which beg the following question: Which rule of international law should prevail when such rules conflict? International human rights norms, as the previous chapters have attested, have a prominent status in the modern international system even though they are not historically as deeply rooted as the principle of diplomatic immunity. The question is, therefore, whether or not the protection of fundamental human rights should prevail over diplomatic immunity. Unless a hierarchy of these two essential rules is established, conflict is inevitable. Diplomatic immunity safeguards accredited diplomatic agents against local jurisdiction; in practice, this guarantee is at odds with the obligation to prevent and prosecute violations of fundamental human rights. Prohibiting fundamental human rights violations are norms

S. Özdan, *The Human Rights Challenge to Immunity in International Law*, https://doi.org/10.1007/978-3-030-92923-7_6

that have been universally recognised as such through State practice and treaties. These human rights are those that have a non-derogable and peremptory nature (see Chap. 3), and, as argued earlier, such prohibitions against torture or slavery are peremptory human rights norms of general international law.

The purpose of this chapter is to consider whether principles of diplomatic immunity should be lifted, limited, or amended when fundamental human rights violations are committed by diplomatic agents. The central argument is that diplomatic immunity, like Head of State immunity, should, on no account, mean impunity when fundamental human rights violations are committed by a diplomatic agent.

On Diplomacy

Diplomacy is an essential instrument of international communication, a tool for managing regular or complex relations among States. It is an official conversation system, creating communications channels between States. Diplomacy, from a State's perspective, is an essential mechanism for implementing, formalising, and managing foreign policy.[1] Diplomacy, as a communication technique, 'is an ancient institution and international legal provisions governing its manifestations are the result of centuries of state practice'.[2]

The concept of diplomacy has always been accepted as crucial for the smooth functioning of inter-State relations. It is 'the application of intelligence and tact to the conduct of official relations between the governments of independent states [...] or more briefly, the conduct of business between states by peaceful means'.[3] States adopt various methods in order to carry out diplomacy with other States. Representation of the State at the highest level abroad is the most substantial task required of diplomacy. This function involves negotiating solutions to difficult international problems and facilitating inter-State affairs through embassies. It follows that the primary purpose of diplomacy is 'to enable states to secure the objectives of their foreign policies without resort to force, propaganda, or law'.[4]

Increasingly tangled issues between States, particularly in respect of human rights, and evolving systems in international relations force States to consider and give weight to their diplomatic channels with other States. As a consequence, the role of diplomatic agents has become more important and their responsibilities have increased. In light of these developments, the international community has sought to draw a framework for diplomatic immunity and to adopt certain principles and rules for diplomatic agents, receiving States, and sending States. The following section analyses significant developments in the codification of diplomatic immunity.

Development of Diplomatic Immunity in International Law

Principles and rules for managing and monitoring the many different features and details of diplomatic relations constitute one of the oldest formulations of international law. In international law, the official status of diplomatic agents has been acknowledged by the international community since ancient times. As Malcolm Shaw remarked, whenever 'in history there has been a group of independent states co-existing, special customs have developed on how the ambassadors and other special representatives of other states were to be treated'.[5]

Strictly speaking, by 1961 it had been recognised that diplomatic agents must bear particular privileges and immunities from any domestic civil or criminal jurisdiction. This arrangement has been accepted as the fundamental rules of diplomatic law. These norms have been substantially developed through customary international law. The words of eighteenth century Diplomat, Emerich de Vattel, articulate the reasons for the immunities and privileges of diplomatic agents:

> A minister is often charged with commissions that are disagreeable to the prince to whom he is sent. If that prince has any power over him, and especially on sovereign authority, how is it to be expected that the minister can execute his master's orders with due fidelity, firmness, and freedom of mind? It is a matter of no small importance that he have no snares to apprehend—that he be not liable to be diverted from his functions by any chicanery—that he have nothing to hope, nothing to fear, from the sovereign to whom he is sent. In order, therefore, to the success of his ministry, he must be independent of the sovereign authority and of the jurisdiction of the country, both in civil and criminal matters.[6]

It follows that diplomatic agents demand special and differential treatment under international law. Without it, those agents may encounter significant obstacles in performing their duties. Ernest Satow also emphasised that historically 'embarrassing incidents, and the growing independence of the courts, made it necessary to enact national laws expressly providing for diplomats to enjoy immunity from civil suits and from execution against their property'.[7]

The need to provide immunity to diplomatic agents has forced the international community to establish and develop particular diplomatic immunities and privileges, for which purpose, some codifications regarding the rules of diplomatic law were enacted. The Havana Convention on Diplomatic Officers 1928 and the Harvard Research Draft Convention on Diplomatic Privileges and Immunities 1932 are regarded as early attempts at codifications. The Havana Convention, which was recognised by only fourteen Latin American States, described itself as a temporary instrument to be used only until more proper and absolute codification was formulated. The Harvard Draft Convention proved unable to modify and adjust the provisions of national law in compliance with diplomatic immunities and privileges.[8] As a result, the international community felt the need for a more effective, universal, and comprehensive system through which to regulate diplomatic functions and relations. This also corresponded with a move more generally within the UN to codify fundamental areas of international law.

When one considers the functions of diplomatic agents, it is easy to justify the granting of diplomatic privileges and immunities. However, a lack of constraint on these diplomatic privileges and immunities has allowed embassies to abuse their diplomatic rights. This chapter addresses such acts and discusses the shaping of the principles on diplomatic privileges and immunities, the UN International Law Commission adopted the Vienna Convention on Diplomatic Relations in 1961 and Vienna Convention on Consular Relations in 1963. The Vienna Convention on Diplomatic Relations, which came into force in 1964, codified and developed the customary international law of diplomacy. The Convention primarily consolidates State practice as it had developed until 1961. It clarified the customary law, 'adjusted its content to modern conditions, and re-launched it in the more impressive form of a multilateral convention'.[9] The 1961 Vienna Convention provides 'a complete framework for the establishment, maintenance, and termination of diplomatic relations on the basis of consent between independent sovereign States' and the Convention 'has established itself as a cornerstone of modern international relations'.[10] The 1963 Vienna Convention on Consular Relations includes a general framework of minimal standards in respect of the conduct of consular relations.[11] Both Vienna Conventions formalise the core of international diplomatic and consular law.

The formulation of the Vienna Convention on Diplomatic Relations was basically a response to the unrestricted immunity customarily granted to diplomats.[12] When the Vienna Convention was adopted on 16 April 1961, it was substantially accepted as codifying the rules of diplomatic law. The Convention was recognised as a milestone development in respect of regulating the principles of diplomatic relations. It was also deemed a watershed of supreme importance in respect of the codification of international law. Unlike the Havana Convention or the Harvard Draft Convention, the Vienna Convention has been recognised by 190 State parties as of February 2016. The Vienna Convention can, therefore, be deemed to enjoy overall consensus. It establishes contemporary international law pursuant to the immunities and privileges of diplomats.

Indeed, in 1936, Montell Ogdon pointed to the need for the concept of diplomatic immunity to be framed and regulated under legal conditions, as he believed that there was increasing opposition to the absolute and limitless immunities held by the diplomatic agents. On this point Ogdon observed that:

> The tide of world-wide revolt against special privilege has gone so far as to make itself felt in the channels of diplomacy and has begun to weaken the foundations of sand on which certain fictions of diplomatic immunity were built. The pressure for invasion of the sacred rights of diplomats may be observed from the Continent of North America to South Africa and from the Orient to Great Britain [...]. It is aimed primarily at the destruction of license and privilege, much of which grew out of a period of jealously and fear between princes and kings who believed themselves to personify the State.[13]

Ogdon implies that there was a need to formulate effective diplomatic law. The adoption of the Vienna Convention on Diplomatic Relations assisted in systematising the practice of hosting diplomatic agents, the institution of diplomatic assignments, and the rules of diplomatic immunity. The Convention designates and regulates certain duties of both sending and receiving States. It also designates the functions of diplomatic missions. The main purposes of the Convention are to maintain international peace and security and to promote friendly relations among States. The Vienna Convention, in its Preamble, provides a rationale for granting immunities and privileges to diplomatic agents on the basis of functional needs. The Convention therefore is not intended to benefit the individual, in their individual capacity; on the contrary, its purpose is to provide and maintain well-ordered relations among States.

The Vienna Convention outlines the responsibility of the receiving State for establishing a smooth environment in which diplomatic agents can carry out their duties. It states that the 'person of a diplomatic agent shall be inviolable. He shall not be liable to any form of arrest or detention. The receiving State shall treat him with due respect and shall take all appropriate steps to prevent any attack on his person, freedom or dignity'.[14] Given that the diplomatic agent is an official representative of his or her own State, all measures taken by the receiving State should be read as protective measures in respect to that diplomat's official position. In light of the purposes of the Vienna Convention, three significant grounds are established for diplomatic immunity. Each is notable for its use as a justification for granting immunity to diplomatic agents abroad. The next section clarifies and criticises these grounds.

Theoretical Grounds for Diplomatic Immunity

Three significant theories have been put forward in order to justify the practice of bestowing immunity on diplomatic agents when performing official duties abroad: these are: (1) Personal Representation; (2) Extraterritoriality; and (3) Functional Necessity.[15]

Personal Representation was the first theory promulgated to justify diplomatic immunity. The representative's privileges 'are similar to those of the sovereign herself, and an insult to the ambassador is an insult to the dignity of the sovereign'.[16] Regarding this theory, Vattel emphasised that the 'respect which is due to sovereigns should redound to their representatives, and especially their ambassadors, as representing their master's person in the first degree'.[17] In other words, according to this theory, a diplomatic agent embodies the sovereign ruler of his or her own State. It follows that any insult to the diplomatic agent constitutes an insult to that agent's sovereign.

L. J. Brett set out the theory of Personal Representation in *The Parlement Belge* case as follows. The immunity of a diplomatic agent from the jurisdiction of the domestic courts to which 'he is accredited is based upon his being the representative of the independent sovereign or state which sends him, and which sends him upon the faith of his being admitted to be clothed with the same independence of and superiority to all adverse jurisdiction as the sovereign authority whom he represents would be'.[18] However, a counterargument to the Personal Representation theory has been raised by some scholars who pointed out that the immunity of a diplomatic agent may not be equal to that of his or her own sovereign.[19] In view of this counterargument, the personal representation theory might seem to be a weak foundation for diplomatic immunity. Nevertheless, this theory cannot be dismissed since diplomatic agents do represent their own sovereigns abroad. In fact, the theory has been reformulated to comply with contemporary international law.

The second theoretical ground for diplomatic immunity is Extraterritoriality. According to this theory, the territory that belongs to diplomatic agents is accepted as the sending State's territory in spite of the fact that the diplomatic agent lives in a foreign State. It follows that the diplomatic agent has no liability under the host State's law because technically the agent does not reside in the host State.[20] In relation to Extraterritoriality theory, Grotius stated that ambassadors were to be outside of the boundaries of the country to which they were sent. Accordingly, they are not subject to the domestic law of the host State.[21] From the perspective of this theory, diplomatic agents benefit from immunity in a foreign territory where they perform diplomatic relations on the behalf of their own States.

Ogdon claimed that the immunity from domestic jurisdiction that is granted to the diplomatic agent's personal property originates in the presumption that 'the domicile of the owner was still in his own country'.[22] Because the diplomatic agent's 'personal effects were sometimes regarded as belonging to, or being closely associated with the domicile of the owner, the fiction was, therefore, extended to render' the diplomatic agent's personal property free from confiscation in the host State.[23]

The final theoretical ground related to diplomatic immunity is that of Functional Necessity. This theory is accepted as the most viable justification for diplomatic immunity, and is the predominant theory in current international relations. According to this theory, diplomatic agents cannot be sued by applying the jurisdiction of domestic courts because if they were, their official functions would be impeded. The theory of Functional Necessity justifies diplomatic immunity for the sake of providing smooth diplomatic relations. Diplomatic agents are considered vital to maintaining mutual relations among States; however, these agents cannot fulfil the object of their assignment unless they are vested with all the prerogatives they require to accomplish their official tasks successfully, securely, and completely. While international conventions obligate us to admit diplomatic agents, they also explicitly bind us to recognise those agents in their entirety, including their personal effects, as possessing all the rights and prerogatives necessary for them to safely perform their official functions.[24]

According to Functional Necessity Theory, from the moment diplomatic agents are admitted to the receiving State's territory, throughout the period of their residence and until their diplomatic duties end in that State, they are entitled to a complete exemption from the domestic both civil and criminal jurisdiction.[25] Wheaton, referring to the functional necessity theory, argued in 1836 that the aforementioned exemption from domestic jurisdiction is based on mutual advantages stemming from the requirement that diplomatic agents 'should be entirely independent of the local authority' in order to perform their diplomatic duties.[26]

The Vienna Convention indicates that diplomatic immunity is vested to ensure and maintain the efficiency of diplomatic functions and also to regulate the framework in which diplomatic immunities are implemented. Thus, the Convention stresses the functionality of the diplomatic immunity. If a diplomatic agent's deeds fall outside the remit of international relations and particularly diplomatic relations, the concept of diplomatic immunity inevitably becomes questionable. Having outlined the theoretical grounds for granting immunity to diplomatic agents in this section, the next section analyses the importance of diplomatic immunity for diplomatic agents and criticises the absolute nature of diplomatic immunity under the Vienna Convention.

Diplomatic Immunity

Diplomatic relations involve the performance of the governmental functions of the sending State on the territory of the host State, with the authorisation of the latter. Crawford remarks that having agreed 'to the establishment of diplomatic relations, the receiving state must enable the sending state to benefit from the content of the [authorisation]'.[27] This directive has led to the development of a branch for immunities and privileges for diplomatic agents.

The roots of diplomatic law date back to ancient history, and it is therefore seen as one of the earliest fields of international law. Diplomatic immunity also stems from the desire to protect envoys or attachés of foreign States in a host country from retaliation during a time of international dispute, and to further and develop peaceful and courteous relations between sovereign States. Diplomatic immunity, in common law, first appeared as State immunity. The need to preserve the State's independence and dignity abroad has raised the question of how to grant protection to the State's diplomatic agents. Towards this end, it was accepted that diplomatic agents should be endowed with a level of immunity tantamount to that of the sovereign State.

The certain privileges and immunities 'related to diplomatic personnel of various kinds grew up partly as a consequence of sovereign immunity and the independence and equality of states, and partly as an essential requirement of an international system'.[28] In this regard, Lord Talbot's statement in the 1736 *Barbuit* case is an apt reference point:

> [T]he privilege of a public minister is to have his person sacred and free from arrest, not on his own account, but on account of those he represents; and this arises from the necessity of the thing, that nations may have intercourse with one another [...] the foundation of this privilege is for the sake of the prince by whom an ambassador is sent.[29]

It is beyond doubt that the protection of diplomatic agents in the foreign country where they serve is regarded as an important function of diplomatic immunity. In this respect, the Vienna Convention confers upon the host State a special duty to take all appropriate measures to protect the premises of the mission against any type of intrusion, and to prevent any disruption to the diplomatic mission or impairment of its dignity.[30] In this sense, the decision of the ICJ on the 1980 *Tehran Hostages* case[31] has been recognised as clearly demonstrating the importance of providing protection for diplomatic agents in relation to their official duties and positions.

In the *Tehran Hostages* case, a group of Iranian students overran the premises of the United States Embassy in Tehran and took more than sixty residents hostage on 4 November 1979. On this occasion, the ICJ remarked that the students' act could be attributed to the State of Iran only if the students acted on the behalf of the State. Although Iran had a responsibility to protect the premises of the United States Embassy under the Article 22(2) of the Vienna Convention, it failed to take all necessary and appropriate measures to guard the embassy and residents. Therefore, the United States argued that Iran had breached the Vienna Convention of 1961 and, furthermore, the Vienna Convention on Consular Relations of 1963. The Court ultimately decided on 4 November 1979 that the

Iranian State and its authorities were unequivocally aware of their responsibilities under the Vienna Conventions of 1961 and 1963, but failed to take all necessary measures to safeguard the premises and diplomatic agents of the United States Embassy.[32]

In the *Tehran Hostages* case, Iran drew attention of the ICJ to the 'deep rootedness and the essential character of the Islamic Revolution of Iran' and asserted that the 'examination of the numerous repercussions of the revolution [...] is a matter essentially and directly within the national sovereignty of Iran'.[33] However, as the ICJ in its Order of 15 December 1979 stated:

> a dispute which concerns diplomatic and consular premises and the detention of internationally protected persons, and involves the interpretation or application of multilateral conventions codifying the international law governing diplomatic and consular relations, is one which by its very nature falls within international jurisdiction.[34]

The ICJ stated that 'Iran was placed under the most categorical obligations, as a receiving state, to take appropriate steps to ensure the protection of the United States Embassy and Consulates, their staffs, their archives, their means of communication and the free movement of the members of their staffs'.[35] Ultimately, the Court found that Iran, by committing continuing violations of the international obligations laid down by the 1961 and 1963 Vienna Conventions and 'applicable rules of general international law, has incurred responsibility towards the United States', that Iran was under an obligation to pay reparation to the United States for the injury caused to the United States.[36] In its judgement, the Court pointed out that 'the obligations laid on States by the two Vienna Conventions are of cardinal importance for the maintenance of good relations between States in the interdependent world of today'.[37] The Court then stated that there 'is no more fundamental prerequisite for the conduct of relations between States [...] than the inviolability of diplomatic envoys and embassies, so that throughout history nations of all creeds and cultures have observed reciprocal obligations for that purpose'.[38] The *Tehran Hostages* case underscores the significance of the obligation to protect diplomatic agents in the foreign countries where they perform their official duties.

Five years later, the Vienna Convention was thrown into crisis by events that took place in London on 17 April 1984, when Libyan opponents of the Government of Colonel Gaddafi held an orderly demonstration opposite the Libyan Embassy. During the demonstration, shots were fired from a window of the Libyan Embassy that led to the death of Police Constable Yvonne Joyce Fletcher who was on duty in the area. Immediately after this event, the Libyan authorities were asked to order those diplomatic staff in the Embassy to leave the building to enable it to be examined for explosives and weapons. The Libyans rejected this request; the British Embassy in Tripoli was subsequently targeted for antagonistic demonstrations and the Libyan authorities unjustifiably arrested and detained particular British citizens. Upon cessation of diplomatic relations between the United Kingdom and Libya, Libyan diplomatic officials, together with those allegedly responsible for the death of the police constable, were permitted to leave the United Kingdom.[39]

Rosalyn Higgins criticised diplomatic law and emphasised that many legislators were extremely disturbed and concerned that the current international law on diplomatic immunity evidently prevented the Libyan Embassy from being searched and those allegedly responsible for the shooting from being detained and arrested. Higgins added that 'it was widely felt that diplomats acting in a way incompatible with their diplomatic status should not benefit from an immunity granted to assist the orderly conduct of diplomatic relations'.[40] The general sentiment was that diplomatic premises which were a base for criminal deeds should not be accredited with inviolability. On this basis, Higgins remarked that 'a proper interpretation of the Vienna Convention would support the view that immunity and inviolability fell away when diplomats and missions abused their positions'.[41] Moreover, if the Convention cannot provide these recommendable outcomes, she argued, the content of the Convention should be amended and adapted in light of the increasing importance of international human rights.[42] Diplomatic immunity under the Vienna Convention may be seen as a questionable principle of international law given the fact that the role of international human rights has been growing.

Efforts to Limit Diplomatic Immunities Provided by the Vienna Convention

According to the Vienna Convention, three possible measures can be taken by a State against a diplomatic agent who abuses his or her diplomatic immunity: (1) declaring that agent *persona non grata* (an unwelcome or unacceptable person); (2) the application of sending State jurisdiction; and (3) waiving immunity. It must be noted that these limitations do not permit any possible redress or compensation for the injured party. The primary objective of these limitations is to deter States and their representatives from exploiting diplomatic immunities and privileges.[43]

First, Article 9 of the Vienna Convention of 1961 permits the host State to declare diplomatic agents *persona non grata*. It states that the 'receiving State may at any time and without having to explain its decision, notify the sending State that the head of the mission or any member of the diplomatic staff of the mission is *persona non grata* or that any other member of the staff of the mission is not acceptable'.[44] *Persona non grata* can be viewed as an important step towards challenging the exploitation of diplomatic privileges and immunities by diplomatic agents. In fact, this measure has been applied very sparingly in response to gross abuses of diplomatic immunity. The declaration of *persona non grata* is generally issued to those who commit acts of terrorism, espionage, or who engage in overt criminality. The provision of *persona non grata* under the Vienna Convention is accepted as a lawful limitation to absolute immunity of diplomatic agents.[45]

In 1958, the International Law Commission also noted that an 'exception arises in the case of proceedings relating to a professional or commercial activity exercised by the diplomatic agent outside his official functions. It was urged that activities of these kinds are normally wholly inconsistent with the position of a diplomatic agent, and that one possible consequence of his engaging in them might be that he would be declared *persona non grata*'.[46]

Second, the Vienna Convention on Diplomatic Relations states that the 'immunity of a diplomatic agent from the jurisdiction of the receiving State does not exempt him from the jurisdiction of the sending State'.[47] It follows that a diplomatic agent may be subject to the jurisdiction of his or her national court for wrongdoings committed in the receiving State. Denza indicated that civil proceedings against a diplomatic agent before the national courts of his or her own State 'do not usually provide a satisfactory remedy for a claimant in the receiving State'.[48] It should be noted that a claimant can neither serve proceedings against the diplomatic agent nor may be able to finance the costs of having legal advice and instituting legal proceedings in the foreign State. In the furtherance of these difficulties, Sir Gerald Fitzmaurice, while at the International Law Commission, indicated that international law did not 'impose any positive obligation on States to allow their diplomatic agents to be sued before their own courts'.[49] It follows that the jurisdiction of the sending State is unlikely to be deemed a feasible means through which to challenge the abuses of diplomatic immunity.

Third, the Vienna Convention states that the 'immunity from jurisdiction of diplomatic agents and of persons enjoying immunity under Article 37 may be waived by the sending State. Waiver must always be express'.[50] In other words, a diplomatic agent may be subject to the jurisdiction of the national courts of the host State, provided that the sending State explicitly waives the diplomatic agent's immunity. On this point, Farhangi remarked that if 'the sending state waives its diplomat's immunity, the receiving state does not infringe upon any of the Vienna Convention's protections when the receiving state acts against the offending diplomat'.[51] Waiver of immunity from jurisdiction on the subject of administrative or civil litigations is not to be taken to manifest waiver from immunity in the matter of the execution of the adjudication, which requires a separate waiver.[52] The Bureau of Diplomatic Security of the United States Department of State has stressed that waiver of diplomatic and consular immunity does not belong to the individual interests; rather, such a waiver can be only realised for the benefit of the sending State.[53] Immunity can only be waived or claimed by the State and not by an individual. When the sending State decides to waive immunity of its diplomatic agent, the agent cannot invoke diplomatic immunity him/herself. Let us now turn to consider some State practices for the application of waiving immunity from diplomatic agents.

On 3 January 1997, Gueorgui Makharadze, who was the second highest-ranking diplomat at the Embassy of Georgia in Washington, District of Columbia, was speeding and under the influence of alcohol when he crashed his car causing the death of a teenage girl, Joviane Waltrick, and injured four other persons. The United States attorney's office for the District of Columbia 'informed the Department of State that its initial review of the evidence indicated that Makharadze could be charged with negligent homicide, involuntary manslaughter, or second-degree murder'.[54] Six days later, the Department of State requested the waiver of Makharadze's diplomatic immunity from criminal prosecution by the Georgian Embassy. On 14 February 1997, the Georgian Embassy transmitted a diplomatic note as follows:

> The Government of Georgia has considered the request of the United States Department of State and according to Article 32 of the Vienna Convention on Diplomatic Relations has waived the diplomatic immunity for Mr George Makharadze, so he can be prosecuted in the United States, for the accident that took place on January 3, 1997, in Washington, DC.[55]

Subsequent to the waiver of his diplomatic immunity by the Georgian Government, George Makharadze was charged with causing the death of Waltrick and injuring four people before the Superior Court of the District of Columbia on 20 February 1997. Makharadze then pleaded guilty and was sentenced to seven to twenty-one years in prison on 19 December 1997.[56]

In 2002, Soto-Mendoza, who was a secretary to the military attaché at the Colombian Embassy in London, was accused of the murder of Damian Broom who had robbed Soto-Mendoza's son. Soto-Mendoza was expected to be interrogated at the London police. He claimed diplomatic immunity to avoid interrogation. After Colombia's president-elect Alvaro Uribe and Prime Minister Tony Blair held an official meeting over this diplomatic issue, Colombia announced that Soto-Mendoza's diplomatic immunity would be waived for the trial. He was found not guilty of murdering Damian Broom and was acquitted at the Old Bailey.[57]

On 18 October 2004, the New Zealand Court of Appeal took into consideration the waiver of diplomatic immunity in the *R v X* case. The defendant, X, was a diplomatic agent. The plaintiff was a nanny working and living in X's house. The diplomatic agent was charged with indecent assault, following an incident in which he entered the nanny's private room in the middle of the night and masturbated to ejaculation. She pretended to be asleep when the diplomatic agent was in her room. After he left her room, the nanny realised that she had semen in her hair. The nanny cut some of her hair off and placed it in a plastic bag for investigation. She made a complaint to the police and provided them with the sample. The police then laid charges against the diplomatic agent. The sending State waived the diplomat's immunity from prosecution.[58] The diplomatic agent, in the District Court, asserted that the semen sample provided by the nanny was inadmissible, relying on Article 29 of the Vienna Convention, which declares that 'the person of a diplomatic agent shall be inviolable'.[59] However, the Court dismissed this application. The Judge then ruled that 'the person of the diplomatic agent did not include bodily fluids which have been discarded by that person'.[60] The case was appealed to the Court of Appeal; however, the Court held that the semen sample was admissible. Article 29 of the Vienna Convention was not breached, in that the hosting State 'had done nothing directly or through its agents to detain or arrest or constrain X in order to obtain the sample'.[61] Since the agent had abandoned his semen, the subsequent acts of the Courts or police in regard to the semen sample could not have violated Article 29. Furthermore, the Court held that the waiver of immunity by the sending State 'extended to all steps which were reasonably incidental to the prosecution of X, including leading evidence of the sample'. Therefore, the appeal was dismissed.[62]

It must be noted that since diplomatic immunities are granted to maintain smooth diplomatic functions, only the State can claim or waive immunity. The purpose of bestowing immunity is not to benefit an individual. Diplomatic agents cannot claim immunity themselves. Aforementioned State practices show that if a diplomatic agent abuses his/her official duties set out by the international conventions, the sending State may waive the immunity of that agent.

Personal and Functional Immunities for Diplomatic Agents

Immunity is a prerogative of governments. Immunity should on no account be attributed to an individual. Given that the rationale for extending immunity to diplomatic agents is based on the theory of functional necessity, it is important to distinguish between personal (*ratione personae*) and functional (*ratione materiae*) immunities. This distinction helps to explain whether or not human rights violations committed by diplomatic agents abroad should be covered by diplomatic immunity.

In customary international law, two forms of immunity from jurisdiction are recognised with regard to State officials: immunity *ratione personae* and immunity *ratione materiae*. These two forms of immunity are distinct legal entities. Immunity 'based on the nature of the act is sometime called *ratione materiae* while *ratione personae* is based on the status of the State that performs the act'.[63]

Immunity *ratione personae* is an absolute immunity in that it protects diplomatic agents from foreign jurisdiction in relation to both their official and private acts. Immunity *ratione materiae* concerns the official acts of diplomatic agents. The difference in the way these two immunities are treated may be attributed to their difference in purposes. In this respect, *ratione materiae* is conduct-based immunity, while *ratione personae* is unconnected to the claimed conduct. The main purpose of immunity *ratione personae* is to avoid any grounds for interference in the actions of a representative of the State; thereby, it both enables and facilitates international relations between potentially distrustful States. When considered from this perspective, immunity *ratione personae* cannot be rendered invalid without the assent of the sending State.[64] The next two sections address these two types of immunities with regard to status- and conduct-based immunity in international law.

Personal Immunity

Diplomatic agents enjoy immunity *ratione personae* when they are accredited to the host State. Immunity *ratione personae* 'is derived from the official's status and the post occupied by him [or her] in government service and from the State functions which the official is required to perform in that post'.[65]

Immunity *ratione personae* provides complete immunity while a diplomatic agent is in office. Diplomatic agents require an atmosphere that is conducive to their official functions for the sake of maintaining inter-State relations; immunity *ratione personae* protects diplomatic agents from criminal proceedings that might impede their functions. Immunity *ratione personae* protects diplomatic agents from foreign jurisdiction in relation to both official and private acts; it therefore provides absolute immunity. This immunity is conferred on diplomatic agents as long as they remain in office.

Functional Immunity

Immunity *ratione materiae* is applicable to State officials in a third State irrespective of their official position in the hierarchy of the State.[66] As has been noted, immunity *ratione personae* 'serves to protect governmental acts of one State from being adjudicated before the courts of another and, therefore, only incidentally confers immunity on the individual'.[67] All State officials in a third State are endowed with immunity from foreign jurisdiction with regard to functions, in their official capacity. In the context of immunity *ratione materiae*, by contrast, the nature of the acts in question is more of a determinative factor than the official who performed the acts. All State officials abroad, regardless of their status, are deemed to represent the State and are considered agents of State power. Immunity *ratione materiae* covers a more limited range of acts than immunity *ratione personae*, but it covers a broader range of actors and also potentially involves the official acts of diplomatic agents.[68]

There are two justifications for bestowing immunity *ratione materiae*. The first is that immunity *ratione materiae* constitutes 'a substantive defence, in that it indicates that the individual official is not to be held legally responsible for acts which are, in effect, those of the state'.[69] Such acts are attributable solely to the State, and immunity *ratione materiae* is an entity that imputes liability to the State.[70] The ICJ, in one of its advisory opinions, emphasised this point that the demeanour of any organ of a State should be recognised as an act of that State.[71] In the *Prosecutor v Blaskic* case, the Appeals Chamber used this rationale in its determination that a subpoena could not be directed to the acts of State agents in their official authority, because such official agents are merely representatives of a State and their official deeds can be accredited solely to the State. The Chamber added that such agents cannot be punished for tortious deeds as these are not imputable to them individually but to the State on whose behalf they perform; therefore, they enjoy immunity *ratione materiae*.[72]

The second justification is that, by vesting immunity in State officials, immunity *ratione materiae* precludes the circumvention of State immunity by way of legal proceedings brought against persons who act on behalf of the State.[73] This rationale was mentioned by Judge Sir George Jessel in 1877 in the *Twycross v Dreyfus* case, in which he stated that 'you cannot sue the agent in the absence of the principal, the principal is the Peruvian Government—you cannot sue the Peruvian Government at all, and, therefore, you cannot sue its agents. There is no question of trusteeship'.[74] This rationale was also highlighted in *Zoernsch v Waldock* in 1964, as follows:

> A foreign sovereign government, apart from personal sovereigns, can only act through agents, and the immunity to which it is entitled in respect of its acts would be illusory unless it extended also to its agents in respect of acts done by them on its behalf. To sue an envoy in respect of acts done in his

official capacity would be, in effect, to sue his government irrespective of whether the envoy had ceased to be *en poste* at the date of the suit.[75]

Regarding the question of whether immunity *ratione materiae* should be lifted for fundamental human rights violations, the following issue should be considered. Immunity *ratione materiae* provides protection for official acts; however, arguments have emerged which state that violations of fundamental human rights may not be deemed as official acts.[76] Therefore, in respect of immunity *ratione materiae*, there is a distinction between official acts (*acta jure imperii*) and private acts (*acta jure gestionis*). In general, if a diplomatic agent has carried out missions in relation to the governmental or sovereign deeds of the foreign sovereign State, then the courts of some European countries and some international courts will not exercise jurisdiction over the dispute.[77]

Diplomatic agents should benefit from diplomatic immunity only in respect of deeds which are regarded as part of their official duties. For that reason, any act that goes beyond the scope of diplomatic duties should be accepted as *acta jure gestionis* (private acts) in character. It follows that private acts can be subject to the host State's jurisdiction. In this sense, the Vienna Convention on Diplomatic Relations outlines three exceptional situations to the immunity granted to a diplomatic agent in a receiving State:

a) A real action relating to private immovable property situated in the territory of the receiving State, unless he holds it on behalf of the sending State for the purposes of the mission; b) An action relating to succession in which the diplomatic agent is involved as executor, administrator, heir or legatee as a private person and not on behalf of the sending State; c) An action relating to any professional or commercial activity exercised by the diplomatic agent in the receiving State outside his official functions.[78]

As fundamental human rights violations cannot be regarded as sovereign acts under international law, they are not listed among the official duties of diplomatic agents detailed in Article 3 of the Vienna Convention on Diplomatic Relations of 1961. Article 3 enumerates five functions regarded as diplomatic mission as follows: (1) representing the sending State in the hosting State; (2) protecting in the hosting State the interests of the sending State and of its nationals, within the limits allowed by international law; (3) conducting negotiations with the hosting State's government; (4)

ascertaining by all lawful means conditions and developments in the hosting State, and reporting thereon to the sending State's government; and (5) promoting friendly relations between the hosting and receiving State, and developing their cultural, scientific, and economic relations. However, the Civil Court of Brussels in the 1982 *Portugal v Goncalves* held that Article 3 of the Convention, 'which determined the functions of a diplomatic mission, set out the general framework of those functions and was to be interpreted as including all incidental actions which were indispensable for the performance of the general functions listed there'.[79]

On the one hand, there is the vital question of whether all deeds of diplomatic agents can be considered to be sovereign acts given that such agents are commissioned by a sovereign State and also represent their own governments. On the other hand, fundamental human rights violations committed by diplomatic agents can in no case be accepted as sovereign acts or indispensable to their performance because such acts are not official in nature and obviously do not fall within the scope of diplomatic functions framed under the Vienna Convention on Diplomatic Relations.

On this point, the position of the Labour Court of Brussels in the 1980 *Castanheira v Commercial Office of Portugal* is notable for reflecting the distinction between *acta jure gestionis* and *acta jure imperii*. The Court found that diplomatic immunity from jurisdiction is based on the sovereignty, independence, and equality of States. What must be determined is whether the deeds performed by diplomatic agents are constituted *acta jure gestionis* or *acta jure imperii*. *Acta jure imperii* concern the foreign State's sovereignty and constitute official acts; by contrast, *acta jure gestionis* 'do not raise any question of the exercise of public power [...] [T]he question which must be decided is whether or not the foreign State acted as a private person or on the basis of its *imperium*'.[80] The Court concluded that diplomatic agents are entitled to diplomatic immunity from local jurisdiction as long as they act in an official capacity.[81]

According to a 1984 House of Commons Foreign Affairs Committee Report in the wake of the Libyan Embassy incident in London, when diplomatic agents commit criminal activities, they forfeit their diplomatic position and accordingly fail to benefit from diplomatic immunity; in such cases they are not regarded as diplomatic agents at all.[82] Given that fundamental human rights violations cannot be considered as a part of the diplomatic agents' official functions, it follows that when diplomatic agents violate those human rights, they can no longer be deemed to be diplomatic officials and therefore they should lose the benefit of diplomatic immunity.

When diplomatic agents are suspected of having committed violations of fundamental human rights which are not regarded as sovereign functions of diplomatic agents, they should be held accountable for violations in question; for this reason, diplomatic immunity should not equate to diplomatic impunity. The following section elaborates on and analyses this position in the light of the issues discussed above.

Diplomatic Immunity Versus Diplomatic Impunity

Before discussing the difference between diplomatic immunity and impunity any further, it must be noted that, for the sake of maintaining smooth functions of diplomatic relations among States, diplomatic agents should benefit from diplomatic privileges and immunities as long as their acts do not constitute any violation of fundamental human rights. As Tim Hillier pointed out, modern diplomatic agents should be 'able to move freely and be unhampered as they report to their governments' and further they 'need to be able to report in confidence and to negotiate on behalf of their governments without fear of let or hindrance'.[83] Notwithstanding that diplomatic immunity for diplomatic agents of foreign States is deemed to be an inalienable rule in international law, diplomatic immunities and privileges have in the past been abused to avoid prosecution for committed human rights violations. This abuse makes diplomatic immunity in cases of violations of fundamental human rights incompatible with international law.

Despite the fact that the Vienna Convention on Diplomatic Relations does not distinguish between human rights violations committed by diplomatic agents in terms of their gravity, for the sake of proving the argument that diplomatic immunity does not equate to diplomatic impunity, the hierarchical relationship between prohibition of human rights violations and the right of diplomatic agents to certain immunities must be placed under the microscope. Any interruption of diplomatic immunity should be avoided unless this interference is in response to the violation of fundamental human rights. The principle of diplomatic immunity must be reassessed when those violations are at stake.

Although the theory of functional necessity has been put forward primarily as a justification for preventing all possible impediments to diplomatic functions, granting diplomatic immunity in cases of human rights violations is a controversial issue under international law. It is difficult to defend immunity for diplomatic agents on the grounds of functional necessity when agents are suspected of such violations. When those violations are at stake, diplomatic immunity should not be the primary focus of discussion. Trindade's crucial statement must be emphasised here and also applied to diplomatic agents. He rightly underscored that human rights violations are anti-juridical acts and those acts violate *jus cogens* norms.[84]

In 1929, Lord Hewart remarked that diplomatic officials 'are not, in virtue of their privileges as such, immune from legal liability for any wrongful acts [...] Diplomatic privilege does not import immunity from legal liability, but only exemption from local jurisdiction'.[85] This articulation of the law sounds unquestionable, and it should be applicable to any wrongful acts irrespective of their character.[86] Diplomatic agents should forfeit the rights provided by diplomatic immunity when they commit violations of human rights. They should no longer be recognised as diplomatic agents. Diplomatic agents should be accountable for those violations, because diplomatic privileges and immunities should not engender impunity.

This position was underscored by the Tokyo Tribunal in the case of General Hiroshi Oshima, who was the Japanese Ambassador to Berlin. Ambassador Oshima was arrested in Japan for war crimes in 1945 and was tried and convicted by the Tokyo Tribunal for conspiring to wage aggressive war in 1948. Even though Oshima held a diplomatic position, the Tribunal found that he was 'one of the principal conspirators and consistently supported and prompted the aims of the conspiracy'.[87] Ambassador Oshima claimed that he had diplomatic immunity and was, therefore, exempt from prosecution in respect of his deeds in Germany.[88] However, the Tribunal rejected this argument and stated that:

> Diplomatic privilege does not import immunity from legal liability, but only exemption from trial by the courts of the State to which an Ambassador is accredited. In any event this immunity has no relation to crimes against international law charged before a tribunal having jurisdiction. The Tribunal rejects this special defence.[89]

It is undeniable that diplomatic immunity has always been regarded as vital for ensuring smooth relations between States; however, it must be noted that diplomatic immunity can be abused and consequently used as a shield to safeguard diplomatic agents from being subject to proceedings, and thus to be held to account. Such abuse reveals itself particularly in respect of torture, slavery, and the inhuman treatment of domestic workers by diplomatic or consular agents. Because these acts are breaches of *jus cogens* norms, an inevitable conflict arises between the diplomatic immunity and the prohibition of these acts under international law. *Jus cogens* norms cannot be set aside or abolished by any other rule or principle unless that rule or principle is of equal hierarchic status to *jus cogens* norms. Otherwise, diplomatic immunity leads to diplomatic impunity.

Over the past two decades, the question of whether fundamental human rights violations, particularly violations related to the enslavement of domestic workers inside the premises of embassies or official residencies, fall within the scope of the commercial activities exceptions under the Vienna Convention on Diplomatic Relations has become critically important. To ask the question in this manner is to answer it. The residual (continuing) immunity principle has been used by domestic workers as a way to bring suit against former diplomatic agents. Residual immunity is justified by Article 39(2) the Vienna Convention of 1961 as follows:

> When the functions of a person enjoying privileges and immunities have come to an end, such privileges and immunities shall normally cease at the moment when he leaves the country, or on expiry of a reasonable period in which to do so, but shall subsist until that time [...] However, with respect to acts performed by such a person in the exercise of his functions as a member of the mission, immunity shall continue to subsist.[90]

Residual immunity has been seen as the sole means through which to bring a suit against diplomatic agents, because it does not apply to the private acts of former diplomatic agents. As the District Court of New York indicated, 'the purpose of immunizing a diplomatic agent's private acts is to ensure the efficient functioning of a diplomatic mission, not to benefit the private individual, and this purpose terminates when the individual ceases to be a diplomatic agent'.[91] Although it is not yet fully fledged, there has been a change in orientation from toleration of diplomatic impunity to diminishing diplomatic immunity. The two positions are analysed in the following sections.

Legal Attitudes in Favour of Diplomatic Agents

Although there is a movement towards diminishing the absolute nature of diplomatic immunity, there is a significant case that took a stance in favour of the diplomatic agent. In 1996, the United States Court of Appeals for the Fourth Circuit, in the *Tabion v Mufti* case, established that a diplomatic agent can rely on diplomatic immunity to avoid accountability when he or she violates the human rights of a domestic worker.[92] This case has led to criticism of the exceptions to diplomatic immunity under Article 31 of the Vienna Convention of 1961.[93]

Corazon Tabion served as a domestic worker for Faris Mufti, a diplomatic agent at the Embassy of Jordan in Washington, DC. Tabion alleged that Mufti confiscated her passport and menaced her with deportation. Tabion subsequently filed suit against Mufti and claimed that he had breached the Fair Labour Standards Act. Tabion claimed that the alleged mistreatment should fall within the scope of the commercial activities exception under the Vienna Convention of 1961.[94] However, the Court of Appeals rejected Tabion's claims and dismissed the case based on diplomatic immunity.[95] Based on the protection of diplomatic immunity, the Court stated, Mufti was safeguarded from the claims made by Tabion. However, the Court failed to take notice that the alleged inappropriate treatment of the domestic worker violated her fundamental human rights.

Recently, the United Kingdom Employment Appeal Tribunal delivered a judgement that further obstructs efforts to hold diplomatic agents accountable when they violate fundamental human rights. This decision was held in the case of *Reyes and Suryadi v Al-Malki and Al-Malki* heard before the Employment Appeal Tribunal on 5 February 2015. In 2011, a Saudi diplomatic agent employed Ms Reyes, a Philippine national, and Ms Suryadi, an Indonesian national, as domestic workers. The United Kingdom Visas and Immigration Tribunal 'has determined that both women are the victims of trafficking'.[96] However, the Court decided that Ms Reyes and Ms Suryadi could not pursue their claims on the grounds that the diplomatic agent in question enjoys diplomatic immunity.[97]

Diplomatic immunity explicitly has given rise to inadequate protection for domestic workers who serve in diplomatic premises and are victims of human rights violations. The abuse of diplomatic immunity by diplomatic agents seeking to avoid prosecution before receiving States' courts also obstructs efforts to compensate victims. Decisions that favour diplomatic agents accused of violating fundamental human rights reveal a conflict between the rules of diplomatic immunity and the protection of those human rights. As interest in international human rights has grown within the contemporary international system, the protection of fundamental human rights has presented a significant challenge to diplomatic immunity. This development begs the question of whether diplomatic agents can be held accountable for violating the human rights of their domestic workers.

There are many conventions and protocols prohibiting human trafficking and requiring compensation for victims of trafficking from perpetrators.[98] Accordingly, on 7 January 2010, the ECtHR decided that human trafficking was not compatible with a modern democratic society and was inconsistent with the European Convention on Human Rights.[99] It follows that any involvement by a diplomatic agent in human trafficking should fall outside the scope of diplomatic functions.

Such decisions (*Tabion v Mufti, Swarna v Al-Awadi* and *Reyes and Suryadi v Al-Malki and Al-Malki*) enable diplomatic agents to hide behind diplomatic immunity when they are accused of violating the fundamental rights. Moreover, these decisions are, obviously, troubling for future victims of human rights violations and for those victims whose legal battles against their diplomat employers are still on-going. Nevertheless, there have been a number of decisions which provide some hope that diplomatic impunity can be challenged if not fully set aside when fundamental human rights violations are at stake. These are now discussed.

Legal Attitudes in Favour of Victims of Human Rights Violations

Although diplomatic immunity shields diplomatic agents abroad from prosecution, there have been several cases which show that violations of human rights committed by diplomatic agents have become problematic issues for the application of diplomatic immunity. Accordingly, the protection of human rights is seen as a great challenge to diplomatic immunity by international society. In this sense, a sending State's waiver of its diplomatic agent's immunity from suit is an important step towards chipping away at the absolute nature of diplomatic immunity in the case of human rights violations committed abroad. This human rights' challenge to diplomatic immunity can be found in State practices which are considered in greater depth next.

A prominent and remarkable decision in respect of diminishing the absolute nature of diplomatic immunity was delivered by the Second

Circuit of the United States Court of Appeals in *Swarna v Al-Awadi* on 24 September 2010.[100] Vishranthamma Swarna, a native of India, had been a domestic worker of Badar Al-Awadi who was a Kuwaiti diplomatic agent in New York City. Swarna had been persuaded that she would receive decent treatment in the United States and obtained several promises from the Kuwaiti diplomat regarding her working and living conditions; however, Al-Awadi was accused of seriously abusing Ms Swarna in the Kuwaiti diplomatic premises.[101]

Ms Swarna was exposed to sexual slavery, involuntary servitude, and forced labour. She was prohibited from making contact with anybody outside of the diplomatic premises and was not allowed to make telephone calls. Letters from her family were withheld. She was both physically and psychologically abused and assaulted. The following statement from the Court's report summarises her wretched situation. She 'was threatened to have her tongue cut out and was dragged by her collar on several occasions. The individual defendants referred to Swarna as *dog* or *donkey*, and forcibly cut her hair—which was an important part of Swarna's identity and sense of self—against her will. Swarna slept in the children's bedroom, she had no privacy and no place of quiet refuge, and she often cried herself to sleep'.[102] Furthermore, Swarna was raped on several occasions and threatened with death if she informed anyone.[103] Indeed, she described her horrific situation in her statement to the Court: 'When I was working in the Al-Awadi's kitchen, I could look out the window and [...] often imagined escaping the Al-Awadi home so that I could jump in the river, drown myself, and end the misery of my life [...]. It was only the enduring need of my sick husband and five children in India that kept me from doing so'.[104] It is obvious that the diplomatic agent violated Swarna's fundamental human rights.

Ms. Swarna managed to escape and eventually filed a motion for default judgement against Al-Awadi, his wife Al-Shaitan, and Kuwait, once Al-Awadi had left his diplomatic post in the United States to continue his diplomatic duty in France. Kuwait and Al-Awadi subsequently asserted that as Al-Awadi was a diplomatic agent, he was immune from domestic jurisdiction. The Court upheld the sovereign immunity of Kuwait under the Foreign Sovereign Immunity Act; however, it ruled against Al-Awadi and denied residual immunity of Al-Awadi and his wife, indicating that he no longer had diplomatic immunity under the Vienna Convention given that the diplomatic post of Al-Awadi to the UN had ended. Although Article 39(2) of the Vienna Convention enables residual immunity to former diplomatic agents, that immunity is limited to those acts performed within the scope of official diplomatic function; and that immunity applies only to a person who was a member of the mission.[105]

Al-Awadi argued that the aim of Ms Swarna's employment was to assist him in mission-related activities; therefore, he claimed that he had diplomatic protection under Article 39(2) of the Convention. The Court held that:

> Ultimately, however, Al-Awadi's argument must be rejected, as it assumes a fact that is not supported by the record. The alleged facts clearly show that Swarna was employed to meet Al-Awadi's and his family's private needs and not any mission-related functions. Swarna worked an average of seventeen hours a day, seven days a week, cooking, cleaning, caring for Al-Awadi's children, and tending to the family's personal needs. Al-Awadi also allegedly raped Swarna. If Swarna's work for the family may not be considered part of any mission-related functions, surely enduring rape would not be part of those functions either.[106]

This decision has impeded the absolute impunity of diplomatic agents who are accused of such human rights violations of slavery. While the Court's decision did not remove all obstacles to the abolition of diplomatic impunity in cases of fundamental human rights violations, it raised an important discussion regarding the lapse of diplomatic immunity and as a crucial step in challenging the current framework of diplomatic immunity.

Swarna v Al-Awadi demonstrated that former diplomatic agents can be held liable for the aforementioned violations, although incumbent diplomatic agents can still enjoy immunity from being subject to local jurisdiction. In fact, the Court's position establishes an important precedent in relation to future allegations against diplomatic agents and leaves the door open to diplomatic accountability for human rights violations.

The *Swarna* judgement is not the only one to rule in favour of victims of human rights violations. Further support for such victims is provided by the case of *Baoanan v Baja*, heard before the United States District Court of New York on 16 June 2009. Plaintiff Marichu Suarez Baoanan held a bachelor's degree in nursing and Norma Castro Baja was a former Philippine diplomatic agent accredited to the United States Mission to the UN from 2003 to 2007. Baja promised Baoanan work as a nurse in the United States, which convinced her to move from the Philippines to the

United States. When Baoanan arrived in New York City, however, Baja's driver took her directly to the Bajas' household at the Philippine Mission.[107]

Baoanan claimed that Baja and his family forced her to work as a domestic servant in the premises of the Philippine Embassy in New York City, having lured her from the Philippines with false promises of employment as a nurse in the United States. Baoanan's allegations that were reported by the Court laid her horrendous conditions in the premises of Philippine Embassy bare: 'During the time Baoanan was a domestic worker in the Bajas' household, she worked approximately 126 hours per week. The Bajas limited her meals to leftovers, forced her to sleep in the basement with only one sheet, prevented her from leaving the household unaccompanied, and verbally abused and denigrated her. [She was also restricted] from using the household telephone'.[108] Ultimately, Baoanan claimed that she was exposed to negligent misrepresentation, conversion, fraud, conspiracy, and trafficking with respect to slavery, forced labour, and involuntary servitude.

Baja's term ceased on 21 February 2007, before Baoanan filed the suit against him on 24 June 2008. Consequently, the Court had to determine whether Baja's alleged actions constituted official acts or private acts in the subject of residual immunity. Baja sought the protection of diplomatic immunity by claiming that the mere act of employing a domestic worker constituted an official act; however, the Court rejected his argument. Having considered Baoanan's claims (forced labour, slavery, and involuntary servitude), the Court held that those actions were performed neither as an official function of diplomatic mission nor on behalf of the sending State. Therefore, the Court rejected Baja's claim to residual immunity because the alleged acts were committed in private capacity.[109] The *Swarna* and *Baoanan* decisions, therefore, provide important support for victims of human rights violations.

Article 39(2) of the Vienna Convention clarifies the limitations in respect of the residual immunity. According to this article, immunity shall continue as long as the acts in question are carried out in the exercise of the diplomatic function. There is a clear distinction between 'functions performed as a member of the mission, and other functions performed by the individual diplomat in question whilst present in the receiving State. Since the immunity is no longer necessary to respect the diplomatic purpose of the mission once the diplomat has retired from that post, but continues by way only of a residual protection', this residual immunity, therefore, may be interpreted 'no more widely than the words require'.[110]

These decisions significantly advance the objective of eroding diplomatic impunity in cases of fundamental human rights violations. Protection of those human rights presents a great challenge to diplomatic immunity. When such violations of human rights are committed by diplomatic agents, diplomatic immunity is not fully withdrawn, but at least domestic workers who are exposed to those violations have an opportunity to maintain their claims after the agents in question leave their diplomatic posts.

Another important step on behalf of domestic workers who have been subjected to human rights violations was taken by the then Secretary of State Hillary Clinton in 2011. Her declaration on the commission of human trafficking by diplomatic agents focused attention on abuses of diplomatic immunity. Clinton remarked that:

> We will [...] begin an annual briefing for visiting diplomats and their domestic workers as part of an ongoing effort [...] to protect domestic workers brought here by diplomats and raise awareness within the diplomatic community. Whether they are diplomats or national emissaries of whatever kind, we all must be accountable for the treatment of the people that we employ. We will also work with federal contractors to identify best practices for preventing trafficking, help them protect victims, and hold them accountable if they do not follow the federal government's anti-trafficking policies.[111]

This statement meant that diplomatic agents can be held accountable when they violate the fundamental human rights of domestic workers who are employed in the embassies' premises. Therefore, Clinton implied her support for the idea of abolishing diplomatic impunity for fundamental human rights violations. Ultimately, absolute immunity should be granted where the employment dispute refers to sovereign deeds performed *jure imperii*; in contrast, absolute immunity may be excluded if the employment dispute concerns deeds performed *jure gestionis*, which do not fall within the scope of the sovereign exercise of power.

Conclusion

This recent legal victory of migrant domestic workers against their diplomat employers provides important grounds for justifying the claim that the protection of fundamental human rights should triumph over the diplomatic immunity when these principles conflict.

For future victims of fundamental human rights violations committed by diplomatic agents, these prominent cases are likely to be recognised as precedents. Furthermore, these decisions in favour of victims of human rights violations may deter diplomatic agents and entities from committing such crimes in future. The growing importance of international human rights in the contemporary world order clearly has had a strong influence on the debate over diplomatic immunity. Diplomatic law must still be revised and amended in respect of modern international law. Nevertheless, the aforementioned decisions in favour of domestic workers may be seen as a harbinger of a new period of diplomatic accountability.

Diplomatic immunity is one of the most recognised and incontestable subjects under international law. However, diplomatic immunity can be regarded as a double-edged sword. On the one hand, diplomatic immunity is an internationally accepted rule essential for maintaining international relations; on the other, it provides certain contentious rights which tend to preclude victims from having a suit heard against diplomatic agents even in cases of fundamental human rights violations. Diplomatic immunity should not be claimed when fundamental human rights violations are being committed. Diplomatic immunity on no account equates to diplomatic impunity. The doctrine of immunity should be secured unless it brings about a transgression of fundamental human rights. When diplomatic agents violate fundamental human rights, they should be held accountable. They should not be allowed to hide behind the shield of immunity and to escape punishment; to do so would provide a basis for diplomatic impunity.

The protection of fundamental human rights has been recognised as an important challenge to the principle of diplomatic immunity, and, accordingly, it might be observed from case law that diplomatic agents who have committed certain crimes have been held accountable. However, case law also has demonstrated that there is a tendency to strict adherence to absolute diplomatic immunity, particularly for incumbent diplomatic agents. This inconsistency shows that, once again, there is no settled system for restricting diplomatic immunity under the current legal framework. Current principles of diplomatic immunity should be re-evaluated and amended in compliance with contemporary international law and in recognition of the growing importance of international human rights. The distinction should be made between diplomatic immunity and diplomatic impunity to prevent the number of victims of human rights violations from rising as a consequence of abuses of diplomatic immunity. If diplomatic immunity is leveraged to cover up human rights violations, diplomatic immunity serves as impunity.

Notes

1. G. R. Berridge and Lorna Lloyd, *The Palgrave Macmillan Dictionary of Diplomacy*, 3rd ed. (London: Palgrave Macmillan, 2012), 97–98.
2. Malcolm N. Shaw, *International Law*, 7th ed. (Cambridge: Cambridge University Press, 2014), 546.
3. Ivor Roberts, ed., *Satow's Diplomatic Practice*, 6th ed. (Oxford: Oxford University Press, 2009), 3.
4. G. R. Berridge, *Diplomacy: Theory and Practice*, 4th ed. (London: Palgrave Macmillan, 2010), 1.
5. Shaw, *International Law*, 545–46.
6. Emer de Vattel, *The Law of Nations, or, Principles of the Law of Nature, Applied to the Conduct and Affairs of Nations and Sovereigns*, ed. Bela Kapossy and Richard Whatmore (Indianapolis, IN: Liberty Fund, 2008), bk. IV: 706.
7. Roberts, *Satow's Diplomatic Practice*, 97.
8. Roberts, 99.
9. Berridge, *Diplomacy*, 110.
10. Eileen Denza, 'Vienna Convention on Diplomatic Relations', *United Nations Audiovisual Library of International Law*, 2009, 3–4.
11. Jan Wouters, Sanderijn Duquet, and Katrien Meuwissen, 'The Vienna Convention on Diplomatic and Consular Relations', in *The Oxford Handbook of Modern Diplomacy*, ed. Andrew F. Cooper, Jorge Heine, and Thakur Ramesh (Oxford: Oxford University Press, 2013), 510.
12. Mitchell Ross, 'Rethinking Diplomatic Immunity: A Review of Remedial Approaches to Address the Abuses of Diplomatic Privileges and Immunities', *American University International Law Review* 4, no. 1 (1989): 180.
13. Montell Ogdon, *Juridicial Bases of Diplomatic Immunity: A Study in the Origin, Growth and Purpose of the Law* (Washington, DC: John Byrne & Co., 1936), vii.
14. 'Vienna Convention on Diplomatic Relations', UNTS 500 (1961) Article 29.
15. David B. Michaels, *International Privileges And Immunities: A Case for a Universal Statute* (The Hague: Martinus Nijhoff Publishers, 1971), 47.
16. Leslie Shirin Farhangi, 'Insuring against Abuse of Diplomatic Immunity', *Stanford Law Review* 38, no. 6 (1986): 1520.
17. Vattel, *The Law of Nations, or, Principles of the Law of Nature, Applied to the Conduct and Affairs of Nations and Sovereigns*, 696.

18. *The Parlement Belge*, 5 P.D. 197 (Court of Appeal 1880) at 207–208.
19. See Clifton E. Wilson, *Diplomatic Privileges and Immunities* (Tucson: The University of Arizona Press, 1967); Biswanath Sen, *The Diplomat's Handbook of International Law and Practice*, 3rd ed. (The Hague: Martinus Nijhoff Publishers, 1965).
20. J. Craig Barker, *The Abuse of Diplomatic Privileges and Immunities: A Necessary Evil?* (Burlington, VT: Ashgate, 1996).
21. Stephen C. Neff, ed., *Hugo Grotius on the Law of War and Peace* (Cambridge: Cambridge University Press, 2012), 263.
22. Ogdon, *Juridical Bases of Diplomatic Immunity: A Study in the Origin, Growth and Purpose of the Law*, 81.
23. Ogdon, 81.
24. Vattel, *The Law of Nations, or, Principles of the Law of Nature, Applied to the Conduct and Affairs of Nations and Sovereigns*, 705–6.
25. Henry Wheaton, *Elements of International Law: With a Sketch of the History of the Science* (London: B. Fellowes, 1836), 272–73.
26. Wheaton, 273.
27. James Crawford, *Brownlie's Principles of Public International Law*, 8th ed. (Oxford: Oxford University Press, 2012), 397.
28. Shaw, *International Law*, 546.
29. *Barbuit's Case*, English Reports Full Reprint Vol. 25 – Chancery (Including Collateral Reports) (1557–1865), 777.
30. Vienna Convention on Diplomatic Relations Article 22(2).
31. *United States Diplomatic and Consular Staff in Tehran, Judgment*, ICJ Reports 3 (1980).
32. *United States Diplomatic and Consular Staff in Tehran, Judgment*, ICJ Reports at 28–33.
33. *United States Diplomatic and Consular Staff in Tehran, Judgment*, ICJ Reports at 18.
34. *Case Concerning United States Diplomatic and Consular Staff in Tehran, Request for the indication of Provisional Measures, Order*, ICJ Reports 7 (1979) at 16.
35. *United States Diplomatic and Consular Staff in Tehran, Judgment*, ICJ Reports at 30.
36. *United States Diplomatic and Consular Staff in Tehran, Judgment*, ICJ Reports at 41–44.
37. *United States Diplomatic and Consular Staff in Tehran*, Judgment, ICJ Reports at 42.
38. *United States Diplomatic and Consular Staff in Tehran, Judgment*, ICJ Reports at 42.

39. See Rosalyn Higgins, 'The Abuse of Diplomatic Privileges and Immunities: Recent United Kingdom Experience', *American Journal of International Law* 79, no. 3 (1985): 643–45.
40. Higgins, 644.
41. Higgins, 644.
42. Higgins, 645.
43. Grant V. McClanahan, *Diplomatic Immunity: Principles, Practices, Problems* (London: C. Hurst & Co. Publishers, 1989), 126–37.
44. Vienna Convention on Diplomatic Relations Article 9(1).
45. See Eileen Denza, *Diplomatic Law: Commentary on the Vienna Convention on Diplomatic Relations*, 2nd. (Oxford and New York: Oxford University Press, 2004), 59–71.
46. International Law Commission, *Draft Articles on Diplomatic Intercourse and Immunities with Commentaries*, vol. II (New York: Yearbook of the International Law Commission, 1958), 98.
47. Vienna Convention on Diplomatic Relations Article 31(4).
48. Denza, *Diplomatic Law*, 265–66.
49. International Law Commission, *Summary Records of the Ninth Session*, vol. I (New York: Yearbook of the International Law Commission, 1957), 105.
50. Vienna Convention on Diplomatic Relations Article 32(1) and (2).
51. Farhangi, 'Insuring against Abuse of Diplomatic Immunity', 1526.
52. Shaw, *International Law*, 560.
53. US Department of State, Office of Foreign Missions, *Diplomatic and Consular Immunity: Guidance for Law Enforcement and Judicial Authorities* (Washington, DC: Government Printing Office, 2015), 21.
54. Sean D. Murphy, *United States Practice in International Law – Vol. 1: 1999–2001* (Cambridge: Cambridge University Press, 2003), 86.
55. Murphy, 87.
56. Murphy, 87.
57. Sue Clough, 'Colombian Official Cleared of Murdering Son's Mugger', *The Telegraph*, 23 July 2003.
58. *R v. X*, 2 NZLR 121 (Court of Appeal Wellington 2005).
59. *R v. X*, 2 NZLR 121 at 123.
60. *R v. X*, 2 NZLR 121 at 123.
61. *R v. X*, 2 NZLR 121 at 121.
62. *R v. X*, 2 NZLR 121 at 121.
63. Hazel Fox QC and Philippa Webb, *The Law of State Immunity*, 3rd ed. (Oxford: Oxford University Press, 2013), 537.
64. Robert Cryer et al., *An Introduction to International Criminal Law and Procedure*, 2nd ed. (Cambridge: Cambridge University Press, 2010), 546.

65. International Law Commission, 'Preliminary Report on Immunity of State Officials from Foreign Criminal Jurisdiction: By Roman Anatolevich Kolodkin, Special Rapporteur', UN Doc. A/CN.4/601 (UN General Assembly, 29 May 2008), 78.
66. Fox QC and Webb, *The Law of State Immunity*, 565.
67. Ilias Bantekas and Susan Nash, *International Criminal Law*, 3rd ed. (Oxon: Routledge-Cavendish, 2007), 101.
68. International Law Commission, 'Second Report on Immunity of State Officials from Foreign Criminal Jurisdiction: By Roman Anatolevich Kolodkin, Special Rapporteur', UN Doc. A/CN.4/631 (UN General Assembly, 10 June 2010), 11.
69. Dapo Akande and Sangeeta Shah, 'Immunities of State Officials, International Crimes, and Foreign Domestic Courts', *European Journal of International Law* 21, no. 4 (2010): 826.
70. Akande and Shah, 826.
71. *Difference Relating to Immunity from Legal Process of a Special Rapporteur of the Commission on Human Rights, Advisory Opinion*, ICJ Reports 62 (1999) at 87.
72. *Prosecutor v. Tihomir Blaskic, Judgement on The Request of The Republic of Croatia for Review of The Decision of Trial Chamber II of 18 July 1997* (ICTY Appeals Chamber 29 October 1997) at para. 38.
73. Akande and Shah, 'Immunities of State Officials, International Crimes, and Foreign Domestic Courts', 827.
74. *Twycross v. Dreyfus*, 5 Ch. D. 605 (Court of Appeal Chancery Division 1877) at 618.
75. *Zoernsch v. Waldock and Another*, 1 WLR 675 (Court of Appeal 1964) at 692.
76. International Law Commission, 'Second Report on Immunity of State Officials from Foreign Criminal Jurisdiction: By Roman Anatolevich Kolodkin, Special Rapporteur', 16–18.
77. Richard Garnett, 'State and Diplomatic Immunity and Employment Rights: European Law to the Rescue?', *International and Comparative Law Quarterly* 64 (2015): 785.
78. Vienna Convention on Diplomatic Relations Article 31(1).
79. E. Lauterpacht and C. J. Greenwood, eds., *International Law Reports*, vol. 82 (Cambridge: Grotius Publications Ltd., 1990), 115.
80. Lauterpacht and Greenwood, 82:102.
81. Lauterpacht and Greenwood, 82:102.
82. Foreign Affairs Committee, 'The Abuse of Diplomatic Immunities and Privileges', H.C. Paper 127, December 1984.
83. Tim Hillier, *Sourcebook on Public International Law* (London, Sydney: Cavendish Publishing Ltd., 1998), 315.

84. Judge Antônio Augusto Cançado Trindade, *The Construction of a Humanized International Law: A Collection of Individual Opinions (1991–2013)* (Leiden: Brill Nijhoff and Hotei Publishing, 2015), 1519.
85. *Dickinson v. Del Solar*, 1 K.B. 376 (King's Bench Division 1930) at 380.
86. Yoram Dinstein, 'Diplomatic Immunity From Jurisdiction Ratione Materiae', *International and Comparative Law Quarterly* 15, no. 01 (1966): 81.
87. Neil Boister and Robert Cryer, eds., *Documents on the Tokyo International Military Tribunal: Charter, Indictment, and Judgments* (Oxford: Oxford University Press, 2008), 615.
88. UN, *Historical Review of Developments Relating to Aggression*, vol. 673 (New York: United Nations Publication, 2003), 213–14.
89. Bernard V. A Röling and C. F. Rüter, eds., *The Tokyo Judgment: The International Military Tribunal for the Far East (I.M.T.F.E.), 29 April 1946–12 November 1948* (Amsterdam: APA – University Press Amsterdam, 1977), 456.
90. Vienna Convention on Diplomatic Relations Article 39(2).
91. *Swarna v. Al-Awadi*, 607 F. Supp. 2d 509 (Dist. Court 2009) at 517.
92. *Tabion v. Mufti*, 877 F. Supp. 285 (Dist. Court 1995); *Tabion v. Mufti*, 73 F. 3d 535 (Court of Appeals, 4th Circuit 1996).
93. Article 31(1) of the 1961 Vienna Convention on Diplomatic Relations reads: 'A diplomatic agent shall enjoy immunity from the criminal jurisdiction of the receiving State. He [or she] shall also enjoy immunity from its civil and administrative jurisdiction, except in the case of: (a) a real action relating to private immovable property situated in the territory of the receiving State, unless he holds it on behalf of the sending State for the purposes of the mission; (b) an action relating to succession in which the diplomatic agent is involved as executor, administrator, heir or legatee as a private person and not on behalf of the sending State; (c) an action relating to any professional or commercial activity exercised by the diplomatic agent in the receiving State outside his [or her] official functions'.
94. *Tabion v. Mufti*, 877 F. Supp. at 285–87.
95. *Tabion v. Mufti*, 73 F. 3d at 538–39.
96. *Reyes and Suryadi v. Al-Malki and Al-Malki*, EWCA Civ 32 (Court of Appeal (Civil Division) 2015) at para 1.
97. *Reyes and Suryadi v. Al-Malki and Al-Malki*, EWCA Civ 32 at para 96.
98. See Article 5(3) of the European Union Charter, Articles 60–92 of the Office of the UN High Commissioner for Human Rights Report on Abolishing Slavery and its Contemporary Forms and Article 2 of The Palermo Protocol (2000). Furthermore, Article 15(3) of the Council of Europe Convention on Action against Trafficking in Human Beings (2005) requires that '[e]ach party shall provide, in its internal law, for the

rights of victims to compensation from the perpetrators'. Council of Europe, 'Council of Europe Convention on Action against Trafficking in Human Beings', ETS 197 (2005) Article 15(3).

99. *Rantsev v. Cyprus and Russia, Judgment*, Application no. 25965/04 (ECtHR 10 May 2010) at para 282.
100. *Swarna v. Al-Awadi*, 607 F. Supp. 2d; *Swarna v. Al-Awadi*, 622 F. 3d 123 (Court of Appeals, 2nd Circuit 2010).
101. The Kuwaiti diplomatic agent Al-Awadi 'promised to pay Swarna $2000 per month; to provide Swarna an annual paid vacation to India to visit her family; and to allow her to take Sundays off to attend church'. *Swarna v. Al-Awadi*, 622 F. 3d at 128.
102. *Swarna v. Al-Awadi*, 622 F. 3d at 129–30.
103. *Swarna v. Al-Awadi*, 622 F. 3d at 130.
104. *Swarna v. Al-Awadi*, 622 F. 3d at 130.
105. See *Swarna v. Al-Awadi*, 622 F. 3d. On this point, the District Court of New York stated that 'residual diplomatic immunity applies to official acts—because such acts are attributable to the Sending State—but does not apply to private acts—because the purpose of immunizing a diplomatic agent's private acts is to ensure the efficient functioning of a diplomatic mission, not to benefit the private individual, and this purpose terminates when the individual ceases to be a diplomatic agent'. *Swarna v. Al-Awadi*, 607 F. Supp. 2d at 517.
106. *Swarna v. Al-Awadi*, 622 F. 3d at 137–38.
107. *Baoanan v. Baja*, 627 F. Supp. 2d 155 (Dist. Court 2009) at 158–160.
108. *Baoanan v. Baja*, 627 F. Supp. 2d at 159.
109. *Baoanan v. Baja*, 627 F. Supp. 2d at 160–70.
110. *Abusabib & Anor v. Taddese, Judgment*, Appeal No. UKEAT/0424/11/ZT (United Kingdom Employment Appeal Tribunal 20 December 2012) at para 29.
111. Hillary Rodham Clinton, 'Remarks at the President's Interagency Task Force to Monitor and Combat Trafficking in Persons' (U.S. Department of State, 1 February 2011). The 2005 Miami Declaration of Principles on Human Trafficking considers human trafficking as a contemporary form of slavery and recognises human trafficking as a violation of *jus cogens* norms. The Miami Declaration of Principles on Human Trafficking, 10 February 2005, *Intercultural Human Rights Law Review* 11 (2006).

References

Abusabib & Anor v. Taddese, Judgment, Appeal No. UKEAT/0424/11/ZT (United Kingdom Employment Appeal Tribunal 20 December 2012).

Akande, Dapo, and Sangeeta Shah. 'Immunities of State Officials, International Crimes, and Foreign Domestic Courts'. *European Journal of International Law* 21, no. 4 (2010): 815–52.

Bantekas, Ilias, and Susan Nash. *International Criminal Law*. 3rd ed. Oxon: Routledge-Cavendish, 2007.

Baoanan v. Baja, 627 F. Supp. 2d 155 (Dist. Court 2009).

Barbuit's Case, English Reports Full Reprint Vol. 25 – Chancery (Including Collateral Reports) (1557–1865), 777–78.

Barker, J. Craig. *The Abuse of Diplomatic Privileges and Immunities: A Necessary Evil?* Burlington, VT: Ashgate, 1996.

Berridge, G. R. *Diplomacy: Theory and Practice*. 4th ed. London: Palgrave Macmillan, 2010.

Berridge, G. R., and Lorna Lloyd. *The Palgrave Macmillan Dictionary of Diplomacy*. 3rd ed. London: Palgrave Macmillan, 2012.

Boister, Neil, and Robert Cryer, eds. *Documents on the Tokyo International Military Tribunal: Charter, Indictment, and Judgments*. Oxford: Oxford University Press, 2008.

Case Concerning United States Diplomatic and Consular Staff in Tehran, Request for the indication of Provisional Measures, Order, ICJ Reports 7 (1979).

Clough, Sue. 'Colombian Official Cleared of Murdering Son's Mugger'. *The Telegraph*, 23 July 2003.

Council of Europe. Council of Europe Convention on Action against Trafficking in Human Beings, ETS 197 (2005).

Crawford, James. *Brownlie's Principles of Public International Law*. 8th ed. Oxford: Oxford University Press, 2012.

Cryer, Robert, Hakan Friman, Darryl Robinson, and Elizabeth Wilmshurst. *An Introduction to International Criminal Law and Procedure*. 2nd ed. Cambridge: Cambridge University Press, 2010.

Denza, Eileen. *Diplomatic Law: Commentary on the Vienna Convention on Diplomatic Relations*. 2nd. Oxford and New York: Oxford University Press, 2004.

———. 'Vienna Convention on Diplomatic Relations'. *United Nations Audiovisual Library of International Law*, 2009.

Dickinson v. Del Solar, 1 K.B. 376 (King's Bench Division 1930).

Difference Relating to Immunity from Legal Process of a Special Rapporteur of the Commission on Human Rights, Advisory Opinion, ICJ Reports 62 (1999).

Dinstein, Yoram. 'Diplomatic Immunity From Jurisdiction Ratione Materiae'. *International and Comparative Law Quarterly* 15, no. 01 (1966): 76–89.

Farhangi, Leslie Shirin. 'Insuring against Abuse of Diplomatic Immunity'. *Stanford Law Review* 38, no. 6 (1986): 1517–47.

Foreign Affairs Committee. 'The Abuse of Diplomatic Immunities and Privileges'. H.C. Paper 127, December 1984.

Fox QC, Hazel, and Philippa Webb. *The Law of State Immunity*. 3rd ed. Oxford: Oxford University Press, 2013.

Garnett, Richard. 'State and Diplomatic Immunity and Employment Rights: European Law to the Rescue?' *International and Comparative Law Quarterly* 64 (2015): 783–827.

Higgins, Rosalyn. 'The Abuse of Diplomatic Privileges and Immunities: Recent United Kingdom Experience'. *American Journal of International Law* 79, no. 3 (1985): 641–51.

Hillier, Tim. *Sourcebook on Public International Law*. London, Sydney: Cavendish Publishing Ltd., 1998.

International Law Commission. *Draft Articles on Diplomatic Intercourse and Immunities with Commentaries*. Vol. II. New York: Yearbook of the International Law Commission, 1958.

———. 'Preliminary Report on Immunity of State Officials from Foreign Criminal Jurisdiction: By Roman Anatolevich Kolodkin, Special Rapporteur'. UN Doc. A/CN.4/601. UN General Assembly, 29 May 2008.

———. 'Second Report on Immunity of State Officials from Foreign Criminal Jurisdiction: By Roman Anatolevich Kolodkin, Special Rapporteur'. UN Doc. A/CN.4/631. UN General Assembly, 10 June 2010.

———. *Summary Records of the Ninth Session*. Vol. I. New York: Yearbook of the International Law Commission, 1957.

Lauterpacht, E., and C. J. Greenwood, eds. *International Law Reports*. Vol. 82. Cambridge: Grotius Publications Ltd., 1990.

McClanahan, Grant V. *Diplomatic Immunity: Principles, Practices, Problems*. London: C. Hurst & Co. Publishers, 1989.

Michaels, David B. *International Privileges And Immunities: A Case for a Universal Statute*. The Hague: Martinus Nijhoff Publishers, 1971.

Murphy, Sean D. *United States Practice in International Law – Vol. 1: 1999–2001*. Cambridge: Cambridge University Press, 2003.

Neff, Stephen C., ed. *Hugo Grotius on the Law of War and Peace*. Cambridge: Cambridge University Press, 2012.

Ogdon, Montell. *Juridicial Bases of Diplomatic Immunity: A Study in the Origin, Growth and Purpose of the Law*. Washington, DC: John Byrne & Co., 1936.

Prosecutor v. Tihomir Blaskic, Judgement on The Request of The Republic of Croatia for Review of The Decision of Trial Chamber II of 18 July 1997 (ICTY Appeals Chamber 29 October 1997).

R v. X, 2 NZLR 121 (Court of Appeal Wellington 2005).

Rantsev v. Cyprus and Russia, Judgment, Application no. 25965/04 (ECtHR 10 May 2010).
Reyes and Suryadi v. Al-Malki and Al-Malki, EWCA Civ 32 (Court of Appeal (Civil Division) 2015).
Roberts, Ivor, ed. *Satow's Diplomatic Practice*. 6th ed. Oxford: Oxford University Press, 2009.
Rodham Clinton, Hillary. 'Remarks at the President's Interagency Task Force to Monitor and Combat Trafficking in Persons'. U.S. Department of State, 1 February 2011.
Röling, Bernard V. A, and C. F. Rüter, eds. *The Tokyo Judgment: The International Military Tribunal for the Far East (I.M.T.F.E.), 29 April 1946–12 November 1948*. Amsterdam: APA – University Press Amsterdam, 1977.
Ross, Mitchell. 'Rethinking Diplomatic Immunity: A Review of Remedial Approaches to Address the Abuses of Diplomatic Privileges and Immunities'. *American University International Law Review* 4, no. 1 (1989): 173–205.
Sen, Biswanath. *The Diplomat's Handbook of International Law and Practice*. 3rd ed. The Hague: Martinus Nijhoff Publishers, 1965.
Shaw, Malcolm N. *International Law*. 7th ed. Cambridge: Cambridge University Press, 2014.
Swarna v. Al-Awadi, 607 F. Supp. 2d 509 (Dist. Court 2009).
Swarna v. Al-Awadi, 622 F. 3d 123 (Court of Appeals, 2nd Circuit 2010).
Tabion v. Mufti, 877 F. Supp. 285 (Dist. Court 1995).
Tabion v. Mufti, 73 F. 3d 535 (Court of Appeals, 4th Circuit 1996).
The Miami Declaration of Principles on Human Trafficking, 10 February 2005. *Intercultural Human Rights Law Review* 11 (2006).
The Parlement Belge, 5 P.D. 197 (Court of Appeal 1880).
Trindade, Judge Antônio Augusto Cançado. *The Construction of a Humanized International Law: A Collection of Individual Opinions (1991–2013)*. Leiden: Brill Nijhoff and Hotei Publishing, 2015.
Twycross v. Dreyfus, 5 Ch. D. 605 (Court of Appeal Chancery Division 1877).
UN. *Historical Review of Developments Relating to Aggression*. Vol. 673. New York: United Nations Publication, 2003.
United States Diplomatic and Consular Staff in Tehran, Judgment, ICJ Reports 3 (1980).
US Department of State, Office of Foreign Missions. *Diplomatic and Consular Immunity: Guidance for Law Enforcement and Judicial Authorities*. Washington, DC: Government Printing Office, 2015.
Vattel, Emer de. *The Law of Nations, or, Principles of the Law of Nature, Applied to the Conduct and Affairs of Nations and Sovereigns*. Edited by Bela Kapossy and Richard Whatmore. Indianapolis, IN: Liberty Fund, 2008.
Vienna Convention on Diplomatic Relations, UNTS 500 (1961).

Wheaton, Henry. *Elements of International Law: With a Sketch of the History of the Science*. London: B. Fellowes, 1836.

Wilson, Clifton E. *Diplomatic Privileges and Immunities*. Tucson: The University of Arizona Press, 1967.

Wouters, Jan, Sanderijn Duquet, and Katrien Meuwissen. 'The Vienna Convention on Diplomatic and Consular Relations'. In *The Oxford Handbook of Modern Diplomacy*, edited by Andrew F. Cooper, Jorge Heine, and Thakur Ramesh, 510–43. Oxford: Oxford University Press, 2013.

Zoernsch v. Waldock and Another, 1 WLR 675 (Court of Appeal 1964).

CHAPTER 7

Conclusion

Fears over whether and how the protection of fundamental human rights recognised as *jus cogens* norms take priority over the immunity of States, Heads of State, and diplomatic agents should not be ignored. There is an unequivocal need to distinguish between immunity and impunity in order to protect fundamental human rights, given that impunity is itself a violation of human rights.[1] While immunity is used to shield those who commit violations of human rights, it must be recognised not only that there is considerable differentiation between immunity and impunity, but also that immunity becomes impunity when violations of human rights are at stake.

This book has argued that in cases involving violations of *jus cogens* human rights, immunity should on no account amount to impunity. While there is as yet no settled conclusion to, or resolution of, the tension between immunity and fundamental human rights, the unjust benefits of immunity should be abolished in order to maintain and enhance human rights. The tension between immunity and *jus cogens* human rights cannot be resolved unless the distinction between immunity and impunity is clearly articulated.

There are two essential interests in international law at stake here: preserving the immunity of States and those who represent them, and protecting human rights. Striking a balance between those interests does not mean providing equal conditions for States and their recognised agents and victims of human rights violations; on the contrary, this balance is achieved by pursuing a policy that prioritises the peremptory norms of general international law. It follows that finding and maintaining the

S. Özdan, *The Human Rights Challenge to Immunity in International Law*, https://doi.org/10.1007/978-3-030-92923-7_7

balance between the interests in question will be helpful in abolishing impunity and promoting human rights. Unlike the use of immunity as a shield against prosecution for human rights violations, fundamental human rights are *jus cogens*, a distinction which highlights the difference between immunity and impunity. It is impossible to disregard those interests in international law; however, it is feasible to impose considerable restrictions on the use of immunity when violations of fundamental human rights are concerned. This issue was explored in Chap. 2, which examined the origins of absolute and restrictive sovereignty. This examination provided the foundation for the analysis of absolute and restrictive immunity in subsequent chapters, as sovereign immunity is derived from the concept of sovereignty.

The non-derogable and peremptory nature of fundamental human rights was highlighted and the distinction between immunity and impunity underscored by the international community after the horrors of the Second World War. However, the implications of this distinction for the protection of human rights have not yet been subject to in-depth analysis by academics. This book has engaged with that contentious issue and analysed the question of State, Head of State, and diplomatic immunity in the case of violations of these human rights. It contends that immunity should not amount to impunity if violations of *jus cogens* human rights are committed. It offers, for the first time, a thorough explication of the distinction between immunity and impunity in the context of *jus cogens* human rights protection. This book has also aimed to expand knowledge and broaden understanding of the distinction between immunity and impunity in light of increasing violations of human rights in the contemporary international order.

Immunity in international law is derived from the sovereign structure of a State, and Chap. 2 described the transition from absolute sovereignty to restrictive sovereignty in parallel with increasing emphasis on human rights. Specifically, the chapter charted the evolution of sovereignty from a Westphalian to a post-Westphalian system, a transformation which reveals the impact of human rights discourse on the structure of absolute sovereignty. The transition from a State-centric perspective to a human-centric perspective of international relations was explored, and indicates an inescapable obligation to protect fundamental human rights by preventing States and their official representatives from abusing the immunity principle, whose origin lies in the need to preserve the smooth functioning of inter-State relations. Chapter 2 unveiled the tension between the protection of a peremptory nature of human rights and absolute structure of sovereignty. This tension explains the human rights challenge to immunities. Noting that increasing concerns over human rights chip away at the absolute sovereign structure of the State, Chap. 2 argued that absolute sovereignty is incompatible with international human rights in the current international order. As such, absolute sovereignty is an outmoded system that inherently limits the essence of what *jus cogens* human rights require: fundamental protection. Accordingly, Chap. 3 demonstrated the increasing importance of human rights in international law after the Second World War. Drawing on Article 53 of the Vienna Convention on the Law and Treaties, which states that if a treaty comes into conflict with a peremptory norm of general international law, it becomes void, Chap. 3 emphasised that fundamental human rights require absolute protection and respect.

The concept of immunity does not imply protection for States, Heads of State, and diplomatic agents by any means; at its core, immunity is designed to facilitate the smooth functioning of relations among States, State organs, and their representatives. In other words, there is a difference between immunity and impunity. This distinction between immunity and impunity was explored throughout this book, with the aim of identifying the source of the tension between the protection of human rights and the bestowal of immunity on States, Heads of State, and diplomatic agents. Although the international community has tended to abolish impunity in cases involving the violation of human rights, this movement is not yet fully fledged and the abolition of impunity is far from assured. Be that as it may, equating immunity with impunity in cases of fundamental human rights violations presents a major handicap against the establishment of justice and the promotion of human rights. This book sought to develop the distinction between immunity and impunity in terms of the adverse impact of impunity in respect of *jus cogens* human rights.

Chapter 4 explored the tension between immunity and impunity in relation to the State itself. While noting the strong roots of the State immunity principle under international law, the chapter underscored the understanding that the law of State immunity has never been static through the evolution of international law. It also considered the controversial exceptions to State immunity and focused on the human rights challenge. In doing so, it illuminated the evolution from a State-oriented approach towards a human-oriented approach to international relations which is finding voice in international law. Chapter 4 set out the tension between the protection of fundamental human rights and the preservation of State immunity. It argued that State immunity should not equate to State impunity if violations of *jus cogens* human rights are at stake. It explored two inescapable interests in international law: the bestowal of State immunity and the protection of human rights. It argued that violations of human rights do not fall within the scope of either acts *jure imperii* or acts *jure gestionis*, that such violations are incompatible with *jus cogens* norms and that the protection of those human rights takes precedence over the bestowal of State immunity. Therefore, immunity should not be used as a shield to cover up human rights violations; otherwise, State immunity becomes State impunity.

A tacit side of Head of State immunity was discussed in Chap. 5. Namely, that such immunity is at variance with the expectancy that international law should be implemented to stimulate respect for human rights and challenge backlash against the maintenance of human rights. It contemplated the question of whether such immunity engenders impunity in practice when transgressions of *jus cogens* human rights are perpetrated by Heads of State. For the sake of maintaining smooth international relations, this chapter accepts and recognises that the role of Head of State immunity is of the essence. However, it claims that exemption from punishment should not be available for Heads of State in the event that *jus cogens* norms are breached.

Bestowing diplomatic immunity on diplomatic agents abroad is a contentious issue when those agents are accused of having committed violations of human rights recognised as *jus cogens*. Chapter 6 argued that under such circumstances, there should be no derogation of the prohibition against violations of human rights; to do so erodes the distinction between diplomatic immunity and diplomatic impunity. This chapter analysed *acta jure imperii* and *acta jure gestionis* to support the argument that violations of human rights fall outside the scope of sovereign or public acts of a State; accordingly, such violations can in no case be deemed as diplomatic functions. Therefore, diplomatic agents should not be allowed to use immunity as a shield to avoid punishment for violations of human rights committed by them.

There is currently no agreed system in law for limiting diplomatic immunity, particularly for incumbent diplomatic agents. Accordingly, Chap. 6 asserts that diplomatic immunity equates to impunity as long as it is leveraged to conceal violations of fundamental human rights. With reference to a number of prominent cases that have favoured diplomatic agents involving violations of those human rights, this chapter noted remarkable deficiencies in international law in terms of promoting human rights. The chapter draws from examples of judgements that have found in favour of the victims of such violations, to support the argument that the protection of human rights triumphs over the principle of immunity for diplomatic agents, despite the fact that efforts to promote human rights are not yet fully fledged.

The ever-changing character of international society has necessitated revision of the concept of immunity. Increasing unease over matters relating to fundamental human rights and the changing dynamics of relations between States have contributed significantly to the formalisation of the concept of immunity in contemporary international law.

The transition from absolute immunity to restrictive immunity is a critical milestone in the campaign to challenge violations of human rights, particularly those committed by States, Heads of State, and diplomatic agents. Part III of the UN Convention on Jurisdictional Immunities of States and their Property[2] is regarded as a crucial foundation of the principle of restrictive immunity. To display the tension between the bestowal of immunity and the protection of fundamental human rights and also to analyse the attitude of international law towards the tension in question, this book adopted the logic of restrictive immunity outlined by the UN Convention. Given that a State is entitled to functional immunity if it engages in the types of activities that fall under the principle of State immunity, it follows that there are certain types of activities that fall outside the scope of the principle of State immunity. Therefore, it is necessary to identify the nature of a State's activities in order to determine whether or not immunity applies to that State and its official representatives. This book contends that while immunity applies in cases of governmental, non-commercial, sovereign, or public acts (*acts jure imperii*), non-governmental, commercial, non-sovereign, or private acts (*acta jure gestionis*) fall outside the scope of activities covered by immunity. This is an important distinction with regards to the transition from absolute sovereign immunity to restrictive sovereign immunity. Violations of *jus cogens* human rights naturally fall outside the scope of official governmental or public activities and thereby no immunity should be available in respect of such acts for States or their representatives.

In time, the tension between immunity and human rights may be reconciled. Whether or not this reconciliation takes place will surely depend on the initiatives of international law, society, and scholars. Sample case studies, effective dissenting opinions, the contributions of international scholars, and so on will certainly play an important role in shaping the future of human rights. To what extent the tension between them is either maintained or resolved depends on whether immunity is differentiated from impunity in relation to violations of fundamental human rights. As expressed in Chaps. 4, 5, and 6, the protection of human rights should triumph over vesting immunity in States, Heads of State, and diplomatic agents, when the two principles clash because immunity should in no case amount to impunity. Such an approach would promote human rights and resolve the conflict between immunity and human rights. Furthermore, asserting that immunity does not amount to impunity would help prevent abuses of immunity by the State or its representatives and thereby support and enhance international human rights.

The strong dissenting opinions, legal holdings, legal regulations, and international conventions on behalf of human rights complement each other and are also powerful expressions of a movement not only to develop human rights but also to chip away at impunity. International public opinion thus far destabilised the tension between human rights and immunity. That said, international law has provided no clear guidance for reconciling this tension. Inconsistent legal judgements prove that there is no fixed opinion on the relative weight of the bestowal of immunity and the protection of *jus cogens* human rights. Differentiating between impunity and immunity is vital to ensure continued progress on human rights and to protect the true purpose of immunities.

Legal opinions in support of domestic workers against their diplomat employers, prominent cases involving Heads of State who were held responsible or were sued for committing human rights violations and triumphant dissenting opinions that stand against human rights violations committed by States or their official representatives provide important guidance and signal a willingness to end impunity and reinforce international human rights. Legal, social, and political support for this position undermines not only the elevation of absolute sovereignty over human rights but also the culture of impunity in international society.

In summary, *The Human Rights Challenge to Immunity in International Law* asserts that immunity should not equate to impunity in cases involving violations of human rights recognised as peremptory norms of general international law. Here, it should be noted that while the doctrine of immunity should be preserved, this doctrine should no longer apply to circumstances in which there has been a transgression of fundamental human rights within the scope of *jus cogens* norms. Violations of human rights by States and State representatives that abuse their immunity rights can only be challenged from this position. Ultimately, the international community should adopt this approach in order to reconcile the competing principles of immunity and human rights and most particularly to develop and protect international human rights in the contemporary international order.

Notes

1. Judge Antônio Augusto Cançado Trindade, *The Construction of a Humanized International Law: A Collection of Individual Opinions (1991–2013)* (Leiden: Brill Nijhoff and Hotei Publishing, 2015), 1589.
2. Part III of the UN Convention describes proceedings in which State immunity cannot be invoked. UN General Assembly, 'United Nations Convention on Jurisdictional Immunities of States and Their Property', A/RES/59/38 (2004) Part III (Articles 10–17).

References

Trindade, Judge Antônio Augusto Cançado. The Construction of a Humanized International Law: A Collection of Individual Opinions (1991–2013). Leiden: Brill Nijhoff and Hotei Publishing, 2015.

UN General Assembly. United Nations Convention on Jurisdictional Immunities of States and Their Property, A/RES/59/38 (2004).

Index[1]

[1] Note: Page numbers followed by 'n' refer to notes.

S. Özdan, *The Human Rights Challenge to Immunity in International Law*, https://doi.org/10.1007/978-3-030-92923-7

I

J

K

L

M

N

O

P

The manufacturer's authorised representative in the EU is Springer Nature Customer Service Centre GmbH, Europaplatz 3, 69115 Heidelberg, Germany. If you have any concerns regarding our products, please contact ProductSafety@springernature.com

Printed and bound by CPI Group (UK) Ltd, Croydon, CR0 4YY
30/09/2026
02225661-0003